COMMON

THREADS

COMMON THREADS

A Parade of American Clothing

LEE HALL

A Bulfinch Press Book   Little, Brown and Company   Boston Toronto London

First Edition

Picture credits appear on page 324.

Library of Congress Cataloging-in-Publication Data

Hall, Lee.
    Common threads : a parade of American clothing / Lee Hall. — 1st
ed.
        p.   cm.
    "A Bulfinch Press book."
    Includes bibliographical references and index.
    ISBN 0-8212-1900-6
    1. Costume — United States — History.   I. Title.
GT605.H35   1992
391′.00973 — dc20   92-3970

Bulfinch Press is an imprint and trademark of Little, Brown and Company (Inc.)

Published simultaneously in Canada by Little, Brown & Company (Canada) Limited

PRINTED IN THE UNITED STATES OF AMERICA

*To my colleague and mentor
Ruth Weintraub
with affection; with admiration for
her mind, spirit, and style; in appreciation
for her abiding interest in this project;
and for her friendship*

Contents

Part III: The Twentieth Century

In the early twentieth century, Native American elders taught children traditional Indian ways, including those of clothing.

Acknowledgments

I am indebted to those friends who encouraged me to develop an idea into this book: Bill Blass, Kathryn Gamble, Diana Johnson, Virginia Lynch, Robert Maloy, David McCoy, Mary McFadden, Joan Patota, David Riesman, Charlotte Sheedy, Rose Slivka, Sheila Smith, John Stevens, Dolores and Jim Zaccaro; and to those who sweetly nourished its development with encouragement, information, and kindness: Mary Kennerly, Nell Eurich Lazarus, Diane Paton, Irma Rabbino, Paula Treder, and Krystyna Wasserman, who have dispensed patient and understanding help throughout the several years given to research and writing.

This book has provided numerous occasions to appreciate the special skills of helpful people and the rich resources of a variety of institutions. For assistance in illustrating the book, I thank: Lisa M. Anderson, New York State Museum; Nat Andriani, Wide World Photos; Tracey Baker, Minnesota Historical Society; Mary Bennett, State Historical Society of Iowa; Ruth Blietz, Des Plaines Historical Society; Nicollette Bromberg, Kansas Collection of the University of Kansas; Pat Carter, Washington State University; Monica Crystal, Historical Society of Pennsylvania; Vicki Cwiok, Sears, Roebuck and Company; Susan Danforth, The John Carter Brown Library; Wilson Davis, University of North Carolina–Greensboro; Janice Dockery, Historical Society of Pennsylvania; Lynn Downey, Levi Strauss and Company; Julie Dumont, John Fitzgerald Kennedy Library; Michelle E. Dzyak, Pennsylvania State University; Ann Farnam, The Essex Institute; Patrick J. Fraker, Colorado Historical Society; Joan Gosnell, The Penney Archives; Catherine H. Grosfils, The Colonial Williamsburg Foundation; Kim Grover-Haskin, Texas Woman's University; Nancy A. Heywood, The Essex Institute; Alan Hirtz, Santa Fe Trail Center; Charles F. Holmes, Memphis State University; Elizabeth M. Hutchison, Lafayette Miners Museum; Peter J. Knapp, Trinity College Library; Deanna Kohlburn, Madison Historical Society; Stacy Krammes, Hoover Historical Center; Rebecca Lintz, Colorado Historical Society: Joyce Luster, Caterpillar, Inc.; Lisa E. Martin, Frontier Historical Society; Nancy P. Martinez, Oshkosh B'Gosh, Inc.; Laurel Nielsen, Lynn Historical Society; Milton F. Perry, Division of Historic Research and Development, Clay County Department of Parks, Recreation, and Historic Sites; Joe M. Pinkston, The John Dillinger Museum; Diane Powers, Picture Collection, New York Public Library; Cynthia Read-Miller, Henry Ford Museum and Greenfield Village; Janet Riley, Frontier Historical Society; E. Philip Scott, Lyndon Baines Johnson Library; Alice Shelton, University of North Carolina–Greensboro; Mary Sylvia Siverts, Brown Group; Chris Steele, Massachusetts Historical Society; Raymond Teichman, Franklin D. Roosevelt Library; Julie Thomas-Lowe, Carnation; Jean Toll, General Mills, Inc.; Elliott Trotta, Eastern Airlines; Kenneth C. Turino, Lynn Historical Society; Mark Woodhouse, Elmira College; and Jonathan T. Zwink, Santa Fe Trail Center.

I extend special gratitude to Steve Ostrow, Mary Ison, and Pam Posz of the Prints and Photographs Division, The Library of Congress, who aided this project beyond calculation, and far beyond the requirements of their profession. I am in their debt for their patient assistance in locating and securing illustrations for this book.

I am grateful to Anne C. Edmonds, Librarian, and to Elaine D. Trehub, Archivist, and Marilyn A. Dunn, Reference Librarian, Mount Holyoke College, for their interest, time, and assistance.

I thank Miriam Williford and Honore David, University of Massachusetts, for their enthusiasm for the subject and for their faith in its significance to education. Jo Anne Olian, Curator of Costumes at the City Museum of New York, provided valuable guidance and good conversation about my research.

George Abbott furnished vital information about the clothing industry, and about manufacturing processes. My colleague Betty Mauceri, at The Academy for Educational Development, read passages and made helpful suggestions; her son and my friend Ben Mauceri contributed insight and information. Steve Moseley, President of The Academy, encouraged this project at every opportunity.

I am especially indebted to Margaret Horsnell for generously sharing her considerable knowledge of American history, and for reading and commenting on large sections of the manuscript.

I thank John L. Hochmann, my agent, who helped in my development of the proposal for this book, and found for it the perfect publisher and perfect editor.

I cannot imagine having completed this book without the guidance, friendship, and skill of that perfect editor, Brian Hotchkiss. I am deeply grateful to him.

South Hadley, Massachusetts, December, 1991

General George Armstrong Custer

Prologue

Clothing touches everyone.

For a time longer than recorded history, human beings have added *something* to their bodies. Some of our ancestors adorned themselves with paint and tattoos; others attached a few animal teeth and feathers, or roughly or cleverly devised garments of skin or fur. With technological advances, Homo sapiens husbanded animals for pelts, grew plants for fibers; we learned to weave and to sew and eventually developed whole industries devoted to making and selling clothing to one another.

Now, as in the past, we humans clothe our bodies — our public selves — in particular ways and for a variety of reasons: for protection against the elements and to meet our social and religious requirements of modesty, to make ourselves attractive sexually and socially, to display our wealth and position through conspicuous consumption, to support the role we choose to play in life, and to perform the physical movement necessary to work or play. In both the articles of clothing we choose and our styles of combining and wearing garments, we conform to or rebel against standards set by society, thus meeting or affronting the strictures of tribe, class, or sect. The private motivations and public conventions that meet in an individual's or group's dress have changed throughout our history; contemporary encouragement of individualism — even exhibitionism — in dress notwithstanding, individuals and groups continue to respond to social, economic, and cultural forces in selecting and wearing clothes.

Each day of our lives, as we paw through our closets and chests, we make decisions that, one way or another, reflect our sense of ourselves. We may look upon dressing as an art form and make our decisions about daily dress as expressions of self and creativity; we may thus ally ourselves with other fine and applied arts. Or we may use clothing to announce our political and social views and to dress in accordance with our beliefs and values in relation to ecology, religion, social propriety, or political theory.

The odds are good, however, that we spend less time examining our reasons for dressing than we spend viewing the results in the mirror. Unless we have a particular interest in history, we are even less likely to ponder clothing worn in the past. Yet clothing — that material closest of all to our beings — is a rich source of intelligence about ourselves and our forebears.

We can look at clothing worn by those who built American culture and better understand the fears, obstacles, and rewards confronted by the human beings whose history we share. In that mood, this book is not a scholarly treatise on the meaning of clothing (semiotics), not a scientific examination of human physical and cultural features expressed in clothing (anthropology), not a systematic review of the processes and products involved in the production and distribution of clothing (business and technology), not a self-help book to enable the reader to impress or control other people (popular psychology), and not an effort to define clothing as art. But the author has drawn from all of these sturdy disciplines, and others as well, to tell this particular story of American clothing, of the common threads that have pulled us together or strung us apart as a country and culture made up of disparate people, amazing feats, good and bad luck, greed and generosity, success and failure.

A piece of clothing is an object, a material substance shaped to meet specific purposes and functions. When isolated from its owner, when tacked up on the wall of a museum or historical society, an article of clothing is treated as if it were an object of art, and may or may not come to life in the imagination of the beholder. But whether clothing is or is not art is less at issue than whether the skills and attitudes used in understanding works of art can be applied to the understanding of clothing.

We are accustomed to looking at the arts of America — architecture, painting, sculpture, decorative and applied arts — for evidence of a distinctive American civilization. We peer into the mirrors they provide, and we believe what we see of ourselves, or our civilization, in the making. Moreover, we expect works of art to inform us, enliven our imagination, or challenge our perceptions and thoughts, and we know that art objects reveal and clarify experience in direct proportion to the viewer's investment of knowledge and empathy in honest quest for the kernel of uniqueness and expression that defines a given piece.

Americans seem uncomfortable with the works of art made by artists of both previous and current generations, at once responding to the evocative authority inherent in art objects and suspicious of experience that is not immediately apparent as practical and rational. Still, Americans pursue art on a massive scale. Even a superficial tally of the numbers of people who visit museums, purchase art books, take courses in art and art appreciation, and watch television programs concerning the arts suggests that a large number of us are interested in reading or interpreting the fine arts as a reflection of cultural and social history as well as a source of personal aesthetic experience.

In addition to the interest of casual museumgoers, the formal or scholarly criticism and explication of art have long been the stock-in-trade of academic disciplines, such as the history of art and American studies, as investigated in educational institutions. But the traditional academic disciplines of art do not fully explore — nor are they obliged to — other material evidences of history and culture. Many classes of objects not included in the fine arts also embody and yield to our view the values and attitudes of the past and grant rich personal enjoyment to the viewer. Many objects that are not included specifically in studies of the fine arts embody or evoke expressive qualities, emphasizing their affinity to art.

American clothing, notwithstanding the influences of practicality and necessity, manifests the history of American life, an epic story of the making of our country and our civilization. Articles of clothing worn by men, women, and children in the long parade of the American past often yield telling glimpses of the people whose lives combined to produce our culture.

Clothing evidences directly the hardships and recreation, the vanities and practicalities of the men and women whose lives converged in the development of the United States. Literally, we have worn our history on our backs, and it is a dramatic, often poignant history. It is ours for a modest investment in empathetic consideration of the objects; in exchange for a meager exercise of imagination, we can follow the common threads of our clothing into the fabric of our history.

In the past, we have assumed that American clothing — as we have also assumed of government and art and other aspects of our culture — began in Europe; we have assumed that clothing was transplanted from that source and rooted in the New World; and we have further assumed that clothing developed, in a linear progression of fashion and technology, an American character that emerged as a marketing force after the Second World War. In this view, our conception of clothing is limited to those articles

shaped by fashion, which, in turn, until fairly recently, when American designers gained prominence, was set in Paris or London or Berlin.

When our sense of clothing is confined to fashion, however, and treated in the same way we treat fine arts, its practicality and vitality are too easily denied; it is robbed of purpose and rendered a thin covering for the whims of the affluent and privileged. Thus, the history of fashion, taken alone, is the story of a small minority, a distortion amplified by the fact that only the elite have had the luxury of not wearing out their clothing; their adherence to fashion has been a major part of their conspicuous consumption. Those Americans in the past who could afford fashion — what we now call designer clothes — could afford to store and save those clothes, or they could afford to give them away.

It is safe to say, however, that most Americans have not enjoyed such luxury and such display of wealth. Over the years, most clothing has been born of necessity, innovation, and practicality; most American clothing has been mended, altered, and often handed down; and most clothing has been used up in crazy quilts, household rags, or other articles related to daily life; in many cases, the tattered threads of exhausted clothing have been abandoned alongside overland trails or in the skid rows of contemporary cities, no longer useful, hardly identifiable as articles of dress.

While it is true that those Europeans who came to the shores of the New World were dressed in Renaissance styles indicative of class, occupation, and gender, it is also true that they encountered Native American clothing and adapted both garments (the moccasin) and materials (the use of buckskin) to their own needs. Moreover, the "progression" of American clothing is neither linear nor confined to the dynamic interaction of fashion (taste or desire) and technology (possibility and availability); rather, American clothing — like our language, system of government, and multifaceted culture — issues from many roots, and it flowers in response to a variety of conditions, both individual and cultural.

The story of American clothing consists of numerous strands, and reflects the ideas and issues that have shaped us. In our presumed classless society, clothing, now as in the past, sets people apart, signals distinction according to class, wealth, gender, and ethnic origin; similarly, it declares rank, whether in the substance of a uniform or in the association of specific garments with particular occupations.

Articles of clothing win acceptance or membership in groups.

Women's early bathing costumes, often in nautical styles, were made of heavy material and didn't provide much ease of movement.

Such articles — silk and lace for the colonial girl, boots for the cowboy, expensive frocks for the lady who lunches — become psychologically necessary; they signal the wearer's identity to the world. Recently, young men in inner cities, persuaded to buy by high-powered advertising directed precisely at them, have been murdered for their expensive sports shoes. Fashion's victims may not always be so tragic or so visible, but few contemporary Americans live totally free of fashion's influence through advertising and marketing, and few indeed are willing to dress solely to please themselves.

Clothing has been used to define masculinity and femininity; in the past, this has meant that garments were designed specifically to support men at work and in sports, and to sustain women at home and in social situations befitting their status. Clothing

in the past limited female activity and empowerment: women stumbled over long skirts, felt the pain of corseting, and teetered on high heels, convinced that each convention in dress was a necessary insignia of femininity. Today, in the wake of the latest feminist movement, clothing still reflects the politics of gender — for males as well as females. In summer heat, most American men go to their offices in suits, tight-collared shirts and ties, and heavy shoes; in winter, women wear only a thin layer of nylon stockings to protect their legs against the cold. Lest they be considered unfeminine, professional women in all seasons continue to wear high-heeled shoes, usually at least a half size too small and narrow, that distort the natural line of the spine, maim the feet, and prevent easy and comfortable walking. High heels, worn with a tailored suit or with trousers, symbolize a woman's decision to limit her activities and to advertise her membership in the "weaker" sex.

But the story of clothing is not confined to reflecting the politics of gender; rather, it shows numerous tensions and struggles as different groups have been folded into America, as influences have been encountered and absorbed cross-culturally, and it mirrors numerous and complicated aspects of identity and status in our culture.

A survey of the history of American clothing does not reveal a civilization in the process of effecting equality for all, or even blind justice for all. Indeed, one part of the story of American clothing pits haves against have-nots and reveals sharp contrasts in the costumes of the empowered and the powerless, presenting both the substance and signs whereby the powerful assert their privileges over the weak. But behind the glimmer of fashion and the combined forces of manufacturing, retailing, and advertising to make consumerism and waste a way of life, there are stories of ingenuity and humor, courage and daffiness, necessity and eccentricity that have contributed to the texture and richness of American clothing.

Clothing may not the person make, but clothing, in addition to its utilitarian functions, reflects a number of highly important and entertaining facets of human life within a given culture, climate, region, profession, or dream of the good life. Not only does clothing signal status or class, occupation or profession, it provides the costumes for personal theater; it promotes drama and fantasy, dreaming and self-expression. Even in the meanest society and under the poorest living conditions, clothing can often enhance and display personality. Clothing provides latitude for individual caprice, for entertainment, and for personal assertion.

3

Part I

c. 1492–1800

6

C. Smith taketh the King of Pamavnkee prisoner 1608

CHAPTER 1

In the Beginning . . .

We do not know what the first Americans who crossed the Bering Strait long before Columbus stumbled onto the New World wore when they settled the mass of land that now includes the United States. Partially as a result of evidence, partially as a reflection of stereotypical thinking about preliterate cultures, we imagine them to have been rudely dressed, probably in skins, and adorned with feathers, beads, and other objects. We imagine that they collected dyes from plants, tanned deerskin and the hides of other beasts, and that they used clothing to protect themselves from the elements, to indicate tribal rank, and for ceremonial purposes.

Although apparently correct in the main, that shadowy image of Native American dress provides one — but only one — arbitrary and conjectural beginning for the story of American clothing. Strictly speaking, the story of American clothing has no one precise beginning, but for us it begins when Native Americans and Europeans first saw each other, when European Renaissance males stepped ashore to see and be seen by men, women, and children who lived tribally, hunting and fishing, worshiping their gods and spirits, practicing rituals and skills that sustained them in communities in the many regions of the land.

Background in Europe

The Commercial Revolution, the Renaissance, and the Reformation transformed the social and economic bases of Western Europe, their influence then crossing the Atlantic and transforming the New World. Each of these major upheavals caused colossal change in Europe, and each, in turn, contributed to the colonization of America and to what would come to be called the "American character."

The Commercial Revolution of the fourteenth century brought luxury items from the Near and Far East — silks, jewelry, spices — onto the European market. Europeans, eager to add these newly discovered fine materials to their lexicon of opulence, supported extension and intensification of trade with the East. Spices, soon regarded as a necessity in those households rich enough to afford them, offered a lucrative enough market to entice adventurers and merchants to seek a sea route to China and India, thus setting the stage for the great explorers and navigators who first ventured across the Atlantic to explore the New World.

The Renaissance stimulated interest in secular rather than sacred learning, spawning discoveries in science and technology. New advances in navigation such as the compass, the quadrant, and the astrolabe made it possible to chart voyages across the seas with more accuracy. That ability to navigate and map, coupled with the Renaissance faith that exploration would yield knowledge, impelled Christopher Columbus and others to investigate the physical world.

Columbus, who set sail for the Orient, landed his little fleet of ships in the Americas in an astonishing navigational blunder that revolutionized human understanding of the planet. For the next century after Columbus's landing in the New World, Spain dominated the conquest and settlement of South and Central America, seeking gold and other riches and killing the aboriginal people with the weaponry of advanced technology, as well as with such diseases as smallpox, typhoid, diphtheria, and tuberculosis; the Native Americans, however, may have reciprocated with the strain of syphilis that plagued Europe for centuries.

During their conquest of Native Americans, the Spanish in-

In this 1603 print, Captain John Smith and Chief Opechancanough struggle as Powhatan bowmen and Englishmen with firearms clash in the background. The depiction of armored European invaders and nearly bare Native Americans symbolizes the imbalance of power as well as the devastating cultural differences between the two groups of people. For both, the surprise and curiosity of first encounter soon turned to suspicion and fear, and as the Europeans seized the lands of Native Americans, relations between the groups deteriorated further.

deed found gold and silver that made Spain the wealthiest of European countries by the end of the sixteenth century. Other countries, including France, the Netherlands, and England, wanted a share of the wealth to be extracted from the lands on the other side of the Atlantic, and set out to settle the New World. Settlers under each European flag thus transported capitalism and the free-enterprise system to the New World.

The Reformation, a dramatic religious movement, was touched off in Germany by Martin Luther in 1519; by the end of the sixteenth century, Europe was divided among Protestant and Catholic countries that competed not only for economic and political interests in the New World but also for the souls of the Native Americans. Under the banners of church and crown, Europeans would invade, plunder, settle, and claim the riches of the New World and the souls of Native Americans for Christianity.

Two Worlds Meet

By the end of the fifteenth century, human beings on both sides of the Atlantic had established patterns of government and worship and had devised values and accrued skills in support of their ways of life. Save in their membership in the same biological species, however, the Native Americans and the European invaders they encountered had little in common and little on which to base communication and understanding. The meeting of the two groups was fated to be dramatic and to be followed by a shared history marked by tragedy.

What did they think of one another on first encounter? It is impossible to imagine groups of people more different in their appearance than the Native Americans and the Europeans who came ashore. While the explorers and colonists recorded extensively their impressions of the natives they encountered in the New World, the natives had no writing systems, and we have virtually no firsthand accounts of their early reactions to the white men. But the tradition of storytelling preserved in tribal memories some of those first Indian perceptions of the strangers, and many of these stories were recounted to later historians.

From Indian stories, handed down through several generations and recounted long after their first telling, ethnographers have learned of several prophecies of European arrival. In one such legend, before the arrival of the Plymouth Pilgrims, a Nauset Indian on Cape Cod dreamed that many strange men would arrive; he described their alien dress — English-style breeches and jerkins that he had never seen. One of the men in his dream, he said, dressed in black, carried a large book, and

stood before the Indians to tell them that God was angry with them for their sins.[1]

Indian stories include descriptions of the actual arrival of Europeans in "moving islands." Seeing men aboard these huge sailing ships, the Indians often prepared wigwams, a customary gesture of welcome, for their new guests, and sent canoes out to the foreign ships to greet the white-faced and curiously bearded strangers who came as their prophets had predicted with long knives, thunder tubes, and giant winged canoes. From both Indian accounts and those of early explorers, we know that the Native Americans were prepared in many instances to receive the Europeans as gods, and almost always to offer friendship and assistance.

Upon examination, the Indians found the Europeans oddly like themselves anatomically; they were humans, only strangely colored and oddly dressed. Often, Indians insisted on very close scrutiny of the white bodies behind the European armor, mail, and weapons, and gravely discussed among themselves the revealed faces, bodies, legs, and arms of their terrified subjects of examination. Since Indians were largely hairless, and customarily extracted or singed visible hair from their bodies, they were fascinated by European beards, furry limbs, and chest hair. In one instance, an Indian tried to remove a sailor's red beard, offering him a variety of pelts from otter, beaver, and skunk in exchange.[2]

The Native Americans quickly had opportunity to inspect a wide variety of the European physical types who came to their land. As exploration and colonization became thriving enterprises, gentlemen adventurers, navigators, thugs, guys on the lam, and men of God gripped the decks of fragile vessels, put their faith in crude navigational tools, and submitted themselves to the perils of crossing the sea in order to claim land for monarchs, to proselytize Christianity among Native Americans, to find gold, to win fame, or to exorcise their private devils in a life of peril and adventure in the newly found strange land. A small store of artifacts contain Indian images of Europeans, particularly carved effigy combs and pipes and woven wampum belts. By the eighteenth century the colonists were occasionally depicted by the Indians as recognizably human figures. Missionaries, for instance, were associated invariably with crosses, while most Europeans were depicted wearing frock coats and tall, wide-brimmed hats.

The beardless Indians found the hirsute white people strange and their heavy clothing bizarre, and there is no doubt that the Europeans were astonished by the appearance of the Native

Americans. European explorers first saw North American Indians wearing skins draped over their shoulders covering portions of the upper body and genitals. During the winter, they saw some of the natives wearing an outer cloak of feathers for additional warmth, and they saw men wearing ceremonial headdresses fashioned from animal skins, feathers, and bones.

Extensive tattooing, in some instances, decorated the almost nude bodies of both men and women. For women, the Europeans learned, the tattoos represented their status in the tribe and the position of their husband. For the men, tattoos denoted rank in the tribe and accomplishment in war.

The aboriginal people of the New World and their attire fascinated people in Europe, who eagerly sought the explorers' reports, as well as the goods they brought back. The publication of illustrated books, then a new enterprise, fanned the appetite for

of the Christians, Hakluyt argued that colonists would naturally enlarge "the dominions of the Queen's Most Excellent Majesty, and consequently of her honor, revenues, and of her power by this enterprise." Moreover, Hakluyt held out the promise of extending the market for "the woollen clothes of England, especially those of the coarsest sort," which would improve "the maintenance of our poor, that else starve or become burdensome to the realm; and vent also of sundry our commodities upon the tract of that firm land, and possibly in other regions from the northern side of that main."[3]

Woodcuts and drawings accompanied Hakluyt's publications; these and other illustrations of Native Americans made as long as a century after the arrival of Columbus indicate European images — ideas based on hearsay as well as observation — of those people. Those drawings and woodcuts made by artists who

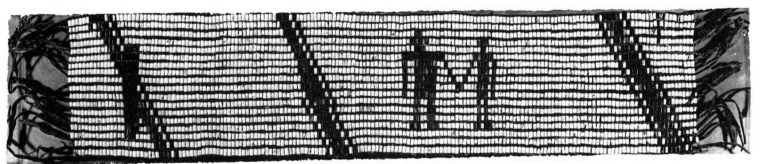

9

information. Moreover, propagandists found that publishing enabled them to spread the word about riches to be gained on the other side of the Atlantic, and to enlist adventurers, colonists, and others hoping to change their lives and fortunes. These published accounts of exploration include European observations of natives, as well as colorful inventories of business opportunities.

In 1564 Frenchman Jacques Le Moyne painted Indian scenes in Florida, in 1582 Englishman Richard Hakluyt published his *Divers Voyages Touching the Discovery of America*, and in the 1580s surveyor and painter John White made a series of watercolor drawings of Indians in Virginia, a rich chronicle of Indian dress and habit. From such material, and from descriptive writing, we see both the varieties of Native American bodily adornment and the Europeans' curiosity about and fear of the people they called "Indians." Richard Hakluyt offered a variety of reasons why the New World should be colonized: for the glory of God, the honor of the Queen, and the enrichment of the English. In meeting the English duty to extend the glory of God by planting religion "among those infidels" and increasing the force

accompanied explorers, and made to record the habits and appearance of the Native Americans, furnish our best evidence regarding the clothing of the Indians at the time of the European exploration of the New World.

An early record of exploration, that of Jacques Cartier's 1534 voyage to the New World, includes a description of Indians, and of trading with them. When Cartier anchored near Port Daniel, in the Gulf of St. Lawrence, Indians in nine canoes paddled near to investigate. Cartier's men set out in two longboats to meet the Indians, who at first ran away but then returned to make signs indicating their interest in bartering. They held up some furs "of small value, with which they clothe themselves." Cartier's men communicated their friendliness, sent two men ashore to offer

Indian depictions of early European settlers are few, leaving considerable room for conjecture as to how the Native Americans viewed the Europeans they first saw. On this early wampum belt, the Indian and European, the latter identifiable by his tall hat and frock coat, hold hands, signifying their treaty of friendship, on the occasion of one of the early land cessions (possibly 1682) from the Delawares to William Penn. In 1857, Penn's great-grandson presented this belt to the Pennsylvania Historical Society.

the Indians some knives and other iron goods, "and a red cap to give to their chief."[4]

Soon the two parties were eagerly trading together. The Indians, to indicate their pleasure in obtaining iron wares and other commodities, danced ceremoniously and threw salt water over their heads with their hands. When the Indians had bartered all they had, including the skins they wore as clothes, they left naked and signing that they would return the next day for more bartering.

Under the British flag, John Hawkins explored the coast of Florida, noting the richness of the earth and vegetation, "also deer great plenty [sic], which came upon the sands before them." He marveled at the ability of the Indians to rub sticks together and make fire, and to build barnlike shelters with "stanchions and rafters of whole trees . . . covered with palmetto leaves." Hawkins described Indian apparel: "In their apparel the men only use deerskins, wherewith some only cover their privy members, othersome use the same as garments to cover them before and behind; which skins are painted, some yellow and red, some black and russet, and every man according to his own fancy."[5]

The Florida Indians also painted their bodies "with curious knots . . . as every man in his own fancy deviseth," and according to Hawkins, the pigment was pressed into scratches and thornpricks in the skin to accomplish a form of tattooing, and to make the decorations permanent. In addition to deerskins, tattoos, and body paint, the Florida women wore garments made of moss, a substance not likely to diminish the insect problems — notably chiggers — that afflicted the people of the Florida peninsula. Both men and women wore jewelry of gold and silver that sometimes included large pearls. Hawkins observed that the Indian women fashioned round gold plates to flatten and "to bolster up their breasts withal, because they think it a deformity to have great breasts."[6]

While circumnavigating the globe (1577–80), Englishman Sir Francis Drake and his men put ashore on the coast of California to encounter Indians who mistook them for gods until, displaying obvious human appetite, they ate and drank. The English mimed their peaceful intentions to the natives and gave them "good and necessary things to cover their nakedness." The Indians, after receiving gifts of shirts and linen cloth from the English, gave to their visitors "divers things, as feathers . . . quivers of their arrows made of fawn-skins, and the very skins of beasts that their women wore upon their bodies." Drake described native clothing:

Their men for the most part go naked; the women take a kind of bulrushes and, combing it after the manner of hemp, make themselves thereof a loose garment which, being knit about their middles, hangs down about their hips and so affords to them a covering of that which Nature teaches should be hidden; about their shoulders they wear also the skin of a deer with the hair upon it.[7]

In 1584, Sir Walter Raleigh sent two ships, commanded by Philip Amadas and Arthur Barlow, on a reconnaissance voyage along the coast of North Carolina. Barlow reported on all aspects of the journey, including the appearance and behavior patterns of the Indians. The sailors on this voyage easily persuaded the first Indian they met of their friendliness, gave him a shirt, a hat, "and some other things and made him taste of our wine and our meat, which he liked very well."[8] The Indian quickly repaid the white men with a large quantity of fresh fish.

The following day, the Indian fisherman returned, bringing several boatloads of tribesmen with him, including the "brother of the king." Barlow found the Indians "very handsome and goodly people and in their behavior as mannerly and civil as any of Europe." The English were invited ashore, where they met the king, expressed friendliness, and returned to trade with the Indians, "exchanging some things that [they] had for chamois, buff, and deerskins." Of all the things the sailors had to offer in trade, the Indian king most liked a "bright tin dish . . . he presently took up and clapped it before his breast and after made a hole in the brim thereof and hung it about his neck, making signs that it would defend him against his enemies' arrows."[9]

Barlow reported that two or three days later the king's brother came aboard the ship to eat and drink with the sailors. A few days later still he returned to the ship, bringing his wife, his daughter, and two or three little children. Barlow judged the wife "very well favored, of mean stature and very bashful." Fascinated by her dress, Barlow wrote: "She had on her back a long cloak of leather with the fur side next to her body and before her a piece of the same. About her forehead she had a broad band of white coral and so had her husband many times. In her ears she had bracelets of pearls, hanging down to her middle and those were of the bigness of good peas."[10]

Other women, he observed, also wore pendants of copper hanging in their ears, "and some of the children of the king's brother and other noblemen have five or six in every ear." The king, though he wore a broad hat of copper or gold, dressed in a manner similar to the women, "only the women wear their hair long on both sides and the men but on one."[11]

The women, organized and supervised by the king's brother's wife, invited the sailors ashore, washed and dried their clothing, and laid a feast of meat, fruit, and vegetables before them. Regardless of their assessment of the sartorial habits of the natives, Barlow and his men expressed appreciation for the good manners and generosity of the people as they left to continue their journey of exploration.

Medicine man — flyer.
The blackbird attached to
the magician's head identifies
him as the possessor of
magical powers. He wears a
loincloth made of skins,
the head of a beast still attached,
and carries the tools of his trade
in a fringed pouch attached
to his waistband.

At the next stop, Raleigh's sailors met Indians "who wondered marvelously when we were amongst them at the whiteness of our skins, ever coveting to touch our breasts and to view the same." These and other reports that emphasized the friendly nature and generosity of the natives and recounted the possibilities for trade, published and widely read in Europe, helped Raleigh enlist colonists to settle in Virginia. By and large, the early colonists expected the Indians to be "most courteous and very desirous to have clothes, but especially of coarse cloth rather than silk; coarse canvas they also like well, but copper carrieth the price of all, so it be made red."[12]

Thomas Harriet, a mathematician and scientist who had tutored Raleigh in navigation, accompanied John White on a second voyage in 1585, intending to prepare and publish a scientific account of the New World. Harriet's subsequent *Brief and True Report of the New Found Land of Virginia* contained attractive descriptions of goods that might be exported profitably from America for the benefit of England, including worm silk. He wrote:

In many of our journeys we found silkworms fair and great, as big as our ordinary walnuts. . . . [T]he country doth naturally breed and nourish them, there is no doubt but if art be added in planting of mulberry trees and others fit for them, in commodious places, for their feeding and nourishing, and some of them carefully gathered and husbanded in that sort as by men of skill is known to be necessary, there will rise as great profit in time to the Virginians as thereof doth now to the Persians, Turks, Italians, and Spaniards.[13]

In time, Virginia colonists, among their many efforts to find an exportable commodity that would yield quick and sizable profit, did attempt silkworm cultivation. But despite trained French workers brought to Jamestown to cultivate silkworms and produce silk, the promised abundance of mulberry trees in the Virginia climate notwithstanding, the experiment failed and the colonists continued to import silk along with other fineries.

Harriet took pains to write "of the nature and manners of the people," insisting that "they are not to be feared, but that they shall have cause both to fear and love us that shall inhabit with them." He described the Virginia Indians as wearing "loose mantles made of deerskins and aprons of the same round about their middles, all else naked," and as being, like English people, of varying heights. Without iron or steel, the Indians depended

11

Indian couple eating from shared bowl

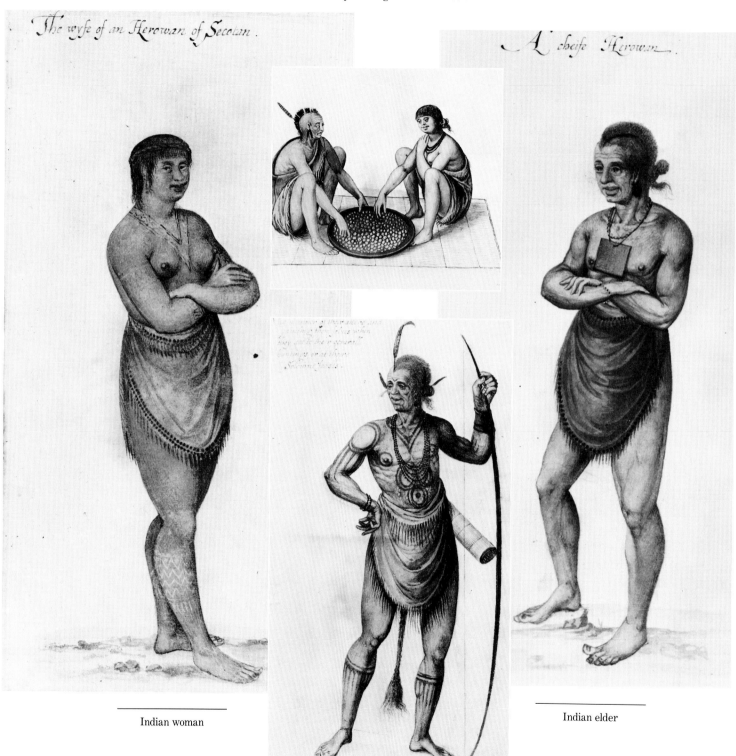

12

Indian woman

Indian with war paint

Indian elder

on bows and arrows. Describing Indian pantheism, Harriet reminded potential missionaries — who, along with colonists seeking to extend empire and wealth, would go to the New World to convert the Indians to Christianity — that "some religion they have already, which although it be far from the truth, yet being as it is there is hope it may be the easier and sooner reformed."[14] Still, few Europeans — missionary or layman — were prepared to acknowledge profound spirituality, let alone an acceptable religion, among the savages who, among other insults to the European God, persisted in nakedness.

Native Americans, tattooed and clad in skins and grasses, generous and friendly toward the first explorers, saw the bearded European men — women were not included in the great adventure until many years later — dressed in the clothes of their countries, religions, and stations in life. Even without narrative accounts of these first sightings of Europeans, we can be certain that the Indians found their dress and general appearance bizarre. Nonetheless, from all accounts, the Indians seem to have been willing to accept the Europeans and offer them hospitality, but they were also eager for every opportunity to investigate the strange bodies and clothing of their invaders.

The Indians saw men wearing the armor and carrying the lethal weapons that accompanied Renaissance dress. Men of means wore richly embellished garments of brocades, satins, taffetas, and velvets, colored by a treasury of dyes made from madder, henna, saffron, and indigo, and further enhanced by the skills of braid-makers, embroiderers, and tailors capable of cutting and fitting the fashions of the day.

Indians and Europeans alike, differing in fashion but not intention, bejeweled themselves ornately; each group displayed the signs and symbols of power and status, and each group found the other exotic; neither group understood the significance of the other's badges and emblems of status.

In those first years when Native Americans met European men, attitudes and issues regarding race, gender, and class were symbolized in clothing; the "languages" of clothing were different for each race, but — as today — the statements were apparent to those who could read them. The story of people in the land that became the United States has been evident in their clothing, which from the beginning has served to articulate the values stitched into the fabric of American civilization. Just as clothing reflected and symbolized the values of Native Americans and Europeans in the early years of European exploration of the New World, clothing also dramatized the tragedy of ethnocentricity and of the cultural clash between the different races.

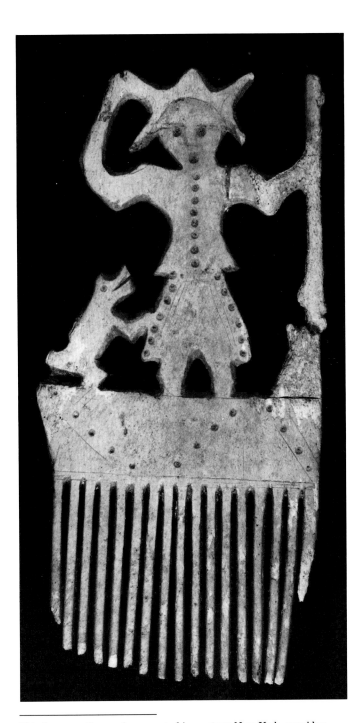

This Seneca antler comb, excavated in western New York, provides an Indian view of a Dutchman. As in other rare examples of Indian renderings of Europeans, clothing classifies the Dutch subject; here the white man wears the hat, buttoned jacket, and pantaloons edged with buttons characteristic of men's clothing in Holland during the seventeenth century. A small dog tries to attract the musket-bearing man's attention.

13

CHAPTER 2

The Seventeenth Century
Mixing Cultures

Competition for the New World grew swiftly. While the Spanish had staked early claim to territories in the Americas, the French, English, and Dutch in turn soon found it advantageous to claim and develop areas of the rich land. Simultaneously, colonial America absorbed Europeans seeking religious freedom, personal wealth, and political security for the enactment of their dreams of a perfect society.

The Church of England colonies in Virginia and the Puritan colonies of New England brought different aspects of English culture to the New World; Lord Baltimore (George Calvert) and William Penn, both English, established colonies of Catholics and Quakers respectively. The Dutch brought still other attitudes and values; each group brought characteristic clothing and, moreover, skills and crafts related to making and maintaining clothing.

Taxation, sumptuary laws, religious belief, and economic realities in each colony, as well as the settlers' pursuit or rejection of Europe's high fashion, influenced clothing in the various colonies during these years. Colonial America was indeed composed of distinct and separate groups who, notwithstanding similarities of indigenous materials available and hardships obtaining in the unfamiliar land and climate, were slow to change the manner of dress they had learned in their homelands. Their rigid adherence to familiar styles resulted in the variety of dress worn in America in the early years of settlement; in turn, the resulting energy and richness of motif contributed to the larger parade of American clothing.

Many would-be settlers read the descriptions of the Indians, their dress and social customs, and read also of the extravagant riches to be had in the New World: the fertile soil, waters teeming with fish, plentiful game and fowl, benign climate, and countless opportunities to acquire wealth. The first European men in the New World — the explorers, trappers, navigators, the naturalist-artists, the swashbucklers, pirates, and soldiers of fortune — only observed and reported the dress habits of the Indians; they and other settlers would later learn from American Indians how to tan deer hide for clothing and shelter and to make moccasins.[1] Similarly, the Indians found it advantageous for a variety of reasons to adopt articles and aspects of European dress. And everyone — European settler and Indian alike — made clothing from substances available to them.

From the beginning of colonization in America, dress varied among the settlers according to gender, national origin, class, religion, and other factors. By popular custom, New England settlers have been described as tending toward plain dress, and Virginians who could afford to do so as copying the dress of the rich English classes, but both trends have been romanticized and stereotyped over the years, and neither view is full or accurate.

In the first years of colonization, the settlers faced the harsh reality of life in the American wilderness. Having survived the hazardous crossing of the Atlantic Ocean, they soon encountered Indians who, pressed by the invaders into territorial wars among themselves and into fear for their lives and habits, became increasingly hostile. Further, scarcity of food, harsh winters, malarial swamps, insects, poisonous snakes, and other hardships threatened the Europeans. Many settlers had come from poverty, prisons, and unadvantageous positions within affluent families, dreaming of worldly riches or of otherworldly

---

William Penn, despite his admonitions against opulence, dressed in lavish materials and enjoyed rich worldly settings. When the Quakers first settled in the New World, they did not distinguish themselves by a characteristic uniform. Later, after years of agreement on the nature and style of "plain dress," the Quakers would be known for their uniform clothing.

reward resulting from service to religious goals, and they expected to transpose familiar styles of living to the conditions of the New World. Moreover, they expected to bend the Indians to their ways quickly, and to exploit them for their purposes.

In 1602, his initial efforts to found a colony, on Roanoke Island off the coast of Virginia, having ended in mysterious failure in 1587, Sir Walter Raleigh sent another group to establish an English colony in North America. Captain Bartholomew Gosnold navigated his small bark around the New England waters, reaching what is now Cape Cod, Nantucket, and Martha's Vineyard, and establishing a temporary settlement on Cuttyhunk Island in Buzzards Bay. Gosnold's group traded with the Indians, loaded a cargo of furs and sassafras roots, and returned home after deciding that neither their number nor their provisions enabled them to attempt a permanent colony. John Brereton, a member of the group, published his report of the investigation of coastal North America, one of the earliest English eyewitness accounts of New England.*

Brereton described an encounter with six Indians who at one point stood on the shore watching the voyagers put down anchor and then sailed in a small boat out to greet the strangers. He was astonished to find that one of the Indians "wore a waistcoat and breeches of black serge, made after our sea fashion, hose and shoes on his feet." Another wore blue breeches; all the rest were naked. According to Brereton, the Indians were tall, grim-looking, and dark-skinned with eyebrows painted white. Other Indians were described as tall and big-boned, "all naked, saving they cover their privy parts with a black, tewed skin, much like a blacksmith's apron, tied about their middle and between their legs behind."[2]

Several days later, the English would-be settlers met a group of Indians, "became very great friends," and traded with them for "furs, which are beavers, martens, otters, wild-cat skins, very large and deep fur, black foxes, cony [rabbit] skins of the color of our hares but somewhat [smaller], deerskins very large, sealskins, and other beasts' skins to us unknown."[3]

Brereton admired the copper chains, earrings, and collars that the Indians wore, noting that

their chains are many hollow pieces cemented together, each piece of the bigness of one of our reeds, a finger in length, ten or twelve of them together on a string, which they wear about their necks. Their collars they wear about their bodies like bandoleers a handful broad, all hollow pieces like the other but somewhat shorter, four hundred pieces in a collar, very fine and evenly set together.[4]

By and large, two waves of colonization, in Virginia and New England, established twelve of the thirteen colonies. During the period, instances of racial conflict born of European ethnocentricity (including a widespread religious conviction that white people were superior to other races) established the tradition of the white people's shameful mistreatment and injustice to Native Americans.

In 1607, George Percy, a "gentleman adventurer," after feasting with Indians on the southeastern coast, watching them dance, and appreciating their physical beauty, described their unfamiliar — and to him, savage — ways:

They hang through their ears fowls' legs; they shave the right side of their heads with a shell; and the left side they wear of an ell long, tied up with an artificial knot, with a many of fowls' feathers sticking in it. They go altogether naked, but their privities are covered with beasts' skins, beset commonly with little bones or beasts' teeth. Some paint their bodies black, some red, with artificial knots of sundry lively colors, very beautiful and pleasing to the eye. . . .[5]

Later, Percy met an Indian prince and his followers, who were

as goodly men as I have ever seen of savages or Christians, the wereowance [prince or king] coming before them playing on a flute made of a reed, with a crown of deer's hair colored red, in fashion of a rose, fastened about his knot of hair, and a great plate of copper on the other side of his head, with two long feathers in fashion of a pair of horns placed in the midst of his crown. His body was painted all with crimson, with a chain of beads about his neck, his face painted blue, besprinkled with silver ore, as we thought, his ears all behung with bracelets of pearl, and in either ear a bird's claw through it, beset with fine copper or gold.[6]

---

*John Brereton, *A Brief and True Relation of the Discoverie of the North Part of Virginia . . . Made This Present Year 1602 by Captain Bartholomew Gosnold, Captain Bartholomew Gilbert, and Divers Other Gentlemen Their Associates by Permission of . . . Sir Walter Raleigh . . .* (1602)

The women of this tribe, according to Percy, like other Indian women observed by earlier explorers, decorated their bodies with raised, brightly colored, and highly complicated tattoos. "[W]ith a sharp iron, which makes a stamp . . . which will never be taken away, because it is dried into the flesh where it is seared," they drew fishes, fowls, beasts, and a variety of decorative patterns over "their bodies, legs, thighs, arms, and faces."[7]

But amid the reports of friendly savages bizarrely dressed and given to odd practices, a few sinister notes began to sound. Captain John Smith's accounts of his troubles with the Indians foretold future strife and enmity. Like others who discovered the New World, Smith, the leader of the colony at Jamestown, was astonished by the richness of nature, and noted that the Indians were "great and well proportioned men" whose

attire is the skins of bears and wolves; some have cassocks made of bears' heads and skins that a man's head goes through the skin's neck and the ears of the bear fastened to his shoulders, the nose and teeth hanging down his breast, another bear's face split behind them, and at the end of the nose hung a paw; the half sleeves coming to the elbows were the necks of bears and the arms through the mouth, with paws hanging at their noses. One had the head of a wolf hanging in a chain for a jewel. . . .[8]

When Smith was held captive by the Indians and was uncertain of his fate, he was required to sit before a fire in a longhouse. There he encountered an Indian,

a great grim fellow, all painted over with coal mingled with oil, and many snakes and weasels' skins stuffed with moss and all their tails tied together, so they met on the crown of his head in a tassel; and round about the tassel was a [headdress] of feathers, the skins hanging round about his head, back and shoulders, and in a manner covered his face.

"With a hellish voice and a rattle in his hand," the Indian danced and chanted.[9]

In 1610, William Strachey was appointed governor of the Virginia colony; like his countrymen who had explored and settled the region earlier, he wrote about his experiences, putting forth "a true description of the people; of their color, constitution, and disposition; their apparel." Noting appreciatively their brown, or tawny, color, Strachey speculated that the custom among the Indians of body-painting might have originated as a means for

repelling insects. Their hair, he noted, was black and straight, their faces beardless. "They are generally tall of stature and straight, of comely proportions, and the women have handsome limbs, slender arms, and pretty hands; and when they sing they have a delightful and pleasant tang in their voices."[10]

Indian clothing, however, was to Strachey less appealing than their physical qualities:

They are sometimes covered with the skins of wild beasts, which in winter are dressed with the hair but in the summer without. The better sort use large mantles of divers skins, not much differing from the Irish faldings, some embroidered with white beads, some with copper, others painted after their manner; but the common sort have scarce wherewithal to cover their nakedness but stick long blades of grass, the leaves of trees, or such-like under broad baldrics of leather, which covers them behind and before.[11]

He noted that the finely dressed skin mantles of higher-caste women were worn with shagged and fringed skirts and painted with "some pretty works or the proportions of beasts, fowl, tortoises, or other such-like imagery as shall best please or express the fancy of the wearer."[12]

Preadolescent girls, he observed, ran naked and without shame. Pocahontas, "a well-featured but wanton young girl, Powhatan's daughter, sometimes . . . got the boys forth . . . and made them wheel, falling on their hands, turning their heels upwards." Once past twelve years of age, however, Pocahontas, like other Indian maidens, wore "a leather apron before [her] belly and was very shamefaced to be seen bare."[13]

Like others who recorded observations of Indian dress, Strachey described the use of beads, tattoos, and all-over body painting with a sticky substance that allowed the Indians to add "the soft down feathers of the carnation [cardinal] bird . . . as if so many variety of laces were stitched to their skins, which makes a wondrous show."[14]

Strachey saw Indian men in ceremonial dress, wearing on their heads deer antlers, copper ornaments, dried hawks' wings, and a variety of skins and feathers. "Their ears," he wrote, "they bore with wide holes, commonly two or three" and hung with chains of copper; or inserted fowls' legs and hangings made of bears' teeth or the claws of small beasts. "And some of their men there be who will wear in these holes a small green-and-yellow colored live snake, near half a yard in length, which, crawling

17

and lapping himself about his neck, oftentimes familiarly he suffers to kiss his lips; others wear a dead rat tied by the tail. . . ."[15]

Waves of settlers came to the New World dreaming of the vast riches and friendly natives described by the first explorers. Meanwhile, many Indian tribes had been uprooted, and their lands settled by Europeans. As dislodged Indians were forced to encroach on the lands of other tribes, disputes grew into tribal wars. Increased friction between white settlers and Native Americans over land ownership resulted in new violence, and soon European fear of Indians had surpassed what began as fascination. White missionaries, serving the purposes of state as well as church, sought to convert Native Americans to Christianity, and to render them peaceable. They also attempted, for the benefit of the settlers, to identify the "safe" Indians by persuading them to symbolize their conversion by cutting their hair and donning European garb.

Over the years of Christian proselytization, letters from the missionaries recount difficulty in persuading the Indians to adapt the cumbersome European style of clothing, which, in addition to being uncomfortable and unfamiliar, had the disadvantage of impeding the wearer's passage through the forest in pursuit of game. (The Indians' light moccasins and breechcloths had allowed them to move swiftly, silently, through dense undergrowth and thick forests.) Moreover, for the many male Indians who customarily squatted to urinate, the European breeches offered only a ludicrous impediment to natural function. By the end of the nineteenth century, the Native Americans, in a desperate attempt to preserve Indian tradition, would adopt the white man's clothing but with varying degrees of modification.

As Europeans claimed land in the New World, Indians were slowly forced to change their patterns of living. As time would show, the first quarter of the seventeenth century marked the beginning of the end of aboriginal life in the New World. During the colonial period, the style was set for Indian treatment at the hands of white people, and clothing carried symbolic significance for both Indians and white settlers, as it reflected the currents of cross-culturalization and the ubiquitous powers of fear and chauvinism.

Conversion to Christianity, the missionaries assured the Indians, promised riches in the life after death as well as the immediate rewards of material goods, including warm and protective clothing. But Christianity required a complete change in Indian life that to the missionary and his sponsors seemed an improvement but to the Indian was a confusing and sad loss of identity and custom.

Free-running and indulged children of Indian converts, under the new social order, had to obey their fathers, respect their elders, wear constraining clothes, and attend to appointed chores as if they were the hardworking children of the English colonials. Peaceful wives with their own interests and powers in Indian society, when converted, subordinated themselves to their husbands; they had to give up their hoes and outdoor work to take up sweeping the hearth, spinning, and the arts of housewifery as defined by the English. The Indian fathers and husbands who enrolled in Christian society were required to dominate the family, and to turn from the honored and sustaining pursuits of fishing and hunting to the supposed stability of agriculture.

Moreover, every converted Indian — male and female, adult and child — had to cover his or her nakedness. No longer were Indian limbs free to move and breasts bare to the air and light; bodies were to be covered to meet English colonial standards of modesty. American Indians, converted and civilized, dressed in closely fitted fashions brought to the New World from urban or peasant Europe. Long Indian hair, shaped to communicate proud accomplishments and tribal standing, was cut. Hard cobbled shoes replaced supple, silent moccasins.

When the Jesuits converted Kittamaquund, in Maryland, "he exchanged his skin garments for clothes made in the English fashion, and made some effort to learn the English language." He also repudiated his many wives and accepted monogamy. But not all of the Indians who converted to Christianity embraced spiritual conversion or cultural modification. Colonials joked about the "wheat and eel" Christians, those Indians who nodded acquiescence to Christianity in exchange for liquor, tobacco, and clothing, and, though costumed as European peasants, continued their Indian ways.[16]

By 1734, a concerted effort was under way to "civilize" the Indians, a process in which the colonists intended to substitute European heritage for Indian religion and customs. A missionary settlement in Stockbridge, Massachusetts, established a school for educating Indian children who were taken from their families and removed from the influences of their tribes; they were dressed as if they were English colonials, and taught to live in the English manner and to speak the English language.

In general and without question, the settlers considered their patterns of life and modes of dress superior to those of the

Indians, and tried diligently to persuade Indians to adopt language, manners, clothing, and styles of life compatible to values and standards shaped in Europe. When diligent pedagogy failed, the settlers often used more forceful means of persuasion. It was, in their minds, God's cause.

Jamestown and the Virginia Colonies

In 1606, the Virginia Company, a private venture capital group in London, with a charter from the Crown, financed colonists who were instructed to find gold, to locate the Northwest Passage, and to provide valuable commodities to strengthen English commerce. The settlers sailed for the New World anticipating a paradisiacal bounty of food, wild fowl, and game, assuming that they would take possession of land, build houses, and establish lucrative trade with the Indians. Some expected to engage the Indians in work for wages of trifling baubles, or, if necessary, as forced laborers. Descriptions of American Indians that had come from the earlier explorers suggested a bizarre, primitive, but essentially peaceful and friendly lot.

Most of the settlers themselves wore European clothing that reflected their status, occupation, and wealth in their homelands. While some came to the New World outfitted with clothes deemed suitable for the travails anticipated, few were fully prepared for the conditions of life in the New World. Even fewer recognized that Indian clothing, in addition to serving symbolic tribal functions, included features particularly appropriate to the conditions of the New World.

Typically, with variation according to homeland or religious conviction, European men brought breeches and frock coats, Monmouth caps, woolen shirts and socks, boots, and handkerchiefs. Women, when they finally began to arrive in the late sixteenth century, brought cumbersome dresses with full skirts, laced bodices over low-cut blouses, capes, petticoats, and aprons.

Once in the New World, industrious colonial women worked long hours to make clothing for their families, and they followed the familiar styles and patterns of Europe. They grew plants for fibers and raised sheep for wool; they carded, spun, and wove fibers and wool into cloth; and they sewed cloth into garments, which they then had to patch and mend and launder as necessary — an unending round of jobs to maintain clothing for large families engaged in hard work, tasks all the more onerous for being entirely done by hand.

Clothes were handed down, made over, and used to their extinction. In those poor years hardworking wives and mothers tolerated little waste, cutting up worn-out garments and stitching the pieces into new life as patchwork quilts. That practice means that virtually no clothing worn by working people from this period exists today; the few garments preserved were worn by richer people.

The early colonists' records and recollections of settling the Virginia region bear little resemblance to the later popular romantic evocations of grand houses, parties, balls, and fine clothes. The life of planters in Virginia began, according to Captain John Smith, with fifty-two "gentlemen adventurers," a preacher, two doctors ("chirurgeons"), four carpenters, twelve laborers, a blacksmith, a sailor, a drummer, four boys, and some others; Smith lamented the preponderance of gentlemen adventurers over men with vital skills.

The Virginia Company sent the men out to the colonies and advised them to provide specific clothing for themselves, the inventory of which today recounts a man's essential wardrobe of the period: a Monmouth cap, three shirts, one suit of canvas, four pairs of shoes, three falling bands, one waistcoat, one suit of

19

frieze, one suit of broadcloth, three pairs of silk stockings, and one dozen pairs of points.

These articles of clothing constituted the uniform, as prescribed by the Virginia Company, for the settlers, and soon became the standard dress for white males in the colonies. The costume may not have been the most practical for the small landholders and indentured servants who struggled to survive, and to plant and cultivate crops that would be financially rewarding, but such clothes, in their reckoning, marked them as superior to the Indians, and superior men of European origin were entitled by natural law to land and prosperity.

Even so, survival was a more immediate issue than fashion, and survival required economic well-being in addition to health, shelter, and safety. The planters needed something to grow; they needed a crop that would provide a steady and predictable income for them. In the 1560s, Sir John Hawkins had introduced the use of tobacco — a plant long used among the Indians — to England, where its popularity would make it the paying crop the planters needed. But long before it was condemned for health reasons, tobacco was not an unmixed blessing; it exhausted land quickly, requiring continual expansions of even large landholdings, and it required extensive labor of the most gruelling sort.

As the Virginia colony expanded, with the arrival of additional settlers, lumbermen, vintners, metalworkers, and the poor of England came to Virginia. All were subject to disease, crop failures, and the debilitation brought about by unending hard work; those living on the fringes of the settlement risked massacre by Indians.

At the end of the seventeenth century, however, a general improvement in colonial life resulted in the possibility of more abundant clothing for most people, and more elegant and luxurious clothing for the few wealthy Americans. In the blush of newly gained riches, a number of colonists displayed their earthly garments, causing the fathers of church and state (at a time when those entities had not been separated by constitutional government) to institute sumptuary laws that were ostensibly intended to offset the tendency of mortals toward the sin of excesses in dress, hairdos, and bodily adornment. In fact, sumptuary laws in the American colonies stipulated clothing according to class, prohibiting those of lower social caste from appropriating finery reserved for the rich and powerful.

America in its infancy, as today, was not a classless society; despite efforts to guarantee religious freedom and to institute democratic processes of government, class definition and related social power significantly influenced the quality and tone of life

in the early American colonies. Clothing, more than any other single entity, symbolized status, wealth, and profession.

At one point, the members of Virginia's House of Burgesses, themselves splendidly adorned and bewigged in the manner of the English House of Commons, passed a series of laws on clothing, including a tax: "Be it embraced that for all public contributions every unmarried man must be assessed in church according to his apparel and every married man must be assessed according to his own and his wife's apparel."[17]

In 1660, Virginia sumptuary law prevented importation of "silke stuffe in garments or in peeces except for whoods and scarfs, nor silver or gold lace, nor bone lace of silk or threads, nor ribbands wrought with gold or silver in them." But such prohibitions notwithstanding, the colonists sought both rich materials and trendy fashions of the day. As the lawmakers and other prosperous males in the Jamestown settlement turned themselves out in London fashions, poorer men did their best to approximate the splendor of the richer colonists. Individuals of both sexes and all classes seem to have attempted to emulate the jaunty and grand style we associate with portraits by the Flemish painter Van Dyck.

The more affluent men often wore short cloaks, or *piccadilles*, over slashed doublets, which, in turn, covered linen shirts. (The name of Piccadilly Street, in London, is thought to be the result of its having been the location of a row of shops devoted to producing *piccadilles*.) Breeches were both fringed and pointed; even boots were decorated with ruffles of lace or softened leather. Rakishly worn hats, the broad-brimmed Flemish beaver with a rich hatband, often flaunted a romantic plume of feathers. This dash and grandeur of the cavalier was further emphasized by swords swung from elaborate baldrics draped from the right shoulder. For somber occasions, when men were required to display their influence and dignity, the wealthy among them wore a luxuriously laced buff coat, sometimes embroidered with gold or silver, and further embellished by a silk or satin scarf tied by a bow over or behind the hip.

During the colonial period, men wore jackets of four basic types: doublet, vest, peascod, and jerkin; all save the jerkin were filled with bombast, a stuffing of seed, straw, or fabric designed both to protect the wearer from the weapons of enemies and to add girth to his silhouette. But men who chose companions carelessly, or provoked rancor, were likely to lose their stuffing — their bombast — and thus to be diminished in bulk and respect.

The breeches of the day — with stylized puffing and slashing said to have originated as a commemorative gesture for soldiers reduced after the Battle of Grandsome (1476) to forming clothing from strips of available material — consisted of two sections joined in the middle by a padded fastening flap, or codpiece. Codpieces, censured by the church, both held the two halves of the breeches together and provided a means for vaunting male sexual organs. European men displayed a variety of sizes and shapes of exaggerated codpieces surrounded by swollen and stuffed breeches, and the early explorers and settlers wore such garments to the shores of the New World.

Workingmen of the colonies, unable to afford the finery of the gentlemen adventurers and requiring clothing that did not interfere with labor, wore loose baggy breeches, pullover loose-fitting blouses, and jerkins of canvas or frieze. Their hose were made of coarse wool, and their shoes of tanned leather tied in the front. Their hats were fabricated from thrums or felt. This laborer's uniform was also worn in Europe at the time.

Almost every colonial workingman wore a long, strong leather apron over his clothing, a garment also seen on Europeans of the period. In North America, however, the Indians taught the settlers to tan deerskin, a plentiful commodity, and to use it for leather aprons and other articles of clothing. Deerskin clothing offered distinct advantages for the colonists: it was tough but supple, comfortable and durable; its coloration provided camouflage for hunters stalking game in the woods.

Women of the period, regardless of class membership, wore costumes similar in cut and styling, but the richer women wore clothing made of finer materials and the poorer women had to settle for homemade linsey-woolsey. The dress for women consisted of a long skirt, a low-cut bodice with square-cut tabs about the waist, and full sleeves that ballooned beneath the elbows and ended in soft lace ruffles encircling the wrists. Women usually covered their shoulders with a wide collar, but they left bare their throats and necks.

Stockings for men, women, and children were made of silk, wool, or cotton thread. The shoes worn by men were usually made of ordinary leather, and the shoe buckles were manufactured of brass, steel, or silver. In the literature of the era there are many references to boots, the popular footwear of the planters who spent much of their time on horseback or walking and required sturdy, protective, and comfortable footwear.

Several inventories of the period include references to serge breeches lined with linen or worsted and fastened with thread buttons; occasionally there are references to calamanco breeches with hair buttons. Rarely, whole suits, often olive-colored, were made of plush, broadcloth, kersey, or canvas, but more often the coat was made of drugget and the waistcoat and breeches of stuff cloth. Men prized lace and silk handkerchiefs for fancy occasions but commonly used those made of blue linen.

Wealthier Virginians ordered their clothing from England, maintaining the symbols of class distinction in their adherence to fashion. But most of the farmers and their families wore homemade clothing or items available from a local merchant.

All in all, and despite the requirements of work and climate in the New World, the typical dress of English colonists in the southeastern settlements resembled that worn in their homeland.

The New England Colonies

New England's early settlers came from the Puritan sect that, decrying the moral corruption throughout English life and the taint of Roman Catholicism on the Church of England, crossed the Atlantic to avoid persecution and to establish a community that would allow them to live in strict consonance with the teachings of the New Testament. They sought simpler religious services and a less hierarchical form of government but, though differing among themselves on matters of church governance, did not separate the powers of church and state. As early settlers in America, the Puritans and the Pilgrims (a still stricter separatist group derived from the Puritan movement) thus intermingled the teachings of the church with the laws governing their communities, a practice that found expression in, among other aspects of life, the sumptuary laws of New England as well as those of the Virginia colonies.

The first English settlers in Massachusetts, the Pilgrims, arrived in December 1620. They stepped ashore at Plymouth wearing clothing that, though somber in color and without decorative knots or embellishments or lace, resembled the fashions worn at the court of Charles I. The 104 Pilgrims included 2 carpenters, a fustian worker and silk dyer, a lady's maid, 2 printers and publishers, a tailor, a wool carder, a cooper, a merchant, 4 seamen, a soldier, 2 tradesmen, 10 adult servants, a lay reader, a hatter, a physician, and a smith.

The Puritans, less austere than the Pilgrims, came to the New World with financial backing from the powerful Massachusetts Bay Company. Better clothed and richer than their Pilgrim brothers and sisters, they settled in Salem.

Seventeenth-century clothing worn by both groups in Massachusetts, despite an abundance of sumptuary laws equaled in number only by the frequent capers in defiance of them, was for the most part plainly wrought of practical materials, and repre-

21

sented sensible response to economy and weather as well as to the prevailing religious teachings. Poverty, however, and not sumptuary laws determined what the multitude of settlers in New England wore, as they struggled merely to provide clothing that would protect them from the elements and secure their modesty. Like their southern counterparts, they wore into extinction their Hampshire kerseys, their Monmouth and red knit caps. If they were fortunate, they had mandilions, fastened with hooks and eyes, to wrap themselves against blustery storms; if they were not blessed with such a serviceable wrap, they sheathed themselves in ragged combinations of clothing and blankets, often binding their feet — whether over or in lieu of shoes — with lengths of woolen cloth.

Poorer women dressed typically in homespun petticoats, short camlet gowns, and long white aprons. For warmth and modesty, they made mittens that left the fingers bare but covered the hands and arms to the elbow. Their short cloaks had attached hoods that could be pushed back for social gatherings. At home, women often wore small caps, sometimes decorated modestly. But women in the New England upper class, eager to appear in the latest English fashions, cherished brocades and silks, furs for trimming cloaks and hoods, and any other ornament to display wealth and station.

During these early years in Massachusetts, numerous efforts were made to control individual tendencies toward the sin of opulence. In 1634, the Massachusetts General Court, driven by Puritan standards, forbade the purchase of "any apparell, either woolen, silke, or lynnen with any lace on it, silver, golde, silk, or thread."[18]

Such restrictions on materials, however, did not prevent the general display of finery, and the courts soon established laws restricting the style of clothing people might wear, preventing indulgence in fashionable grandeur by forbidding ordinary citizens to "make or buy slashed clothes, other than [those with] one slash in each sleeve and another in the back . . . there shall be no cutt works embroid'd or needle work'd capps, bands, and Rayles; no gold or silver girdles, hatt bands, belts, ruffs, beaver hatts."[19]

The sumptuary laws did not limit the taste of all citizens, but, as intended by the lawmakers, served to further separation and visual distinction among classes. Under such laws, clothing served to identify those persons of power and prestige in the community. The laws were invoked, therefore, to suppress ostentation on the part of people not entitled by wealth and rank to finery; those persons with estates of less than two hundred pounds were strictly prohibited from wearing fine dress.

In Newbury, in 1635, two women were assessed taxes for wearing silken hoods and scarves, but upon proving that their husbands owned two hundred pounds they were released. In 1636, the wearing of lace was forbidden save for a very small binding on the edging of linen.

In 1639, the Massachusetts court declared its "utter detestation and dislike" of men and women of "mean condition, education, and calling" who would wear the "garb of gentlemen." They prohibited Puritan men of low estate from wearing "immoderate great breeches, knots of riban, silk roses, double ruffles and capes," and forbade women of lower ranks to wear silk hoods and scarves, or short sleeves "whereby the nakedness of the arms may be discovered."[20]

The sumptuary laws served to order society perhaps more practically than they effected their stated purposes of promoting morality and preventing sin, but not all citizens adopted Puritan standards with equal zeal, and some enjoyed the mischief of flaunting their fine clothing. In Salem, for example, in 1652, a man was "presented for excess of bootes, ribands, gould and silver laces, and Ester Jenks for wearing silver lace."[21]

22

In 1675, in Connecticut, thirty-eight women were charged with wearing clothing deemed beyond their social station. One defendant, a young girl, was accused specifically of "wearing silk in a flaunting manner, in an offensive way and garb not only before but when she stood presented." During the same period, thirty young men were arrested for wearing silk and long hair. The Puritans kept proper distinctions between the sexes, and Massachusetts forbade men to wear long hair — "the manifest pride openly appearing amongst us in that long hair, like women's hair, is worn by some men, either their own or others' hair made into periwigs." Hannah Lyman and a group of other young women in Northampton, Massachusetts, fell into trouble with the courts when, in 1676, they were arrested for overdressing (they wore hoods). Hannah, defiant rather than contrite in court, was censured and fined. Thus, through a series of proscriptive laws promulgated by courts that combined the authority of church and state, the Puritans established an American dress code in the first half of the seventeenth century, and they affirmed that theirs was not a classless society.[22]

Puritans were also diligent in policing modesty and morals among their members. In 1679, a Puritan synod, noting the rise in the incidence of bastardy, and an attempt to establish a brothel in Boston, laid part of the blame on clothing, commenting on the sinful visibility of necks and arms "or, which is more abominable, naked Breasts."[23]

Even so, many upper-class Puritan women's tastes were influenced by eagerly sought news of fashions in Europe, and they exposed arms and breasts in the latest fashions they could afford, wearing tiffany hoods, broad-brimmed hats, silk, and lace. Poorer women embroidered clothing, a relatively small indulgence in opulence, and adopted as many fashionable aspects of clothing as their budgets would support.

True believers among the Puritans viewed clothing as the outward evidence of the inner spirit, and they dressed in an honest and simple manner, hiding their nakedness, at once denying voluptuousness and waste. In 1638, the Massachusetts General Court, vigilant against even the slight tendency toward nudity that bare female arms might suggest, ruled: "No garment shall be made with short sleeves, and such as have garments made with short sleeves shall not wear the same unless they cover arm to wrist; and hereafter no person whatever shall make any garment for women with sleeves more than half an ell wide."[24]

During the seventeenth century, children were dressed like their parents. Little bodies in rich families, limited in freedom of movement, were shaped by uncomfortable materials and fashions, by stomachers, ruffles, lace, necklaces of pearls, and other displays of finery; poorer children, dressed in the simpler and more practical styles and materials of their parents, enjoyed somewhat greater freedom.

Alice Morse Earle, an historian of Early American clothing, observed that available infants' clothing consisted of the "better sort" of garments, not everyday articles of clothing but ceremonial items such as christening robes, finer shirts, and caps and petticoats. Displaying her prejudice for wool as the only suitably warm substance for children's clothing, she wrote:

23

left

Gloves, generally made locally, were constructed of yarn or tanned ox, lamb, buck, dog, or sheepskin. These dress-up gloves with gold and silver threads woven through the cuffs, dating from about 1645, were worn by Governor John Leverett of Massachusetts.

above

In this 1673 portrait Sir John Leverett, governor of the Massachusetts Bay Colony, dressed in a buff-colored leather coat with decorative fasteners and a linen falling collar tied with tassels, holds a pair of gentlemen's embroidered gloves. The cavalier-style hat on which his right hand rests would have completed the outfit. The rich and powerful Governor Leverett dressed in the manner of the gentlemen adventurers of the Virginia colonies.

above

This heavy ox-hide coat, made in England, was worn by Governor
John Leverett in the 1673 painting of him. Its original clasps
were made of gold or silver. Garments of this sort were designed originally
to be worn under armor; when it was learned, however, that the
thickness and toughness of the hide alone dulled bullets and blunted
arrowheads, the coat was worn with only a belt and sword.
Bloodstains and holes on the arms and skirts reveal that Leverett may
have been wounded while wearing the garment.

center

These children's garments, finely made of rich materials, were worn
by the offspring of wealthy New Englanders. Their styles
resemble those of adults, however, and reflect the pervasive attitude
of the period that children, in fact, were merely smaller adults.

Colonial tanneries also provided leather for shoes, which were made of leather or fabric; some had wooden soles and heels. Ties and buckles provided opportunity for both men and women to add decoration to footwear. Both shoes in a pair, without regard to differences in left and right feet, were generally built on the same last.

Early in the colonial period Lynn, Massachusetts, developed as a center for making shoes. While the uppers of shoes were commonly leather or fabric, the heels were wooden; shoes were held on the foot with straps and buckles. Women's shoes, more often than men's, were made of fabric — either fine wool or silk. In 1648, the first labor organization, the Shoemakers of Boston, was authorized by the Massachusetts Bay Colony and permitted to meet and elect officers. In 1676, the Massachusetts courts set the price on shoes: "Five pence half penny a size for all pleyne and wooden heel'd shoes, and above seven pence half penny a size for well wrought french falls." (McClellan, p. 95.)

Linen formed the chilling substructure of their dress, thin linen, low-necked, short-sleeved shirts; and linen even formed the underwear of infants until the middle of [the nineteenth] century. These little linen shirts are daintier than the warmest silk or fine woollen underwear that have succeeded them; they are edged with fine narrow-thread lace, hemstitched with tiny rows of stitches, and sometimes embroidered by hand.[25]

The Dutch and New Amsterdam

In 1609, Captain Henry Hudson anchored *The Half Moon* alongside Manhattan Island and directed his English and Dutch sailors in exploration of the contiguous lands. When he returned to the Netherlands and reported that the area teemed with fur-bearing animals, Dutch merchants organized and backed trapping expeditions to the New World. It was not until 1621, however, that Holland chartered the Great West India Company, which, in turn, backed Dutch settlers in the New World.

In 1626, Peter Minuit led colonists, supplied with cattle and household goods, to settle Manhattan. The Dutch settlement planned to enjoy the comforts of home that could be provided by skilled tradesmen and workmen and by women adroit with needle and cloth, clever and frugal in the requirements of housewifery. But despite Washington Irving's later romanticized portrayal of Dutch domestic life, the home was not the driving force behind Dutch life in the New World: the colony developed around the requirements of merchants in search of profits.

Under the Dutch, Manhattan soon became a lively commercial center, profiting from taverns and brothels as well as from trapping and trading. The pleasure-loving and practical Dutch did not impose sumptuary laws, and the settlers enjoyed the styles of clothing that they could afford.

The Dutch traded among themselves, buying and selling the clothing materials they made: raw flax, linen, laces, and linsey-woolsey. Using these and imported goods, the Dutch housewives made most of the clothing worn in the colony.

A Dutch woman, simpler garbed than her European counterpart, probably wore short woolen petticoats and a loose jacket of red cotton or blue Holland, a white kerchief around her shoulders, a long white apron, and a fitted white cap. Wealthier Dutch women dressed in petticoats and loose jackets that reached the knee, their elbow sleeves turned back and faced.

Richer men wore clothing of velvet, satin, and silk trimmed with lace or fur. Peter Stuyvesant, a typically attired rich and powerful man of the time and place, has been described as

25

never otherwise than faultless dressed and always after the most approved European standard. A wide drooping shirt collar fell over a velvet jacket with slashed sleeves displaying full white linen and shirt sleeves. His breeches were also slashed, very full and fastened at the knee by a handsome scarf tied in a knot, and his shoes were ornamented with large rosettes.[26]

Dutch workingmen, with smaller wardrobes of clothing homemade from simpler materials, dressed in accordance with their occupation and rank in society. A Dutch "rattlewatch" in the middle of the seventeenth century was described as wearing his special costume of blue cloth, trimmed in orange. With his lantern and rattles, he patrolled the town by day and night. Other workmen, without benefit of the trappings of public office, dressed in simple homespun suits of linsey-woolsey, hand-knit hose, and Monmouth caps or thrums. Laborers wore red leather aprons. Both men and women of all classes displayed ornate buttons when they could afford them.

Dutch children, unlike the progeny of the English settlers, wore clothing quite different from that worn by their parents. Upon birth, Dutch children were swaddled; that is, they were so tightly bound with strips of soft cloth that they could move neither hands nor feet, and were then placed in an elaborately embroidered pocket, or pouch, which was either laid in a cradle or hung on a nail in the wall. Even the ears of Dutch babies were tightly bound to the head by a close-fitting, tiny cap. Swaddling, or binding, it was believed, protected the infants, set the skeleton for good posture, and promoted health. The color of the frills and ribbons decorating the pouch, cap, and other articles associated with the baby reflected the sex of the child, blue indicating a boy and white a girl.

Pennsylvania and the Society of Friends

The Society of Friends, like the Puritans, separated from the Church of England. Like the Puritans, they were persecuted in England. With a charter from the Crown, in 1681 William Penn led a small band of Quakers — as members of the Society of Friends were called — to the New World, where they founded and shaped Pennsylvania.

When Penn and his group of Quakers came to the New World, they dressed in the old-fashioned way of English working people of the period, a practice that symbolized their objection to the extravagance and decadence of society. Sturdily, practically, and inexpensively clad, the Quakers concentrated on their inner spiritual lives.

But Penn, equally the wealthy and aristocratic son of an English admiral and the spiritual leader of a band of Quakers, wore clothing made of costly materials, drew a bright blue sash around his middle, and chose opulence over simplicity in his personal attire as in his grand home on the banks of the Delaware. His rich style of dressing was matched by the fine furniture and silver, heavy rugs, and curtains that ornamented his stately house. Penn even traveled sumptuously, journeying into town on a twelve-oared barge. His personal preferences, however, did not prevent his urging his followers to live simply, reject all vanity, and attend to the inner spirit.

Penn admonished his followers to save themselves from the dangers of excessive food and drink, luxury of any form, pride, and avarice. In his book *Some Fruits of Solitude*, the Quaker leader advocated simplicity of dress in a chapter devoted to "apparel." He reminded his followers that "excess in apparel is another costly folly," and advised them to "Chuse thy cloaths by thine owne Eyes, not another's. The more plain and simple they are, the better. Neither unshapely, nor fantastical; and for Use and Decency, and not for Pride. If thou are clean and warm," he wrote, "it is sufficient; for more doth but rob the Poor and please the Wanton." In keeping with the Friends' beliefs, Penn affirmed the importance of minds over bodies, adding that "Meekness and Modest are the Rich and Charming Attire of the Soul: and the plainer the Dress, the more Distinctly, and with greater Lustre, their Beauty shines."[27]

Penn's passionate argument against finery, however, never brought him to codify laws or even to make specific suggestions as to appropriate dress for Quakers. Rather, in keeping with the tenets of the religion, he insisted that each Friend, abiding by his or her own conscience, turn from vanity, false pride, and ostentation. In time, the shared observations and discussions of communal living led to a uniform that stressed plainness and simplicity of style rendered in good materials. Eventually, the Friends wore somber colors, and shunned decoration save in the form of silver shoe buckles or a bit of lace. Unlike Penn, his followers translated their religious values into exact standards of dress, and insisted that individual Quakers conform.

By the nineteenth century the Friends had adopted the style of clothing illustrated on the packaging for today's Quaker Oats and now widely identified with the clothing codes of the religious group. This Quaker uniform, however, was born slowly, and not as an immediate consequence of Penn's requirements for his followers. Eventually, Quaker men uniformly wore buckles on shoes and stocks, enjoyed linen ruffles at waist and collar, and favored formal, somber suits. Altogether, they presented a dignified and elegant style of clothing. The austere Quaker hat, derived from those worn at the court of King Charles II, sat level and rigid upon the wearer's head, and was tipped neither to women nor in salute to men of rank.

Quaker women's simple dresses, cloaks, and bonnets were made with lavish care from good, plain fabrics, the effect being both attractive and dignified.

THE QUAKERS MEETING

The Early French Settlers

The first settlers in the areas of Louisiana and the Missouri Valley failed pitifully. Nonetheless, in 1680, under the leadership of René-Robert Cavalier, or Sieur de La Salle, the French set out to claim for France a waterway linking the Atlantic and Pacific oceans, believing that such a passage would provide its owner with great power among nations. "In the Name of Louis the greatest King of France and Navarre, fourteenth of that name," La Salle took possession of a vast area he called Louisiana — "from the mouth of the river St. Louis and along the river

Colbert, or Missouri, from its source beyond the country of the Sioux as far as its mouth."[28]

La Salle, according to records, dressed grandly, even in the wilderness. He appeared at Mass "very well dressed in his scarlet cloak trimmed with gold lace."[29] His followers, unimpressed by the grandeur of his clothing and wearied by the dangers to which he exposed them, mutinied and killed La Salle.

But La Salle had planted France's flag in the New World and, in 1698, Louis XIV sent four ships, with about two hundred colonists, to the territory of Louisiana. The artisans, laborers, adventurers, ex-soldiers, and their families, provided with clothing and other necessities, settled in remote areas of the vast region. In 1704, twenty unmarried women, chaperoned by nuns, also crossed the Atlantic to join the colonists and to marry the bachelors.

The early French settlers dressed in the clothing available to them, a mixture of homemade items and those that could be brought from Europe. Like those who came from other parts of Europe, they dressed, to the degree possible, in the familiar styles of their homeland. Settling along waterways and in small villages, where they lived close together, the French enjoyed the friendship of the Indians, and often converted them to Christianity. In this amicable intermingling of cultures, the Indians supplied the colonists with buffalo skins; the French settlers taught the Indians how to cultivate crops. Many of the French settlers married Indian women, a practice seemingly accepted by both groups.

In summer, where the climate permitted, French colonists went barefoot, wore wooden clogs, or adopted the Indian's soft leather moccasins, decorated with quills, shells, and beads, which they wore for festivities and in winter. The men wore homemade shirts, long vests, and buckskin or rough woolen leggings. In winter, they added heavy capotes, or hooded and caped overcoats. In warm weather, they wrapped their heads in kerchiefs to protect themselves from sun and mosquitoes. Typically, the women wore bodices, short handmade woolen gowns, and bright kerchiefs decorated with ribbons or flowers.

New Orleans, founded in 1717, quickly grew in commerce, and attracted a population that developed a social life to mirror the conventions and pleasures of the French court. The rich Louisiana colonists in New Orleans, dreaming of the balls and banquets of France, clung to European fashion and resisted the influences of Native American materials and styles in clothing.

27

Styles of dress for men, women, and children changed very little during the colonial period. Very few garments exist from the early colonists, but excellent reproductions based on authentic documents may be seen at both Plimoth Plantation, in Massachusetts, and Virginia's Colonial Williamsburg. Pilgrim men and women dressed in the European styles of the period. Men wore knee breeches, hose, and tied shoes. Large collars and cuffs adorned their coats. Women of the time wore several layers of clothing. Both men and women wore hats with broad brims and fairly tall crowns. Children, for the most part, wore smaller versions of adult clothing.

In 1634, the Puritans in Massachusetts forbade the wearing of clothes with silver, gold, silk or lace, and limited the slashing and decoration that might appear on clothing. The men of New England, eager to display the colorful attire of fashionable Europe, were forbidden to wear "immoderate great breeches," broad shoulder bands, capes, double ruffles, and silk roses on their shoes. Similarly, women were directed toward modesty and away from elaborate ornamentation. Such sumptuary laws, ostensibly to guide the faithful in adherence to New Testament teachings and to further the purposes of the church in the New World, by restricting display of finery to the privileged, also served to define class according to station and wealth.

CHAPTER 3

Birth of a Country
The Eighteenth Century

The eighteenth century in America culminated in a successful revolution and the birth of the United States, the forces of evangelical, nonconformist Protestantism, classical republicanism, and enlightened liberalism combining to overthrow the inequity and resulting economic hardship and political powerlessness consequent to British rule. But even as the new nation was being shaped to emphasize the equality of humankind, the brutal mistreatment of Native Americans and the country's growing economic dependence on black slavery sowed the seeds for bitter conflict and traumatic social upheaval among its citizens.

As American settlers began to move westward across the Appalachian Mountains, into the lands that would become Tennessee, Kentucky, West Virginia, and into the more distant regions of the Ohio River valley and the territories of the old Northwest, they claimed and settled land that Indian tribes had occupied and hunted for centuries. The Native Americans, displaced and often cruelly mistreated, became a further threat to the safety of homesteaders.

In the tobacco, rice, and indigo plantations of the South, black slaves had become the main labor force by the end of the 1600s, but their numbers would increase dramatically a century later when, in 1763, Eli Whitney invented the cotton gin, a machine that made the cultivation of short-fiber cotton profitable for the first time. In the minds of the plantation owners, slave labor was ideally suited for the cultivation of cotton; thus slave-trading and human bondage became expedient resources for the development of the country.

By the middle of the eighteenth century, all English colonies had developed governments that were representative, if not democratic in the modern sense. These legislative bodies were controlled by the landed gentry and wealthy merchants much as they had been in English political patterns·and in the classical republican tradition of Greece and Rome, which restricted political participation to those persons with enough property to look beyond their own needs to those of the common good. As the English colonists debated the proper relationship between the colonial legislative bodies and the royal government in London, they viewed the policies of the royal government as destructive to their best economic interests and to their political freedom.

In 1776 the colonists broke with England when the Second Continental Congress, which served as the nation's governing body from 1776 until 1781, promulgated the Articles of Confederation, establishing the first formal union of states and declaring independence. The Northwest Ordinance of 1787 was one of the outstanding achievements of the government under the Articles of Confederation, providing a structure by which territories would be admitted into the union of the original thirteen states as separate but equal entities.

The years of the Articles of Confederation (1781–87) are sometimes called the Critical Period, because during this time the new republic was faced with serious financial problems, including constantly escalating national and state debts and an expanding trade deficit. To compound matters, the central

clockwise from left

When Benjamin Franklin visited Paris, it is said that he wore a coonskin cap to identify himself with the American frontier.

Samuel Adams, a Massachusetts patriot and leader of the Boston Tea Party, wore the typical clothing of an eighteenth-century male, though he and the men who boarded the British ships in Boston Harbor would disguise themselves as Indians.

Thomas Jefferson, unlike George Washington, cared very little for his dress and, during his presidency, was known to wear bedroom slippers, a comfortable old robe, and corduroy breeches to receive important representatives from foreign states. When portrayed by artists, however, he was costumed in the knee breeches, waistcoat, and frock coat of the late eighteenth century.

When Washington called on the widowed Martha Dandridge Custis — later to become Mrs. Washington — he may well have worn the clothing assigned to him by the artist who made this print. Mrs. Custis and her children, like Washington himself, wear clothing typical of the period and of their class.

government did not have sufficient power to enforce its treaty provisions with foreign nations or its laws on state government. To many people, among them George Washington and James Madison, it seemed that there was too much liberty and not enough emphasis on order and stability in the state and national governments.

These political and economic problems led to a call for a new constitutional convention in 1787. Delegates at this convention produced a document that replaced the Articles of Confederation and that has lasted for more than two hundred years with the addition of only twenty-six amendments — the first ten of which were adopted in 1791 as the Bill of Rights.

With the Constitution of 1787, the people became the ultimate source of power in this republican system of government. But "the people" were defined as property-holding white males. Women, blacks, and Indians were excluded from participation in the political arenas of the new republic. Although women were excluded from public life, the Revolution did pave the way for the redefinition of the role of women in American society. In the new republic women were given the responsibility for training the young to become virtuous citizens, giving motherhood the celebratory status of the flag and the Constitution.

As settlers moved westward toward Ohio, existing styles of clothing were tested against new conditions; soon new adaptations and conventions in clothing would be born of the necessities of back-country life. Though influenced by the harsh realities of colonial life, American clothing at the end of the eighteenth century still derived from European roots. Rich Americans still prized clothing imported from Europe and looked longingly toward Paris, dreaming of possessing fine clothes in the latest styles. But patriotism and taxation checked Americans' pursuit

of European fashion, and at least obliquely contributed to the development of an American idiom in clothing. In the nineteenth century, distinctly American styles would emerge.

During the 1700s, American men dressed in clothing similar to that worn by Englishmen. Affluent American men adopted the styles of the English gentry, while poorer men dressed in the same simple articles of clothing worn by the English lower classes. The tricorn hat was worn throughout the eighteenth century, until, in the wake of the French Revolution, the bicorn hat (shaped like a crescent) associated with the revolutionary came to prominence. In the 1780s the forerunner of the top hat appeared, made of various materials, beaver being especially popular.

Until the end of the eighteenth century all men wore snug-fitting, knee-length breeches and silk stockings held up by garters or bows at the knee. But with the Revolution in France trousers — first worn by patriot sansculottes ("without breeches") to distinguish themselves from aristocrats — began to replace the short breeches.

Shoes were also modified during these years. Heretofore both men and women had continued to wear shoes with red heels and buckles or rosettes in the front. But the buckles, rosettes, and heels disappeared with the Revolution, leaving a heelless slipper fastened with plain string and worn with white or striped stockings. Also to become popular with the patriots during the Revolution were English jockey boots. They were soft, highly polished black leather, with light brown leather turn-down cuffs,

This gold-colored ribbed silk waistcoat (1750–74) is embroidered with silver thread. Though made in England, it was worn in the colonies and was typical of the finer clothing that America imported.

In 1774, men, women, and children rallied in Boston to tar and feather a Tory tax collector. The figures illustrated at the left wear upper-class clothing. Others, however, are dressed in the garb of common people.

worn with short breeches at first and later with long, snug-fitting trousers.

As the colonials became Americans, debating the merits and functions of liberty and authority in government and manifesting both deep patriotism and colorful — sometimes comic — chauvinism, they continued to measure their clothing against European styles. The rich ordered clothing from European centers; the poor, using materials at hand, made their own versions of fashionable clothing. Thus a lady in Virginia and her maid dressed in the same style, though their clothing differed in materials and, in some instances, decoration. Similarly, men almost uniformly wore breeches, frock coats, vests, and pullover shirts. The materials used in workingmen's clothing included

above

As a young man, George Washington surveyed lands in Ohio, traveling with both Indian guides and members of his surveying team. In a print issued long after the event, he is shown wearing a cape over his suit, a costume that, in the artist's treatment of the event, signifies his position. It is unlikely, however, that even Washington's fondness for fine dress would have been manifested in clothing so unsuitable for the wilderness.

above right

Waistcoats were commonly sleeveless, similar to this example made from brown silk damask specifically woven for the cut of the garment. Faced with brown twill weave silk and lined with linen, the coat opens down the center back and was closed by tying the attached tapes, while the front was decorated with buttons and elaborate buttonholes.

buckskin, linsey-woolsey, and other materials generated at home, while richer men, no less fashion- and status-conscious than women, ordered their clothing, or the materials from which their clothing could be constructed, from Europe.

Other Americans understood the symbolic power of clothing. George Washington exercised the power of military uniform to establish authority. When soldiers on guard duty failed to recognize him as their general, Washington added a brilliant blue satin ribbon to his uniform to signal his position. While he rejected royal status, Washington employed many of the trappings — a sword carried in a brilliant green scabbard, gold braid, rich materials, costly buttons and buckles, elegantly powdered wigs — of nobility.

Thomas Jefferson, who apparently gave little thought to his own clothing, was amused by women's fashions as well as aware of the forces of geography and climate, religious dress codes and social stratification, and the availability of materials and skills that influenced clothing in both rich and poor households. In 1783, he wrote a letter describing the then-current fashion among women: hairstyles that made the "head . . . as flat as a flounder," dresses that put the shoulders "where the chin used to be" and the hips where the shoulders used to be. He observed, "The circumference of the waist is the span of the lady's own hands in order to preserve due proportion. All the residue of the figure is resigned to the possession of a hoop which at each angle before projects like two bastions of a fort."[1]

34

Men of the
eighteenth century
wore waistcoats
such as this
elaborate article
(1705–20).

The weave in this garment
is known as "bizarre"
and consists of a
fanciful pattern of gold
and silver threads
with pink silk damask
in the upper back and
upper sleeves.

Finely worked
buttonholes on the cuffs
and for the front opening,
as well as the skillful
tailoring of the body
and sleeves, attest to the
maker's talent as well
as the owner's wealth.

By the middle of
the eighteenth century,
men wore suits, often
similar to this example of
brown uncut velvet.
The small spotted design of
the material adds
richness to an already
luxuriant material.

The outfit,
which would have
been worn with white
linen, consisted of a coat,
waistcoat, breeches,
stockings, and shoes
with decorative
buckles.

Men's suits in the
eighteenth century were
frequently ornate.
This suit, cut from red velvet
woven in a lattice design
with black floral sprigs, was
worn during the period
1765–75, and is
believed to have been
made in France.

36

Women often remade valuable articles of clothing, such as this gown, originally designed in 1727 but reworked during the American Revolution to extend its life. The material is green silk lampas, and the dress is thought to have belonged originally to Sarah Pierpont, wife of Jonathan Edwards, the Connecticut theologian.

This yellow silk gown and petticoat with self trimmings was made toward the end of the eighteenth century and worn with the skirt open to reveal a matching petticoat. The edge-to-edge front closure could have been fastened with straight pins attached to stays hidden underneath. An opening on either side of the robe and petticoat allows the wearer to reach a pocket — a separate article — attached beneath the clothing.

below

Throughout the eighteenth century, women wore hooded cloaks similar to this example made of prized scarlet wool and trimmed with shag. The cloak was constructed to allow its Stonington, Connecticut, wearer to bare her head or to pull the hood up as protection against the elements.

37

Part II

The Nineteenth Century

CHAPTER 4

Overview
1800–1899

By the onset of the nineteenth century, the United States, having survived the travails and gore of the Revolution and having effected constitutional rule, settled to the long process of maturation as a government and as a people, continuing a course of social and political policies and actions that would bring the century to the bloody Civil War and its long-festering aftermath. As the young republic strengthened its capitalistic structure through the development of industry and commerce in the first half of the century, the promise of wealth impelled the formation of massive transportation facilities including roads, bridges, and canals, as well as the transcontinental railroad, completed by 1869. The urgency of national expansion, the burgeoning of capitalism, and the increasing ease of transportation opened vast opportunities to some Americans, and established the West in the collective imagination as the promise of prosperity, freedom, and adventure.

What was for white Americans a culture of economic prosperity worked, however, to ensnare African-Americans in slavery, which, despite protests, was tolerated as an expedient means for wresting goods from the southern soil and meeting the demands of northern manufacturing. By the 1830s all white males, regardless of property, enjoyed political democracy; they were assured the right to participate in the electoral process. Blacks and women, however, with or without property, were excluded from political participation and were shut out of the public life of the new republic. Blacks, both free and in bondage, turned mainstream society's crumbs into a subculture of survival.

As white America sustained a wealthy class, those women who benefited from it turned in large numbers to voluntary associations to further their interests and to organize public support for a variety of causes. During the 1830s and 1840s, owing largely to the zeal of American women — often supported by like-minded men — a remarkable array of social organizations took aim at

objectives intended to better the human condition as reformers urged abolitionism, vegetarianism, temperance, and women's rights and suffrage. These reform efforts often included specific calls for change in the dress of women to free them from the restrictive, cumbersome, and sometimes dangerous clothing of the period.

At the same time, drawn by the promises of a better life, adventure, and gold, people from northern and southern Europe, Asia, and uprooted families from the eastern part of the United States moved into the untamed western lands. Suffering great hardships and risking death, they flooded into the Mississippi River valley, the Great Plains, and the far West. These new immigrants found other people — in the Southwest, the Spanish settlers; in the Northeast, British and French settlers; and throughout the entire region, Native Americans — who also laid claim to this vast land and its riches. As the region became a fierce battleground between competing peoples, the Indians were slaughtered and their culture all but destroyed by the United States government.

On this western stage of violence, lawlessness, brutality, and dreams of freedom and wealth, a variety of costumes would come to identify the actors, to further their real and imagined roles. Though varied to reflect the wearers' lives and times, the eccentric, whimsical, and practical clothing worn by the adventurers came to be associated in popular imagination with the mythic figures of the American West — lawmen, saloon girls,

---

Fashionable ladies and gentlemen of the early nineteenth century disported themselves in a variety of fine clothes, often reflecting the tastes and styles of London and Paris. In this 1827 Currier and Ives woodcut illustration of a velocipede demonstration on Pennsylvania Avenue in Washington, D.C. — the new capital of the United States — men are shown wearing the knee breeches of an earlier time, and women are depicted in the capacious gowns and cloaks that had also been popular at the end of the eighteenth century.

rustlers, miners, explorers, drunks, and deeply religious pioneers — the stock characters of American novels and movies of a later time.

In the years before the Civil War, Americans, no longer content with European modes of life, perhaps dizzied by the possibilities and resources of their own country and able to adapt materials and styles to meet necessity, reflected in their dress the visions, economic forces, social values, and energies of a new country. While European fashions still allowed richer Americans to parade their wealth, both the home-stitched clothing and the manufactured clothing of America initiated new attitudes and styles of dress. These were the decades during which an American idiom in dress began to form and spread.

Inventions and technological advances would influence both materials and styles of clothing. In some cases, seemingly small adjustments were destined to precipitate enormous changes in clothing design and manufacture; in other cases, revolutionary inventions immediately made new styles possible and new clothing available. Noteworthy inventions and technological advances of the period include the development of waterproofing for cloth, the combination of rubber and fabric to produce elastic, the improvement of buttons, and the invention of common, or straight, pins.* The period gave birth, too, to the sewing machine and paper patterns, to the Stetson hat, and to Levi's. But despite such deep and abiding advances in styles and materials, the nineteenth century also saw the failure of the dress reform associated with the bloomer costume.

42

On the Missouri frontier, homesteaders wore the typical rural, or frontier, clothing of the era.

During the first years of the nineteenth century many women wore the earlier style of ample dresses over several petticoats with hooded capes and shoes of cloth or leather. Others, however, influenced by the Empire styles of France, turned to the modern look of the time — dresses with a high waistline that emphasized the breasts, and skirts that ended in decorative patterns. The neckline, usually rounded, could be cut high or low.

Women's clothing tended to reflect modifications of the bodice and skirt worn with many petticoats that had been in style in the seventeenth and eighteenth centuries. In addition to petticoats, a woman's undergarments might consist of a chemise, a corset with stays, knickers, stockings, hoop, bustle, and bandeau (precursor of the brassiere). Drawers — the precursor of "step-ins" and panties — were uncommon until the middle of the century. Corsets, however, appeared around 1810; by the end of the century corsets cinched the waist for the fashionable hourglass silhouette. As nineteenth-century American women accepted the fashionable styles of postrevolutionary France, modeled on ancient Greek and Roman styles, the hoopskirt disappeared and women began to expose a portion of their legs.

Women in all parts of the country, in urban and rural areas, dressed according to their station in life and to mark the character of the day or occasion. Dress-up clothing, as well as workaday garb, varied in pattern and material. Most clothing was made at home, making sewing skills a factor in determining the quality of clothing available to women.

---

* In 1804, Rudolph Ackerman, in London, first patented his method for making rubberized cloth, and in 1823, E. Mackintosh's name was affixed to a process for waterproofing. With these inventions, the raincoat would become a standard item in almost every wardrobe.

In 1820, an Englishman by the name of Hancock produced the first elastic fabric with rubber in it and called it "webbing." Elastic soon replaced garters and the ribbons that secured all slippers at the time and became a popular ingredient in the home sewing basket.

In 1807, the metal button formed of two discs locked together by turned edges and the metal-shanked shell button were developed in England. In 1827, Samuel Williston of Easthampton, Massachusetts, patented his invention for a machine to produce cloth-covered buttons. Buttons quickly replaced "frogs," clasps, lacing, ties, and a variety of difficult-to-make and often inefficient means for closing openings in clothing; those more tedious and old-fashioned means for closing material became, in turn, part of the decorative vocabulary of clothing design in later years.

In 1831, John Ireland Howe made a machine for producing common pins that permitted a seamstress to pin up a piece of clothing and test its fit before final stitching, a practice that allowed for more intricate design and elaborate craftsmanship in sewing.

The workingman's costume at the beginning of the nineteenth century included such items as leather apron and sturdy shoes, warm woolen shirts, simplified knee breeches, caps, and pocket handkerchiefs. For people dependent on the agricultural economy of either the North or South, clothing reflected the conditions of climate and weather. Shorter skirts and looser sleeves enabled women to work outdoors, for which men might also choose looser sleeves and trousers.

Footwear varied in style, construction, and degree of torture inflicted. Affluent American men, in accepting changing fashions, not only accepted ill-shaped breeches but also uncomfortable shoes. Before the middle of the century, women often wore fabric slippers that provided neither support nor protection. Rural women and children found leather moccasins sturdy and useful. For special occasions, richer men wore thin leather or fabric slippers, often decorated with bows or embroidery.

Americans who lived in rural areas, or on the frontier, wore clothing adapted to the environment, and determined by frugality. Women sewed endlessly, making and mending garments for themselves and for all members of their families.

43

By the middle of the nineteenth century, Americans who lived in cities dressed in similar styles. San Franciscans, in this engraving from the Reverend William Taylor's *California Life*, wear clothing similar to that worn by contemporary men and women on the East Coast.

Men prized pantaloons and vests that were practical, well-made, and fashionable. These garments, worn together, were made of tan wool. A watch pocket is neatly tailored into the pants; straps fit under the instep to keep the pants taut. The fall — the portion of the trousers designed to drop, a precursor of the modern fly front — is wide, reaching from side seam to side seam, and held in place by four buttons under the waistband.

The wide-wale cotton corduroy pantaloons of the period show similar features in tailoring but have a narrower fall, half closed with three buttons aligned under the central three buttons of the waistband.

Other trousers of the 1800s, like these of coarse cotton in a twill weave, also have a narrow fall — this one held closed by three buttons aligned under the one central button of the waistband — but no instep strap.

44

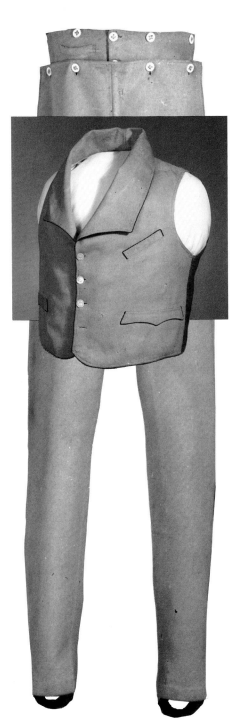

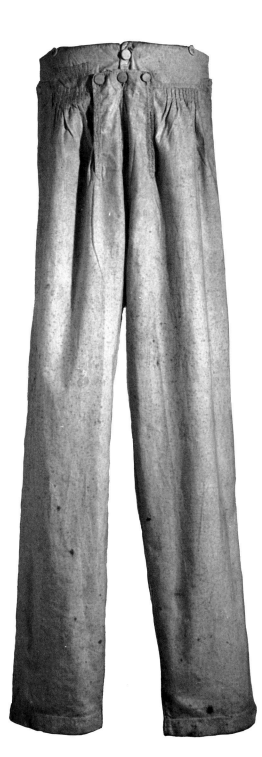

This well-tailored double-breasted "great coat" of tan wool
featured the fashionable high collar of the period around 1820.

Men often chose dress shirts made of white cotton; some, like
this one, had linen collars, cuffs, and fronts. The gathers at waist and
yoke created fullness, or volume, in the shirt that obtained
even when pressed into pleats.

45

This white cotton dress
is intricately embroidered at
top and bottom. The short sleeves
are also embroidered.

Low-necked with a high waist, this frock
is made of sheer white cotton and woven yellow
wool stripes ending in three tiers of ruffles that
touch the floor. The lines of the stripes emphasize the
roundness of the bust and shoulders, and
suggest a columnar figure.

This plum-colored silk dress, worn around
1830, has enormous leg-of-mutton sleeves and
a V neckline above a high, banded waist.

This gold-colored figured silk satin dress,
with its wide neck opening and intricate shaping
of the bosom and sleeves, has a full skirt
flaring from a V-line waist.

48

near right

near right

In the early 1840s, the Hutchinson family of New Hampshire formed a traveling singing group, billed as "a nest of brothers with a sister in it." They are depicted on the cover of sheet music, in clothes of the day. The men wear matching outfits consisting of light-colored trousers with straps under the instep, striped waist-coats, dark coats and ties, and white linen. Abby wears a demure dark dress with high, rounded neck and long, simple sleeves.

far right

As a rule, older people and those living in rural areas wore clothing that had been fashionable at an earlier time. Made around 1860, this photograph shows a woman, in a dust cap and long dark dress, who also practices crafts even then associated with previous periods.

THE OLD GRANITE STATE,

Judson.   Abby.   John.   Asa

A SONG,

COMPOSED, ARRANGED AND SUNG, BY

THE HUTCHINSON FAMILY.

Price 50 Cts Nett.

The bicycle, which became
popular toward the end of the
nineteenth century, required
special clothing for both
men and women.
"Mr. Porter," a machinist in
Lynn, Massachusetts, wore
tight-fitting clothing and
a small cap with a short bill
designed to minimize wind
resistance. His knee
breeches button decoratively
at the knee, and are worn
over knit stockings.

As the bicycle gained favor
among men and women,
it influenced changes in
clothing that favored
simplicity, utility, and safety.

50

51

above

On a bicycle outing in 1890, Laura B. Hunt, Annie Simmons, Mabel Paul, Ada Paul, and Corine Coburn of Lynn, Massachusetts, rested and mended a tire. The bicycles have been designed to accommodate women's skirts, both in the open area between seat and front wheel and in the fanlike shield from back axle to fender to guard against catching the skirt in the wheel. These women wear simple clothing — jackets with full upper sleeves, blouses with assorted neckwear, full skirts, and jaunty hats — considered appropriate for women enjoying the leisure-time activities of walking or cycling in the country.

left

Mrs. Eva Davis, of Junction City, Kansas, posed with her bicycle for this photograph. The high handlebars and low-cut frame between seat and front wheel made the bicycle usable by women wearing long skirts. Mrs. Davis, in a dark tailored suit appropriate for cycling, used hatpins to hold her hat firmly against the wind.

52

Between 1876 and 1881, only one telephone existed in Lynn, Massachusetts, a statistic repeated in many small towns along the eastern seaboard. By 1885, however, the telephone had become a vital business tool, requiring switchboards, or exchanges. In 1896, Hattie E. Bolster (*left*), Lizzie Hunt, and Frank Drew, the regular operators, were photographed at the Lynn telephone exchange; another seventy-five substitutes stood ready to help the switchboard operators keep the exchange active during all working hours.

Operating switchboards was deemed suitable work for women. Female telephone operators of the day were often called "hello girls."

Even women who worked at telephone exchanges or in offices wore constricting corsets designed to shape the body into an hourglass silhouette.

far left

These workmen's garments were exhibited by the U.S. Fisheries at the Great International Fisheries Exhibition in London in 1883. The shirt is made of a multicolored plaid cotton in a plain weave. The shirt cuffs button, but the front of the pullover shirt is laced. The pants, also made of multicolored plain cotton, flare slightly at the bottom of the leg and have a fly closing.

left

Men who could dress fashionably by day could also afford special nightshirts. This white, plain-weave cotton garment, worn during the last decade of the nineteenth century, features machine-made embroidery on the collar, front button placket, cuffs, and pocket.

Not all men at the end of the nineteenth century could afford the latest fashions. As dress-up clothing showed wear, men customarily adapted shirts, waistcoats, trousers, and jackets to their daily needs in the workplace. Special work clothing, itself a luxury, had not found its way into such places as the Stockton Wheel Company, built in 1883. Benjamin Holt (*front row, far left*), the president of the company at the time of this 1883 photograph, appears in a full suit that befits his status as boss. The workmen, almost all wearing hats or caps, display a motley collection of trousers, vests, shirts, and aprons.

For the most part, informal, or sports, clothing did not exist at the end of the nineteenth century, but prototypes for it could be seen in both the working garb worn on the frontiers and in the modifications made to city clothing for leisure activities. Around 1895, this group posed on the deck of the steamboat *Sidney* in Iowa. The younger women have chosen the smart neat attire of the Gibson girl, the popular office look of the period, while the older women don dark clothing. The men wear suits and hats or caps, the boy a cap and long jacket, a flowing tie, and calf-length trousers over stockings and high-lace shoes.

At the end of the nineteenth and beginning of the twentieth century, Charles Dana Gibson, an American illustrator noted for his crisp black-and-white drawings in popular magazines of the period such as *Harper's*, *Scribner's*, and *Century*, pictured small-waisted women with massive upswept hair wearing neat, tailored shirts and toe-length skirts. The idealized "Gibson girl" resulted in a new fashion, almost universally popular in America. Women in all parts of the country could order the Gibson girl look by mail.

The Gibson waist, a basic blouse styled like a man's shirt with a stand-up or turn-down collar often ornamented with a small black tie, offered either straight or leg-of-mutton sleeves. The popular garment was available in lawn, satin, and other fabrics, and could be elaborately decorated with tucks, lace, or insertions to feminize the masculine tailoring of its style.

Office workers at the end of the century — both men and women — were expected to dress in a dignified manner. These workers, posed in the 1890s in the drafting room of the Boston Machine Works, epitomized in their costume the ideals of dignity and efficiency in the office. The woman wears sleeve protectors over her white blouse and an apron over her full skirt, which falls to about four inches above the floor, enabling her to walk easily; while it is full, it is not worn over crinolines. This utilitarian skirt, along with the neat blouse and tidily pinned-up hair, typified the popular Gibson girl office look of the period.

Men in the office took off their jackets and rolled up their sleeves but did not loosen ties and collars.

56

Rural and small-town women across America, here shown voting in the Wyoming Territory in 1888, dressed up in modest long skirts, long-sleeved jackets, and hats.

Caring for clothing
required work and time.
This two-piece dress of white
cotton with printed black floral
stripes and a detachable belt
was advertised as a "wash dress"
because it could be laundered easily.

57

"Wash dresses" soon became popular with women of all ages and in all save the highest social classes. Made of cotton and designed for comfort and easy care, they were often hemmed three or four inches above the floor.

Late-nineteenth-century men's ready-made clothing was available in a variety of styles, including the black worsted evening suit with satin-lined coat and vest, as well as the black Prince Albert and clerical suits. Gentlemen with less-somber tastes could outfit themselves in "crash suits," featuring white duck trousers worn with different-colored vests and jackets, and often accompanied by a jaunty straw hat.

58

By the end of the nineteenth century, bathing suits for both men and women appeared, as Americans enjoyed the shore in decorous and modest attire. In Rhode Island, in 1897, a man wearing a two-piece dark wool suit shows legs and arms. Two women companions, however, wear stockings and bathing suits that resemble shortened dresses.

CHAPTER 5

Manufacturing and the Work Force
Industrialization and Clothing

In nineteenth-century America, the forces of the worldwide Industrial Revolution and the continuing assault on the frontier combined to alter life in nearly every aspect. The men and women who moved from farm to factory not only performed new types of work on machinery theretofore unknown, but they also learned to wear new modes of clothing appropriate to their jobs and their new styles of life. Moreover, industrialization relocated the center of clothing manufacture from home to factory and laid the groundwork for vast supporting systems of advertisement and distribution. Finally, factory-produced clothing furnished new styles of dress to people in all walks of life.

The Industrial Revolution, however, meant different things to different parts of the country; in the North, factories sprang up around water that provided energy to run machinery; in the South, slavery became ever more necessary to growing the cotton sold to northern textile mills. As mill and plantation owners contended for profit within the capitalist system, they pressed hardship upon the slaves and sharecroppers who worked the cotton-producing land as well as the farm workers — often young women or children — hired by mills as cheap labor. As textiles came to dominate the American economy, the North and South, distinct in social organization and values, remained joined in the pursuit of profit from cloth.

In the industrialized North, cheap transportation and increasing opportunities for free education provided working people, especially New Englanders, with a degree of social mobility unavailable to the African-American slave or the poor rural farm worker in the South. Yet industrialization and the resulting northern way of life depended in large measure on the South's cotton kingdom.

By and large, New Englanders who made the shift from farm to factory also made the shift from homemade to factory-produced clothing, in effect trading time and labor for wages and wages for goods that would previously have been made at home. Manufactured clothing, the result of repeated application of specific processes to given materials, tended toward uniformity in style and quality. Handiwork — embroidery, cutouts and lace insertions, and other individualizing embellishment — was reserved for the professional dressmaker's garments for the well-to-do; off-the-rack clothing, however uniform in styling and workmanship, was inexpensive enough to allow wage earners to vary their wardrobes by purchasing more garments than they might previously have owned.

Styles changed for men and women, and, more significantly, expectations and desires for clothing changed radically during the period of industrialization. With the new prosperity of the

---

Increasingly, an American work force congregated in cities to be near factories. In Lynn, Massachusetts, people worked in the numerous shoe factories in and around the town. The growth of footwear manufacturing had followed a path similar to that of mechanized clothing making. Lynn's Micajah Pratt pioneered the centralizing of labor in shops to produce women's shoes and cheap brogans for slaves. In 1812, Pratt employed only a few workers in a flimsy wooden building; by 1850, however, he had moved his operation to a large brick structure and hired more than five hundred workers. Pratt's factories, with steam-powered sewing machines and McKay stitchers, became a highly prosperous enterprise.

Similarly, the Varney Brothers Boot and Shoe Makers, and D. Moulton and Sons, also in Lynn, attracted men and women to manufacture the children's boots and shoes that they advertised "for the Southern and Western trade." Boxes in front of the building, packed with shoes ready to ship, are addressed to Chicago and Cleveland.

industrialized North, men, women, and children expected to own more and better clothing.

To understand the magnitude of changes that occurred in nineteenth-century America, it is important to view them alongside the preceding period. In the 1700s, the New World yeoman in the northern states, with his vast arsenal of trades and skills, had made and used tools with equal facility; he had built and mended houses, barns, fences, wagons, and shoes. He and his family had husbanded animals for wool; his wife had carded, spun, woven, and stitched clothing. Children, who had furnished a necessary source of labor on early farms, had learned all of the skills necessary to grow and preserve food, husband animals, and maintain buildings and tools. On the foundation of composite skills and trades, the eighteenth-century yeoman's family had been nearly self-sustaining, and the American farm had operated with relative assurance of perpetuity. During the nineteenth century, however, with the progression of

below

62

Dressed in hats, shirts, and pants with suspenders, or overalls similar to those worn by generations before them, these farmers in the late nineteenth century harvested their crops. Their lives were not greatly changed by the Industrial Revolution, despite the availability and popularity of machine-made tools and garments.

commerce, transportation, and cities in the wake of industrialization, self-sufficiency gave way to the security of regular wages; homemade articles, including clothing, were replaced by manufactured goods, and people clustered in cities, rather than on family farms, to be near their sources of income.

In the first years of the nineteenth century, homemade articles — petticoats, dresses, and cloaks for women as well as shirts, pants, and coats for men — figured prominently as materials for barter or sale. The garments traded were generally utilitarian, but evidencing the maker's surplus material and better-than-average talents as seamstress or tailor. Cash, always in short supply, was traditionally reserved for taxes, purchase of land, and for ensuring land and dowry for children who married. Thus, in anticipation of earning cash by selling goods and services, farmers planted extra crops, housewives spun extra cloth from the flax they grew and processed or from the sheep they tended and sheared.

With cash earned from selling the extra gains of their work, the early-nineteenth-century family purchased the goods and skills it was unable to provide for itself, or that were better provided by specialists. Homemade clothing, for example, sufficed for daily wear, but those who could afford better garments for special occasions spent cash on professionally made garments. In response to the rural market for such commodities, itinerant craftsmen with special skills — tailoring or fine dressmaking among them — plied their services in small villages or in rural settlements. These traveling clothes makers often hawked their wares as examples of "city" styles, or high fashion.

The same people who valued professionally made clothing for its quality as well as its status would later buy factory-made clothing. The Industrial Revolution would not only change lives, economy, and government, it would also precipitate a revolution in values, status, and consumerism for individuals and for families.

One of the first industries to develop in the United States was the manufacturing of cotton cloth, a staple widely used in the making of clothing. By 1820 the manufacturing of cotton cloth simultaneously made the spinning and weaving of cloth at home unnecessary and ensured the need for workers in American mills. Mill owners, concluding that it was easier to attract single

right

Some families, in response to opportunities afforded by industrialization, lived in communities near new work. Poor families dressed in outfits combining homemade and manufactured garments. Girls wore shorter skirts than mature women, their feet and legs protected by sturdy shoes and heavy stockings. Adult women wore cotton dresses, usually homemade, with aprons. When affordable, men wore manufactured pants and shirts.

farm women than their fathers or brothers, opened the work force to women, thereby setting in motion yet another dynamic upheaval in American life, as women entered the mainstream work force, earned money, and gained new dimensions of independence.

Not only women but large numbers of children, too, eagerly entered the work force, hoping to escape the exhausting labor and economic uncertainty of small farms and to gain the security of regular wages for steady work. Slaves were often rented by their owners to work in southern mills. For them neither wages nor economic security beckoned, but all who worked in the mills toiled long hours in difficult and increasingly dangerous surroundings.

While the great issues of labor — safety, length of workday, wages, unionization, and right to strike — were born in the United States during the nineteenth century, free workers in the early years of the period strove for personal advancement. These white Americans who left the farm for the factory became, in effect, a work force of expectant capitalists, ingrained with the values of hard work leading to prosperity and believing that every worker was potentially a plutocrat.

As mechanization evolved and factories were built in many sections of the country, workers — especially those who joined the industrial force — were increasingly specialized in their jobs and stratified socially. As the jobs became more narrowly defined by the various discrete functions of the manufacturing process and by the products made, men and women wore clothes that enabled them to perform the functions and handle the products effectively. For example, women who moved from farm to industry, from hearthside to factory, undertook significant changes in clothing — prompted by increased affluence as well as concern for efficiency on the job — that quietly brought about lasting changes in female dress in America.

The changes in dress were inextricably meshed with the development of the modern textile industry, and had little to do with the dress-reform efforts of a variety of groups. The importance of the manufacturing of clothing in America grew in an almost predictable line once Moses Brown, born in 1738 into a wealthy Providence merchant family, turned away from the slave trade in which he had made his fortune. Just prior to the

invention of the cotton gin, Moses and his son, William Almy Brown, began to weave cloth from cotton, which, ironically, was probably picked in the South by the Africans that Brown had sold into slavery — one enterprise in the triangle of molasses, rum, and slaves.

With the yeomen workers they hired in the North, the Browns developed a spinning and weaving industry. Recognizing the limitations of their system, and the potential for riches if they could mechanize the process, Moses hoped to appropriate English methods of production. He soon found Samuel Slater, an English immigrant and skilled mechanic who knew how to build a factory.[1]

The Slater-designed and Brown-financed factory, little more than a shed in Pawtucket, Rhode Island, employed nine children as laborers who carded raw cotton and spun it into yarn. By 1800, the Brown business employed over a hundred workers who produced yarn and thread that was sold all over New England.*

Brown's success was soon surpassed by Boston's Francis Cabot Lowell, who took a page from Brown's book but improved upon his manufacturing techniques and developed stronger financial backing and management. Lowell's mills spread across New England, and, in 1826, the textile mills in Lowell, Massachusetts, hired women to meet the needs of the factories for laborers. Taking young females from rural homes in large numbers, and promising them a secure social situation as well as wages, the mill managers exploited the women eager for an option that had not been available in the past.

In the Lowell mills, the women lived in company-run boardinghouses and were encouraged in good manners, literary interests, and uplifting hobbies. Required to dress neatly and deport themselves in the seemly fashion of the day, these young women used machinery to accomplish the same tasks they had earlier done by hand. They earned paltry wages for working grueling schedules in dangerous and unhealthful circumstances, but they manufactured an increasingly important commodity — textiles.

The young women who worked in the Lowell mills were sometimes identified as "show workers" because mill owners pointed to their health and happiness as evidence that mill labor offered attractive opportunities to Americans willing to work. Their actual importance to the mill management was revealed, however, when they lost their jobs to male immigrants from Ireland and Canada.

Mill owners devised a system for training workers, regardless of age, gender, or national origin. Like women and immigrants, teenagers were viewed as an exploitable source of labor. All who entered the mills as apprentices spent three to seven years learning the skills of manufacturing. Given room, board, and modest support from their families, workers usually lived in strictly controlled conditions; their masters might punish them for insubordination but were expected to protect them from outside authority. Unscrupulous factory owners abused the system, taking on youngsters without any intention of providing the training that would allow them to progress, and cruelly using them only as cheap and dispensable labor.

In the beginning of the industrialization of America, factories were situated in small towns, along rivers that supplied power. Later, factories existed in cities, with workers — a new class of urban poor — living in crowded conditions in their proximity. The growth of an urban work force made possible by 1820 the development of the sweated labor system, which divided manufacturing processes among individual workers who performed the same job over and over. The processes of garment manufacturing, for example, included cutting and sewing, functions that were soon divided and subdivided into specializations that could be jobbed out.

The resulting system of "outworkers" flourished in urban centers where a supervisor could employ dozens of clusters of laborers and could deliver work to be done and retrieve the completed materials in small geographic areas. Outworkers, furnishing their own working spaces in attics and garrets in thickly populated cities, helped owners keep overhead down and, further, worked for very low wages.

After 1850, the sewing machine would have great impact on the manufacturing of both clothing and shoes in the United States. Isaac Merrit Singer's machine, modified for specific purposes in factories, encouraged job specialization and set the stage for future industrial development.

---

* In 1790, a year before the Brown-Slater mill opened, South Carolinian Hugh Templeton established America's first mechanized cotton mill in Spartanburg. Templeton rented slaves from plantation owners who in turn reclaimed them for harvesting, financially undermining Templeton's enterprise. Slaves, however, were often used in textile work — derogatorily identified as "nigger work" — a practice that would outrage poor whites who wanted the work and wages available in the mills.

right

Machine operators could stitch about eighty pairs of shoes a day. In order to keep the machines fully employed, mill owners simplified jobs and hired other workers to perform the manufacturing steps leading to final stitching. By 1860, about forty steps could be identified in the making of shoes. At the Brophy Brothers Shoe Company, as illustrated in this photograph, c. 1898, some men wore ties and protected their clothing with aprons or smocks. Women, in long simple skirts and neat blouses with long sleeves, wore aprons.

The seventeenth president of the United States, Andrew Johnson (1808–75) is better remembered for his near-impeachment and controversial role in the Reconstruction following the Civil War than for his earlier career as a tailor, but born into poverty, Johnson prospered and gained social status by tailoring.

His father died when Johnson was only three; at fourteen, he was apprenticed to a tailor in his native Raleigh, North Carolina. Young Johnson worked ten to twelve hours a day, the then standard workday, learning to use scissors, needle, thread, and fabric. Illiterate, and armed only with the partial skills of a tailor, he broke the law when he ran away from his indentured apprenticeship.

Settling in Laurens, South Carolina, Johnson worked as a tailor and fell in love with a local young woman whose mother rejected him as being unfit and without prospects. Before the heartbroken suitor left town, he conferred a token of his love and the emblem of his trade upon the object of his desires: he gave her his heavy iron goose, or tailor's iron.

Rid of the heavy iron, if not of his heavy heart, Johnson walked across the Appalachians to begin a new life in Tennessee. After working for six months for another master tailor, Johnson opened his own shop in Greenville. His success multiplied when, in 1827, he married Eliza McCardle, who taught him to read and write, coached him in oratory and debating, and encouraged his ambition.

Johnson, now an expert tailor, took pride in his work and in the satisfaction of his customers. He provided the wealthier gentlemen of the area with the then fashionable Prince Albert–style coats, a double-breasted variation on the knee-length frock coat. As he fitted his clients, many of them powerful and interested in politics, he impressed them as an intelligent man with sound ideas for social order.

Johnson charged average prices for making garments: $1.50 for a vest, $1.50 for pants, $4 to $7 for a coat, and $8 for a great coat. In keeping with the custom of the time and region, he often bartered with his clients, accepting flour, beef, wood, and other goods in exchange for well-made and well-fitted garments.

Only a few examples of Johnson's skill as a tailor survive.*

———————————

* For discussion of Johnson as tailor, see Sue Gibson Dryad and Mary Frances Drake, "Andrew Johnson, the Tailor President," *Dress* 11 (1985): 77–88.

Andrew Johnson's iron, or goose, and a coat made by the young tailor when he lived in Laurens, South Carolina, attest to his early trade.

Johnson's tailor shop became a center for political discussions, establishing its proprietor as a leader and resulting in his being elected to public office.

66

Andrew Johnson, Tailor and President

68

Communication and the Cult of Womanhood

Fashion magazines and their spawn — style magazines — directed toward a large audience, sway current (and probably majority) attitudes and values about topics as diverse as sexual practices and bargain-conscious shopping, as significant as home-buying and career-planning, and as voyeuristic as the love affairs of public figures and the wardrobes of the famous and rich. These publications relegate nothing to an out-basket marked "trivial": every consumer good is Important! Exciting! New! Articles, often written in a tone of breathless certainty about the components of success and personal power, are also often driven by advertisers.

The magazine chronicles consumerism; the magazine publisher is servant to the producer of consumer goods. For example, the publisher who rakes in stacks of dollars from manufacturers of women's handbags is not likely to encourage writers to call attention to the impediment of the purse and to lament the paucity of utilitarian pockets in the design of women's clothing; and one whose wealth is increased by advertising furs and cosmetics is not likely to give favorable (or fair) attention to the views of people who oppose killing animals for their furs or maiming them in order to test the safety of cosmetics. Moreover, products advertised are also likely to be products recommended, mentioned, lauded, and described in the editorial segments of style magazines.

Judging by the popularity and potency of style magazines, it seems unlikely that the public believes that advertisers and magazine publishers join forces to create a market for goods, or, if so, that their expectation of collusion diminishes the influence of the magazines on the American consumer, and on American life. The twentieth century may have coined the term *hype*, but the practice took root in the nineteenth century, when magazines were born.

At that time, with the conquering of the frontier and increasing emphasis on the importance of the family, gender-related social roles were codified, and, as well, a widely accepted standardization of dress arose to differentiate between men and women, and among members of the various economic and social classes. Just as clothing for men and women differed completely, so clothing among groups of people signaled class attitudes about — if not precise position on the ladder of — wealth and power. This process of rigid classification of men and women, and stratification of classes in American society, was both reflected and furthered by publications for an expanding consumer market, and by the early stages of mass communication.

Impelled in part by the Protestant work ethic and by a high regard for the appearance of probity and rectitude in the conduct of business, men in the nineteenth century were expected to be ambitious, to gather capitalist steam and charge ever onward toward greater riches. It was understood that Providence rewarded a man for his cleverness, and that one of his rewards was an admirable wife.

Thus, while men became more somber, more formal and stately in their dress, it fell to their wives to dress so that the world might know that they were married to rich and powerful men. Social pressures encouraged women of the upper classes to adorn themselves in ever more outrageous fashions that might show them to be the well-kept chattel of the wealthy, to be the protected and indolent spiritual centers of families, and to be incapable of all save the least demanding physical activities. Idleness, after all, is the visible measure of freedom from the necessity to work.

In the eighteenth century, a great respect for motherhood and womanhood had been nurtured; in harsh circumstances, it was a gentling attitude — though sometimes highly sentimental —

From *Arthur's Home Magazine* (1875)

70

that even struck chivalric responses in the ruder quarters of bachelor cowpunchers and the isolated encampments of lumbermen. In America women came to be at once esteemed as wives and mothers and prevented from economic independence by the strictures of the day; women were expected — if not forced by economic and social pressures — to marry. In exchange for the security of wedlock, women offered skills in homemaking and child-rearing; they provided gentility and respectability to families; in the nineteenth century, it became a wife's work to claim and cultivate social position appropriate to — if not actually exceeding — the wealth and power of her husband.

Until recently, this view of womanliness pervaded American advertising, the fashion industry, and women's magazines. If this theme did not actually begin with Sarah Josepha Hale's editorial policies and articles for *Godey's Lady's Book*, it was

honed and honored by her and the publication that she led. Hale (1788–1879) began her reign over *Godey's Lady's Book* in 1837, the year Queen Victoria assumed the throne. "Victoria's reign will be one of the longest in English annals," the new editor wrote. "She may so stamp her influence on the period in which she flourishes that history shall speak of it as her own. . . . Victoria we consider as a representative of the moral and intellectual influence of woman."[1]

Sarah Hale, like Queen Victoria, was a widow who dressed elegantly in black. Throughout the Victorian period, she nattered at Americans about their manners, dress, and values, winning a wide readership for *Godey's* and building the base for the worship of women that, over the years, has kept them from full participation in society, learning, business, and government.

In 1830, *Godey's Lady's Book* was first published in Philadelphia. The prototypical women's magazine, popular for years throughout the country, it illustrated the latest fashions, often French, encouraged sewing, and, more than anything else, deified womanhood while urging women to dress themselves, their children, and their husbands fashionably. Now understood as an important record of the tastes and attitudes of its day, *Godey's Lady's Book* also established the genetic code of the style magazines popular today, encouraged the development of the fashion industry in America, and contributed to the momentum of consumerism in the industrialized United States.

Godey's presented a dream view of American womanhood, manhood, and childhood. Ideal women appeared as perfect images of femininity, children as small adults or adorable dolls, and men as pillars of strength and success. In *Godey's* world, a woman's highly evolved spirituality both evidenced God's expectations of her in a sinful world and provided the inner resources she needed to overcome her physical frailty. A woman, in the *Godey's* view, was to be above concerns for money; through good works and good example she was to increase virtue in the home and in society.

When *Godey's Lady's Book* pressed on its readers an editorial policy based on belief in women's natural spiritual superiority, it advanced the cult of womanhood that, until the present time, has given both vocabulary and attitude to advertising. Dress, of course, manifested a woman's femininity, her membership and precise status in the cult of womanhood. In Hale's domain, Woman was the keeper of virtue, Mother the first teacher; the character and spirit of every human being improved under the influence of Woman. This paragon of spiritual virtue, in Hale's

GODEY'S LADY'S BOOK.

THE ONLY LADY'S BOOK IN AMERICA!

GODEY'S LADY'S BOOK FOR 1869.

THE CHEAPEST OF LADIES' MAGAZINES, BECAUSE

IT IS THE BEST!

EDITED BY MRS. S. J. HALE AND L. A. GODEY.

It is hardly necessary for the proprietor of GODEY'S LADY'S BOOK to issue a prospectus every year, as but little can be done to improve the Book, and its long-continued prosperity (*thirty-nine years*) as the friend of woman, the arbiter of fashion, the encourager and publisher of the best literature of the day, the pattern from which all others copy, being unmistakable evidence that it is appreciated all over the country. LITERATURE, FASHIONS, and ART are equally treated, and the publisher is proud to say that his is the oldest magazine in this country. It is published and edited by the same person who commenced it, and issued the first number on the first of July, 1830.

THE BEST WRITERS IN THE LITERARY WORLD

will contribute to the pages of the LADY'S BOOK during the year 1869. The following unequalled array of talent have been engaged:—

MARION HARLAND, author of "Alone," "Hidden Path," etc.
INO CHURCHILL, author of the celebrated story of "Unrest."
MISS LOUISA S. DORR, a Favorite Contributor the past year.
MRS. VICTOR, MRS. DENNISON, MARY W. JANVRIN.
MISS S. ANNIE FROST, MRS. C. A. HOPKINSON.
And a Host of Others.

The O. FOGY PAPERS will be continued in the Volume for 1869.

BEAUTIFUL STEEL PLATES.

Of these the LADY'S BOOK contains *fourteen* each year, superior (we challenge comparison) to any published in this country, either in book or periodical.

OUR FASHION PLATES.

The original Double Fashion Plates will be continued. Please compare them with the other so called fashions of our contemporaries. We give more figures, better engraved and colored, and truer fashions. After our colored fashions are completed, if anything new should be received from our attentive European correspondent, we give it in a wood engraving in the same number. This always brings our fashions down to the latest date.

MODEL COTTAGES.—The only magazine in this country that gives these designs is the LADY'S BOOK. They are drawn expressly for the Book by I. H. HOBBS, Architect.

DRAWING LESSONS.—In this we are also alone, no other magazine giving them.

ORIGINAL MUSIC.

This department is under the superintendence of J. STARR HOLLOWAY, Esq., and GODEY'S is the only magazine in which music prepared expressly for it appears.

GODEY'S INVALUABLE RECEIPTS UPON EVERY SUBJECT.

We were the first to make this department an object of interest to the public. In it will be found information of value for the Boudoir, Nursery, Kitchen, House, and Laundry. Articles manufactured from receipts taken from the LADY'S BOOK have often received premiums at fancy fairs.

Tinted Engravings.—This is a series of engravings that no one has attempted but ourselves. They give great satisfaction.

LADIES' FANCY WORK DEPARTMENT.

The illustrations in this department consist of designs for
EVENING, WALKING, MORNING, AND BRIDES DRESSES, HEADDRESSES, HAIR-DRESSING, CAPS, BONNETS, CLOAKS, MANTILLAS, RIDING HABITS, ROBES-DE-CHAMBRE, UNDERSLEEVES, SLIPPERS, WREATHS, COLLARS, CHEMISETTES, EMBROIDERY, KNITTING, NETTING, TATTING, CROCHET, AND FANCY ARTICLES OF ALL KINDS.

And everything new, as soon as it appears in Europe, is at once transferred to GODEY. Some of these designs are printed in colors, in a style unequalled.

Terms for 1869.

One copy, one year $3 00
Two copies, one year 5 00
Three copies, one year 7 50
Four copies, one year 10 00
Five copies, one year, and an extra copy to the person getting up the club, making six copies 14 00

Eight copies, one year, and an extra copy to the person getting up the club, making nine copies . . . $21 00
Eleven copies, one year, and an extra copy to the person getting up the club, making twelve copies . . . 27 50

Godey's Lady's Book and Arthur's Home Magazine will be sent one year on receipt of $4 00.
Godey's Lady's Book and Once a Month will be sent one year on receipt of $4 00.
Godey's Lady's Book and The Children's Hour will be sent one year on receipt of $3 50.
Godey's Lady's Book, Arthur's Home Magazine, and The Children's Hour will be sent one year on receipt of $5 00.
Godey's Lady's Book, Arthur's Home Magazine, Once a Month, and The Children's Hour will be sent one year on receipt of $6 50.

☞ CANADA subscribers must send 24 cents additional for every subscription to the LADY'S Book, and 12 cents for either of the other magazines, to pay the American postage.

☞ The money must all be sent at one time for any of the clubs, and additions may be made to clubs at club rates. The LADY'S BOOK will be sent to any post-office where the subscriber may reside, and subscriptions may commence with any month in the year. We can always supply back numbers. Specimen numbers will be sent on receipt of 25 cents.

HOW TO REMIT.—In remitting by Mail, a POST-OFFICE ORDER or a DRAFT, on Philadelphia or New York, *payable to the order of L. A. Godey*, is preferable to bank notes, as, should the Order or Draft be lost or stolen, it can be renewed without loss to the sender. If a Draft or a Post-Office Order cannot be procured, send United States or National Bank notes.

Address,

L. A. GODEY,
N. E. corner Sixth and Chestnut Streets, Philadelphia, Pa.

POSTMASTERS FURNISHED AT $2.50 A YEAR, FOR ANY NUMBER OF COPIES THEY MAY ORDER.

philosophy, was to resist inclinations and persuasions to induce her to think she had a right to participate in the public duties of government; argument, debate, even thought would be injurious to womanhood.

An ideal American wife and mother of the period dressed in accordance with the fashions of the day; she let it be known by the decorous way in which she wore costly clothing that her husband, her lord and master, possessed money and power. And in order to dress in the styles presented in *Godey's*, a woman required a rich husband.

Once a woman was armored and costumed in *Godey's* styles, she played a role in which there was no stage space for the onslaughts of everyday low concerns that plagued the less privileged, the less well turned out. Corseted, her body rigid within the circumscription of stays, she looked beyond the subspiritual matters of food and shelter and clothing, of imperfect children, of slovenly servants, and of unfaithful husbands who might frolic happily in brothels to the decidedly unspiritual cadence of a widely practiced double standard. For husbands, sexuality, aggression, physicality, and capitalistic captaincy were cloaked in the sober threads of the Lincolnesque figures of the period. Wives atoned for their husbands' transgressions; shunning lowness and baseness, denying the nature and needs of their own bodies, they settled on a matching outward inhibition, on clothing that caged their movements in hoops, held their bodies rigid and breathless in tightly laced corsets, dug into their flesh with stays, and distorted their feet in uncomfortable shoes. The ideal woman, so attired, could expect to achieve a quasi-religious euphoria, as much the result of pain and oxygen deprivation caused by her clothing as by sex-determined saintliness.

Children, too, were idealized and categorized during this

right

The early magazines and advertisements presented images of women and children dressed in fashionable clothing that signified wealth and social standing. In such attire, neither women nor children could move freely in work or play, but both served as symbols of the wealth and power of their husbands and fathers.

left

As the economic strength of the country increased, workingmen continued to wear trousers, shirts, vests, and coats, but more financially successful men spurned colorful clothing and unmatching articles, instead choosing the somber, dark uniform of power, social position, and wealth. To dress in the style of the rich — whether possessing wealth or not — made personal worth apparent. And those men who were not actually successful nonetheless sought to appear that way, as the staid, dark look associated with Lincoln — and evidenced by the men in this portrait — became the aspired style for men of all walks of life in the United States.

73

time. Pigeonholed according to sex and class, their clothes reflected both biological and social identity. A poor boy was a distinctly different creature from a rich girl, and both were expected to dress in accordance with their sex and station in life. The poor boy would dress in what was available, hand-me-downs and semirags, if necessary, and would get a job as well. Urchins often appear in pictures of the time, little bodies in the ragtag clothing of destitute and beaten men. Rich little girls, however, crowned with tediously styled curls, wore clothing that required the devoted attention of laundress, seamstress, and nurse as well as the tasteful oversight of an upright mother. The experiences of life varied as much as the clothing: poor children, boys or girls, could expect less protection, less care, and harsher experiences; rich children, as their clothing indicates, could expect a degree of physical and material comfort and care.

As publishing, advertising, and consumerism developed in the late nineteenth century, numerous articles on clothing appeared and reflected the concerns of the age. The progressive editors of *Arena* called for dress reform and railed against "fashion's slaves," calling for "The Next Forward Step for Women, or, The Movement for Rational Dress" and reporting on the activities of a dress-reform symposium. *Spectator* published articles on dress versus clothes and a discussion of the "old extravagance."

74

CHAPTER 7

The Sewing Machine and the Paper-Pattern Empires

Until the middle of the nineteenth century, clothing for men, women, and children was made entirely by hand. For the most part, women made their own clothing and that of their husbands and children, though roving tailors and dressmakers plied their craft among those who could afford better clothing, finding ample opportunity in the small towns and villages of the country. By the 1850s, newly invented and manufactured sewing machines became generally available both to homes and to industries, giving rise to widespread expectation that clothing could be more fashionable, less expensive, and better constructed. Men soon preferred the better-fitting garments that factories produced and, when they could afford it, bought suits and coats from factory-made stock. By the 1860s, factory-made clothing competed with homemade clothing in quality and cost, and fashion — already seen as a symbol of status — would grow as a separate industry.

Women learned to construct elaborate costumes with the aid of the sewing machine, consulting such publications as *Godey's Lady's Book* for guidance in the latest fashion. Merchants stocked lace, buttons, braids, and other decorations along with cloth and thread, enabling women who sewed to realize their fantasies in their dress. Americans believed that by using paper patterns they could home-make clothing that would set them at the forefront of the fashion world, regardless of their actual geographic location, regardless of their income, and regardless of their social class and daily activities.

As historians reckon it, the great Parisian couturier Charles Frederick Worth laid the background for the fashion phenomenon when, in 1858, he added his name — what we now identify as a designer label — to his work. It was a woman, however, who would see an opportunity in the new possibilities for home sewing, developing and marketing paper patterns that would enable women across the United States to make fashionable garments. In Brooklyn, New York, also in 1858, a milliner from Saratoga Springs, Ellen Curtis, married rich publisher and staunch abolitionist William Jennings Demorest. Their marriage would encompass a lucrative business partnership and shared efforts for social reform.

Ellen Curtis Demorest (1824–98) was thirty-three when she married the older publisher; she owned a successful hat-making business and knew the tastes of rich women, having grown up in the fashionable spa town of Saratoga. There, young Ellen — or, Nell, as she was known — watched the ladies strut their clothing and persuaded her affluent father (himself a hat manufacturer) to back her in establishing her own millinery business. Soon, Nell's acumen brought her enough money to take her business to New York.

When she married, Nell set her business interests aside, intending to devote full time to her role as wife of an important man. One day, somewhat bored, she idly watched her maid laboriously pin down pieces of wrapping paper to cut out a dress. She knew in a flash that she could provide accurate paper patterns that would allow women to home-make clothes in the latest styles. She reasoned that anyone skilled in sewing would be able to use such patterns to construct Paris fashions.

While home seamstresses had long employed the practice of using paper outlines to guide in cutting the pieces of a garment and to assist in basting, Nell conceived the idea of packaging

75

As soon as the first sewing machines appeared, women across America saw them — even the most primitive early versions — as a vital tool for making clothing at home. Sewing machines saved hours and provided stronger stitching than most seamstresses could accomplish by hand.

precut paper patterns based on the latest fashions. She and her sister, Kate, had dreamed for some time of making a chart to assist seamstresses in the then hit-or-miss process of fitting clothing. Now, Nell thought, she could take advantage of the mass production of cloth, the sewing machine, and a growing interest in fashion. She could make fitting easier, and could provide an invaluable aid to the home-maker of clothing.

Nell presented the idea to her husband, who, immediately grasping the commercial opportunities, encouraged Nell in her entrepreneurial project. As an amateur inventor, he had tested a system for cooking and heating with gas, had even toyed with gadgets that could be added to sewing machines to yield fancy decorative stitches, and he appreciated the possibilities of the new product.

Nell and William included Kate in their plans. Soon the industrious trio produced scaled paper patterns that answered the needs of a variety of body sizes and shapes; they folded, labeled, and inserted them in paper envelopes with attractive pictures — much like those to be seen in *Godey's Lady's Book* — and marketed their new offspring to the women of America.

Paper patterns were an instant success. They allowed for the making of better-fitting home-sewn clothing, and they created an appetite among their users for a continuous supply of new designs, new possibilities, new costumes with which to realize their dreams of social success and wealth. The need for designs in turn propagated the fashion business in America, where, in opposition to the couturier-based industry of French fashion, desire for style was born in parlors across the country, and was the child of paper patterns and sewing machines.

The Demorests had a shared genius for promotion, and they fully appreciated the snob appeal of French couturiers and of European fashion. Overnight, Mrs. William Demorest became Madame Demorest. Noticing that *Godey's Lady's Book* elicited interest in and yearnings for the styles it showed, Nell brought out *Mme. Demorest's Mirror of Fashions*, featuring illustrations of dresses that could be made from its namesake's marvelous paper patterns. The Demorests priced their publication lower than *Godey's*, correctly planning to make up the difference, and more, on the sale of paper patterns.

In addition to promoting the patterns through their own publication, which soon had more than fifty thousand subscribers, the Demorests, by the 1860s, had established a nationwide distribution system of more than two hundred door-to-door saleswomen — mostly widows and spinsters who needed to earn money. Soon the Demorest empire offered not only paper pat-

terns but also accessories such as creams and lotions, luggage, jewelry, hats, and false hairpieces — all available by mail as well as through the buyer's local representative.

The Demorest patterns, including clear instructions for cutting and helpful suggestions for selecting materials and decorations, found an eager market among America's women in small towns, on lonely farms and homesteads, and in frontier boomtowns. With the guidance of the paper patterns, women in almost any location or circumstance could present themselves in the clothing they believed women of wealth and leisure wore in Paris and New York, thus adorning their husbands and families. Decked out in the latest styles, they could proudly exemplify standards of taste to their communities.

The Demorests also opened their "Emporium," where New York's rich ladies were custom-dressed in the fashions reflecting the latest styles of Paris. Nell, like her husband, was a zealous abolitionist, and the Demorests hired black and white women to work side by side, for the same wages, as seamstresses. If this practice offended customers who disapproved of the mixing of races, so be it; the Demorests stood by their political convictions.

The Demorests believed in equality for the races and for women, and supported Jenni June Croly's* editorial voice in their publication for almost thirty years. Croly's column mixed feminist sentiment with personal advice. Unlike Sarah Hale, Jenni June importuned women to demand equality in education, employment, and marriage. Women, she said, should be doctors or anything else they want to be. Jenni June Croly and Nell Demorest financially backed several women who started their own businesses.

Mme Demorest, perhaps with assistance from William, also developed a line of clever gadgets that were sold by mail through the fashion magazines, including a bosom pad built around spiraled wire, a shoulder brace that improved posture and held garments in place, a working-girl's corset that was purported to be comfortable, cheap, and serviceable, and an "Imperial dress elevator" to raise or lower the skirt so that sidewalk filth could be avoided.

---

* Jane Cunningham Croly (1829–1901), writing under the pseudonym Jenni June, was born in England and came to the United States at twelve years of age. One of the earliest women to enter the field of journalism, editing *Demorest's Quarterly Mirror of Fashion* (later known as *Demorest's Illustrated Monthly*) and specializing in articles on women's issues, she was one of the first journalists to syndicate her columns. In 1868, with Nell Demorest, she helped found Sorosis — an important woman's club, and, in 1889, she initiated the New York Women's Press Club. She wrote *The History of the Woman's Club Movement in America* (1898).

William Demorest patented most of the gadgets he invented himself; neither he nor Nell, however, sought a patent for the paper pattern, and the Demorest enterprise died with Nell and William. But the paper-pattern industry did not die with the Demorests. During their reign, another pattern-maker had been building his own empire.

In Sterling, Massachusetts, Ebenezer Butterick watched his

wife cut gingham for a dress for their baby. He, like Nell Demorest watching her maid cut material for a dress, tumbled to a realization of the possibility of mass-producing and mass-marketing paper patterns for the home seamstress. Butterick began with a line of men's clothing, presumably reasoning that women — the seamstresses in most instances for their husband's clothing — would welcome assistance in fitting and constructing men's shirts. Also like the Demorests, he based his pattern on a system of graded sizes, preparing the paper patterns for market in his little shop in his hometown.

By 1863, the Buttericks moved from Sterling to the nearby and larger town of Fitchburg, where Ebenezer added to his line of men's shirt patterns some paper patterns for children's wear. The Buttericks' business grew rapidly, employing relatives and neighbors to manufacture, fold, and package the patterns. In 1864, Ebenezer opened an office on Broadway in New York City.

Like the Demorests, Butterick and his associates published magazines to entice women to buy paper patterns. In 1867 the firm issued *The Ladies' Quarterly Report of Broadway Fashions*, and in 1868, the monthly *Metropolitan*; the two were combined in 1874 to become *The Delineator*. The first editor of the *Metropolitan*, Jones Warren Wilder, had recognized the lucrative nature of women's patterns and persuaded Butterick to enter that field. With that piece of sage advice, Wilder became the creative force within the business and, moreover, the editorial voice in the publications.

Wilder's personal values did not pervade the Butterick publications as those of Hale's did *Godey's*, nor did his views have the force of Croly's feminist passions in the Demorest publications. Nonetheless, Wilder's pronouncements carried fashion news to women all over the country and won customers to Butterick patterns, creating a demand that required branch offices in Chicago and Montreal.

Butterick had sold six million patterns by 1871, and in May 1872 the company moved to larger New York quarters. At that time it had a hundred branch offices and about a thousand sales agents throughout the United States and Canada. By 1876 Butterick was marketing patterns in London, Paris, Vienna, and Berlin.

It was Butterick, not the Demorests, who patented the paper pattern, and it was Butterick's company that survived as the basis for the paper-pattern and home-sewing industry in the United States.

Nineteenth-century advertisements such as these helped put sewing machines in most American homes.

CHAPTER 8

Dress Reform

With few exceptions, women of the nineteenth century wore the clothing assigned to their sex by society. Despite evidence that long skirts unsanitarily brushed up filth and prohibited easy and safe negotiation of stairs, and that they hampered a woman's ability to move freely and comfortably, rich and poor women wore them. Despite widespread discussion of the physical harm caused by corseting, women of society and women of the streets tightly laced their bodies into undergarments intended to constrict their waists and produce an exaggerated silhouette. According to doctors and dress reformists, such constriction also resulted in injuries to ribs, lungs, livers, stomachs, and intestines. Despite the number of women disfigured or killed as a result of burns suffered when their voluminous skirts caught fire without their noticing until they were engulfed in flames, women were slow to relinquish hoops and crinolines.

All the while that women wore uncomfortable, unsanitary, unhealthful, and inconvenient clothing, a variety of groups of women and men active in promoting social improvement attempted to bring about dress reform, arguing for practicality over fashion, for health and comfort over convention, and for rationality over conformity. Dress reformers cited the authority of God and church, they preached the lessons of nature and the spiritual and physical rewards of the simple life, and they invoked the mystery and powers of scientific reasoning.

When the smoke of fiery sermons died away, the pamphlets arguing rationally and scientifically for change read and forgotten, only a few moderations in dress measured the small success of the dress reformers. At the end of the century, women continued to dress in heavy, cumbersome, impractical garments.

The dress reformers nonetheless had planted seeds that would flower in the 1920s as a revolution in women's clothing, and it would be the bicycle, the factory, and the office that would provide the rich soil for those seeds. High fashion, cultivated to display wealth and power, required idleness, or at least the appearance of idleness. Clothing for work in office and factory, however, required practicality; a working woman needed clothing appropriate for her job as well as clothing that could be easily afforded, cleaned, and mended.

Dress-reform efforts, not surprisingly, were often linked to political action for women's rights. The women's suffrage movement of the nineteenth century peaked in 1848, when Elizabeth Cady Stanton and Lucretia Mott organized a meeting held in Seneca Falls, New York. The meeting produced the Seneca Falls Declaration of Independence, which demanded equal citizenship and equal political rights for women. While little in society changed as a result of the Seneca Falls meeting, its spirit flowed through much of the last half of the century, gaining currency if not potency, and setting the stage for future visible and measurable changes in the role of women in the United States. Issues of women's rights that informed the Seneca meeting were reiterated at the time of the World's Columbian Exposition in 1893, in the early 1900s, and in the final quarter of the present century, when the women's movement again found force. In every instance of feminist activity, women's clothing has been examined as both a symbolic and literal reflection of women's inequality in society.

In 1851, owing in large part to the fervent discussions that had accompanied the Seneca Falls meeting, abolitionist and social reformer Amelia Bloomer appeared in oriental trousers with a very short tunic, her prescription for dress reform. Bloomer (1818–94) proposed revolutionary change to free women from the unhealthful and restrictive clothing of the period. In all of its varieties the bloomer costume, as it was quickly labeled, reflected nineteenth-century attitudes about women, and was doomed to failure. For men, bloomers were an easy target for sexist jokes; for conservative women, they represented the work of the devil that threatened femininity and, therefore, personal identity and security — as well as Motherhood and Family. But the costume proved valuable for rebelling women — those who adopted the latest fashion as an indication of personal outra-

The bloomer costume

79

geousness as well as those who defied fashion for reasons of social and political statement — and for women simply engaging in physical activity.

Bloomers, when flouted as fashionable garb, sometimes attracted wonderment and curiosity. In San Francisco in 1851, a journalist enthralled with the avant-garde fashion he observed on an attractive woman described a green merino fitted overgarment and "loose, flowing trousers of pink satin, fastened below the ankle," adding that three such costumes had been ordered by local ladies:

"Mrs. Cole, who has a ladies dress store on Clay Street, has received the patterns and not only has a figure in the window with the dress on, but wears one herself in the store. It is really very pretty."[1]

Later in the story the costume was identified by name:

The city was taken quite by surprise yesterday afternoon by observing a woman in company with her male companion, crossing the lower side of the Plaza, dressed in a style a little beyond the Bloomer. She was magnificently arrayed in a black satin skirt very short, with flowing red satin trousers, a splendid yellow crepe shawl and a silk turban a la Turque. She really looked magnificent and was followed by a large retinue of men and boys, who appeared to be highly pleased with the style.[2]

Not all Californians, however, favored bloomers. One woman, having seen some women wearing the dress-reform costume, wrote: "How can they so far forget the sweet shy coquetries of shrinking womanhood as to don those horrid bloomers? I pin my vestural faith with unflinching obstinacy to sweeping petticoats." Even she, however, praised women for wearing the bloomer dress, "frightful as it is on all other occasions," in crossing the plains. "For such an excursion, it is just the thing."[3]

Indeed, the bloomer costume appeared at an opportune time for the many women who were crossing the plains during the gold rush period and the booming fifties. Objectively, it would appear to have been exactly the right garment for women needing both protection from the windswept and sun-baked plains and freedom for the physical movement needed to cook over open fires, tend children, care for the sick, and keep a semblance of family life within crowded, rolling covered wagons.

Moreover, the bloomer outfit would seem to suffice for women desiring a costume distinctive from that worn by men, yet one that maintained contemporary standards for female modesty. Many did praise the bloomer costume and adopt it for overland travel; others, however, scorned it as an abomination against femininity and, by inference, against God.

Many women, attired in bloomers to make the arduous journey across the country, elicited the approbation of other women as well as the scorn and jokes of men. Cora Wilson Agatz, traveling west with her prosperous Iowa farm family, noted "the gymnasium costumes" worn by some of the women.

Short gray wool skirts, full bloomer pants of the same, fastened at the knee, high laced boots, and . . . white stockings which were changed often enough to be kept spotless. Large straw hats finished these picturesque and sensible costumes. When compared with the long, slovenly, soiled calico gowns worn by the other women of the train, these simple costumes elicited many commendatory remarks.[4]

Other diarists identify bloomers with the fashion of the day, and therefore a style that caused other women on the trail to view them as emblems of snobbery. One woman records her pleasant surprise in taking a long walk with a woman who "notwithstanding her bloomer dress we found to be a sensible pleasant woman."[5]

The bloomer costume, ideal for travel and physical activity, found an unusual champion in Brigham Young, president of the Mormons and patriarchal exponent of male superiority. Young, a brilliant administrator, planned every aspect of the Mormon westward migration from Ohio to Utah, which began in 1847, an exercise of his genius that guaranteed a high level of success and safety for his followers. He attended to all details, including the dress to be worn by the migrants. Appointing himself dress designer for the women of his group, he urged bloomers for the hardship of trail crossings, and once the Mormons settled in Utah, Young introduced a new variation of Bloomer's design, calling it the "Desert Costume."[6] It consisted of bloomers worn under a loose shapeless sacque and with a narrow-brimmed hat eight inches high. Once in Utah, however, few Mormon women heeded Young's urging, and most returned to the long, full skirts they had known in the East, thus affirming their femininity, helplessness, and subservience to the male-dominated sect.

Ironically, and despite Young's efforts to standardize women's dress, the desire for fashionable clothing may have contributed to the dissolution of polygamy among the Mormons. As expensive clothing became available to those who could afford it, and desirable as evidence of affluence, the economic implications of clothing several wives mitigated as strongly against polygamy as did the law. In the 1870s, one traveler in Utah reported his conversation with a Mormon gentleman who noted that his wives no longer settled easily for the rustic styles of the frontier. He told the visitor:

Our women want new bonnets. They pine for silk pelisses and satin robes, and try to outshine each other. All this finery is costly; yet a man who loves his wives can hardly refuse to dress them as they see other ladies dress. To clothe one woman is as much as most men in America can afford. In the good old times, an extra wife cost a man little or nothing. She wore a calico sunshade which she made herself. Now she must have a bonnet. A bonnet costs twenty dollars, and implies a shawl and gown to match. A bonnet to one wife, with shawl and gown to match, imply the like to every other wife.

The Mormon continued ruefully, "This taste for female finery is breaking up our Mormon Homes. Brigham Young may soon be the only man in Salt Lake City rich enough to clothe a dozen wives."[7]

In the 1870s the Oneida community of central New York, a perfectionist group of little more than two hundred members at the height of its prosperity, not only eschewed monogamy but sanctioned "free love." Under the leadership of John Humphrey Noyes, the Oneidans believed that men and women were equal, and that they must be freed of materialist and competitive behavior, including the usual patterns of courtship and marriage. His doctrine of the "complex marriage," in which all males and all females of a community were married to each other, and in which sexual intercourse between different consenting partners was approved by the community, led the world to identify the Oneidans as exemplars of free love and little more.

Lith of T. Bonar 124 Nassau St*

| *1* | *2* | *3* | *4* |
| The Plain Dress. | Lady of Fashion. | Partial Reform. | The Extreme of Innova: |

The bloomer costume was varied to express different attitudes about dress reform and fashion, and to provide opulence or simplicity.

Visitors to the community remarked on the clothing of the women — loose trousers under tunics, a variation of the bloomer suit. The Oneida women, as they moved closer to men in social freedoms within the community, insisted that elaborate dressing in bustles, crinolines, and tight girdles prevented them from working freely. The Oneida costume, probably born as much of practical considerations as of religious conviction, had little influence beyond the community; for the most part, outsiders considered Oneidans a menace to the social order — if not absolutely immoral — and refused to adopt any aspect of their doctrine.

The utopian community at New Harmony, Indiana, similarly allowed women to wear a variation of the bloomer costume in an effort to establish and emphasize equality between the sexes. But even in that "Community of Equality," women were limited to the activities of the housewife and chose to dress much as other American women of the period.

In preparation for the World's Columbian Exposition of 1893, to be held in Chicago, a federation of a number of women's societies* organized the National Council of Women, whose mutual concerns were enunciated in the preamble to their constitution:

82

We, women of the United States, sincerely believing that the best good of our homes and nation will be advanced by our own greater unity of thought, sympathy and purpose, and that an organized movement of women will best conserve the highest good of the family and the State, do hereby band ourselves together in a confederation of workers committed to the overthrow of all forms of ignorance and injustice, and to the application of the Golden Rule to society, custom and law.[8]

In addition to improving the political and social climate of the country, the National Council undertook concerted action to overthrow the "ignorance and injustice" of women's clothing, and plotted to reform women's dress. Frances E. Russell, of St. Paul, Minnesota, was appointed chairman of a committee mandated to study and design an "every-day dress" for women, "suitable for business hours, for shopping, for marketing, house work and other forms of exercise."[9]

---

* Organizations and women involved in the meeting included the National Woman's Christian Temperance Union, under the presidency of Emma Willard (the founder, in 1821, of the first female seminary), the National Woman's Suffrage Association, headed by Susan B. Anthony, the National Kindergarten Union, of which Sarah B. Cooper, of San Francisco, was the chief officer, and Sorosis, the famous New York woman's club, with Dr. Jennie M. Lozier as president.

DELEGATES

DWIGHT ILL'S
JUNE 27-28 1893

83

Even women united in political action were slow to accept the tenets of dress reform.

The National Council's executive board and the special Committee on Dress Reform conspired to use the occasion of the world's fair to inaugurate and popularize new clothing for women. They speculated that women visiting the fairgrounds would be physically aware of a need for clothing that enabled them to move freely and comfortably, and they reasoned that the many foreign costumes visible at the fair would provide evidence that considerable variety in women's clothing already existed in the world, and that American women could change their style of dress without sacrificing femininity or modesty.

The committee determined to design actual styles of garments, to advertise the advantages of the new styles, and to present the garments by having them modeled by prominent women from around the country. Businesswomen and college girls, both groups identified with intelligence and independence, were encouraged to attend the fair and, wearing the clothing of the coming century, to signal a new freedom for women. In brief, Frances Russell and her committee planned to launch a fad.*

---

* The plan called for securing the specific approval of many of the most influential women of the day, including such well-known reformers as Clara Barton, Harriet Beecher Stowe, May Wright Sewell, Elizabeth Stuart Phelps Ward, Grace Greenwood, and Marian Harland, many hundreds of women less prominently identified with reform and more connected in public perception with conventional and fashionable society, and — it was hoped — thousands of women teachers and students from various colleges.

The women steering the project were aware of the history of dress reform; they warned one another that they might have to incur a slight temporary martyrdom for their cause. In order to win support, Mrs. Russell reported in a popular journal of the day, their plan rested on a concerted action that would protect individuals from "coming out alone publicly in costumes so unlike the Parisian as anything sensible must be, as they are almost sure to be condemned as ugly at first sight."[10]

While conventional wisdom of the day held that the bloomer costume had failed because it was ugly, Mrs. Russell and her colleagues believed that it was deemed ugly merely because it was new. Thus the women of the National Council understood the power of the status quo but were determined to provide "examples of something better." They cited the evils of fashion and the humiliation it inflicted on its slaves. They deplored the social pressures that caused young girls to distort their bodies with corsets, to wear bustles, and to feel themselves ugly if they did not conform to the styles of the day. Yes, they told themselves and those sympathetic to their rational arguments, there were a few — themselves among them — who insisted that dress was a totally individual concern, who imagined that they might dress just as they chose; but as they reminded one another, those free choices were constantly modified by the fashion of the day, and sooner or later an avowed individualist would feel very uncom-

Women leaving Lynn, Massachusetts, shoe factory, 1895

fortable if she did not or could not conform to the general standard of beauty. Against this tyranny, Mrs. Russell appealed to her peers, the privileged and educated women of the United States:

Let every woman who lives a sheltered and easy life think of the many who are obliged to go out in all weathers, to their shops, school rooms, offices, or in the care of their families, and who cannot afford to add to the cares of their lives the nervous strain that comes of a consciousness of general disapprobation of their appearance. If these sheltered, unburdened women will wear for a part of the time, for walking, for summer outings, for activity of any kind, some style of dress which leaves hands and feet entirely untrammelled by drapery in going up and down stairs, they will do for all a lasting service by helping to make a reasonable exercise dress so common as to attract no attention.[11]

The call for sisterhood included a plan to persuade women of influence, especially women's clubs and societies, to sponsor public events and entertainments where the participants might appear in reform dress. The committee expected to induce a great many women to wear their short suits — or walking dresses — at the world's fair, and to make them seem unexceptional, if not fashionable.

"The essentials," according to Mrs. Russell, "of a proper World's Fair dress are a degree of looseness which allows every part of the body its natural action, and a degree of shortness which relieves the hands from the necessity of keeping the skirts out of the way of the wearer's feet and other people's feet in going up and down stairs."[12]

The styles recommended by the committee can be considered revolutionary only if measured against the burdensome styles of the nineteenth century. For the most part, the dress-reform styles were conservative, modest, and consonant with the prevailing attitudes about femininity. But they were different enough to threaten those who found security in conformity, and they failed to catch the imagination of the majority of women.

The frontier of dress reform, targeted for action by several nineteenth-century efforts to improve society, remained an exotic if not forbidden land, unclaimed by women until the 1920s, when the flapper cut her hair, raised her skirts, rolled her stockings, and danced to a new beat. The conservative styles espoused by the early dress reformers scarcely prophesied the flapper's costume, or the changes in clothing that followed.

As women began to work in offices and factories and to ride bicycles and engage in sports, they adopted simpler and more functional clothing. Still corseted and long-skirted, still tightly buttoned and shod, women abandoned the crinoline and hoop in order to play and work.

CHAPTER 9

Masters and Slaves
Southern Hierarchy and Clothing

Prior to the abolition of slavery in 1865 by ratification of the Thirteenth Amendment to the Constitution, an extreme social hierarchy existed in the southern states; there, some Americans bought, sold, and traded other human beings who were used as the primary labor force in the cultivation of cotton and other commodities. Those individuals, usually black men and women wrenched from their homes in Africa to become slaves, owned nothing and had no rights in the American legal system. The slave owners, clinging at all costs to their privileges of fortune and leisure, controlled all aspects of slaves' lives, including their clothing. To measure the relative *good* or *bad* treatment of slaves would be to ignore the essential wickedness of slavery, the very concept of one human being owning and controlling another. Nonetheless, as gauged by degree of physical comfort, slaves fared better or worse according to the households to which they belonged. Clothing played a significant role in defining or manifesting hierarchical position in the complicated social order of the antebellum South, and in symbolizing the stations of slaves, slave owners, and non-slave-owning whites.

Trustworthy reports of life in the antebellum South are rare, and, for the most part, neither northern censuring nor southern apology provide contemporary glimpses of clothing worn by different classes of people. But a journalist on his way to becoming a great landscape designer invested a keen eye and sense of social organization in his accounts of travels in the region, and furnished a vivid picture of clothing in the South.

Frederick Law Olmsted, traveling by horse and on foot through the deep South in 1853–54, recorded in his journal (intended for publication) his impressions of life among the rich and poor, among slave owners and slaves. A careful observer, Olmsted often described clothing worn by those he encountered,

noting the materials and styles exhibited as indicators of both individual character and condition.

Lodging in a "small but pretentious" hotel in a court town where all of his fellow guests wore black cloth coats, black cravats, and satin or embroidered silk waistcoats, Olmsted described the gaggle of small-time southern politicians as "sleek as if just from a barber's hands, and redolent of perfumes, which really had the best of it with the exhalations of the kitchen." Understanding the potent social language of clothing, Olmsted continued, "Perhaps it was because I was not in the regulation dress that I found no one ready to converse with me, and could obtain not the slightest information about my road from the landlord."[1]

Near Natchez, Mississippi, on a sweltering afternoon, Olmsted had occasion to observe further evidence of the southern social hierarchy in clothing. Two ladies, "prettily dressed, but marble-like in propriety, looking stealthily from the corners of their eyes without turning their heads," rode in an open carriage. A woman dressed as a French bonne held a "richly belaced baby." But the dignity of the turnout, according to Olmsted,

chiefly reposed in the coachman, an obese old black man, who should have been a manufacturer of iced root-beer in a cool cellar, but who had by some means been set high up in the sun's face on the bed-like cushion of the box, to display a great livery top-coat, with the wonted capes and velvet, buttoned brightly and tightly to the chin, of course, and crowned by the proper narrow-brimmed hat, with broad band and buckle; his elbows squared, the reins and whip in his hands, the sweat in globules all over his ruefully-decorous face, and his eyes fast closed in sleep.[2]

87

A photograph taken just after the Civil War shows a black family still clad in the clothes given to them by plantation owners. Men, women, and children wear garments similar to those described by Frederick Law Olmsted in the journal of his southern journey.

The clothing of servants, free or enslaved, signifies the refinement and wealth of the master. Or, as the fourth-century hermit St. Jerome asserted, "Sometimes the character of the mistress is inferred from the dress of her maids."[3]

On a visit to a plantation in Mississippi, Olmsted noted that the white overseer wore no waistcoat and carried a pistol "without thought of concealment." A gentleman of the time and of the region — as distinct from a man hired to do the slave owner's bidding — would have both worn a waistcoat and concealed a firearm.

At the onset of a downpour, Olmsted watched a whip-carrying driver order a gang of forty large, strong women slaves from the fields.

They were all in a simple uniform dress of a bluish check stuff, the skirts reaching little below the knee, their legs and feet were bare; they carried themselves loftily, each having a hoe over the shoulder, and walking with a free, powerful swing, like chasseurs on the march. . . . The men wore small Scotch bonnets; many of the women, handkerchiefs, turban fashion, and a few nothing at all on their heads.[4]

When Olmsted asked another slave manager why a gang was so dirty, the manager explained, "Negroes are the filthiest people in the world . . . [some] would not keep clean twenty-four hours at a time if you gave them thirty suits a year." Olmsted learned that there were no helpful rules for maintaining cleanliness, but that "sometimes the negroes were told at night that any one who came into the field the next morning without being clean would be whipped."[5] The threat of the lash for dirtiness gave no trouble to those who were habitually clean; to others, however, the shadow of the lash caused all-night laundering and bathing, a source of racist amusement to the overseers.

Olmsted learned that each slave on the plantation was given two suits of summer clothing and one of winter clothing each year. The manager volunteered that, in addition, "most of them got presents of some holiday finery [calico dresses, handkerchiefs], and purchased more for themselves, at Christmas." Olmsted wrote: "One of the drivers now in the field had on a splendid uniform coat of an officer of the flying artillery. After the Mexican war, a great deal of military clothing was sold at auction in New Orleans, and much of it was bought by planters at a low price, and given to their negroes, who were greatly pleased with it."[6]

Olmsted learned, however, that most clothing for slaves was

below

Costuming in *Gone with the Wind*, a popular movie even today, reflects a romanticized view of clothing worn by both blacks and whites in the antebellum South. Rhett and Scarlett are dressed in the clothing of rich white people.

right

Scarlett O'Hara, the heroine of *Gone with the Wind*, appeared in tattered finery and the working woman's sunbonnet to signify her reduced social and economic circumstances.

homemade, some by slaves themselves, but more often by the women and girls of the plantation household. He described a visit to a loom house in a slave quarter, where "a dozen negroes were at work making shoes, and manufacturing coarse cotton stuff for negro clothing. One of the hands so employed was insane, and most of the others were cripples, invalids with chronic complaints, or unfitted by age, or some infirmity, for field work."[7] Slave labor, after all, was too valuable to be spent profligately on making clothes for other slaves. Such work was suitable only for those who had no use in the fields.

As he traveled into northern Mississippi, Olmsted visited another plantation where he found a group of black women spinning and weaving coarse cotton shirting with an ancient rude hand loom. The white mistress of the house, herself spinning in the living room, asked him "what women in the North could find to do, and how they could ever pass the time, when they gave up spinning and weaving." She boasted that she made the common everyday clothing for all her family and her servants; her family bought only a few "store-goods" for their dress-up clothes. Moreover, she kept the black girls spinning all through the winter, and at all times when they were not needed in the field.[8]

Olmsted's curiosity extended beyond the plantation to include a number of individuals and groups with special places in the southern social hierarchy. For example, he took considerable interest in a black preacher, a "tall, full-blooded negro, very black, and with a disgusting expression of sensuality, cunning, and vanity in his countenance . . . [who was] dressed in the loosest form of the fashionable sack overcoat, which he threw off presently, showing a white vest, gaudy cravat, and a tight cutaway coat, linked together at the breast with jet buttons."[9]

When he journeyed into the Tennessee mountains, Olmsted found a large, neat white house with "negro shanties and an open log cabin in the front yard." There he met "a stout, elderly, fine-looking woman, in a cool white muslin dress [who] sat upon the gallery, fanning herself." When her husband arrived, Olmsted saw that "he was very hot also, though dressed coolly enough in merely a pair of short-legged, unbleached cotton trousers, and a shirt with the bosom spread open — no shoes nor stockings."[10]

Climate, as well as hierarchy, influenced clothing in the South. "I was informed," wrote Olmsted, "that a majority of the [poorer] folks went barefoot all winter, though they had snow much of the time four or five inches deep, and the man said he didn't think most of them about here had more than one coat, and they never wore any in the winter except on holidays."[11]

Making and maintaining clothing occupied most of the waking

89

Hattie McDaniel, as Mammy, wore a standardized "peasant costume."

hours of most women in the South, no less than in the North, in the years prior to the Civil War. The women of southern households, however, sewed for the slaves of the plantation, as well as for themselves and their families. While the production of clothing was only part of the southern woman's duty to care for and manage servants, clothing manufacture reveals the complex relations between mistress and slaves.

Young upper-class women learned to sew early, the needle and pincushion serving as accessories to their passage to maturity and wifehood. Typically, a young woman made chemises, pantalets, nightgowns, and nightcaps for herself and her younger siblings. Even though she sewed most of her own everyday clothing, her parents purchased dress-up clothes for her. She was expected to be interested in clothes, to know the value of materials, to know the principles of dressmaking, and to be able to dress fashionably and in accordance with her social standing.

Elizabeth Fox-Genovese, a more recent student of the role and symbolic portent of clothing in the antebellum South, echoes many of Olmsted's observations.[12] She found that the women of plantation households made clothing for the slaves; they often worked in groups, sometimes overseeing slave assistance to the project. In a typical plantation household, huge bolts of cloth had to be bought, transported, cut, and stitched into two sets of clothing for each slave, each year.

Some women noted in their journals or letters to friends that they enjoyed making special items of clothing as gifts to favorite slaves or their children. But in general, the master of the household distributed clothing among the slaves, an activity that symbolized his supremacy if not his generosity.

Younger unmarried women were instructed not only in the rudiments of sewing but in the art of dressing fashionably. Just as they were taught to sew by their mothers, they were instructed in the manners, responsibilities, and privileges of their class; and they were instructed in the importance of fashion in chronicling their status and in the competition with other women for the attention of men.

Clothing occupied such an important part of the rich southern woman's attention, and played such a profound role in establishing her identity in southern society, that brothers and fathers, too, were expected to impart fashion's conventions to the belles of the family. The daughter of a plantation household learned early that a lady identified herself by her dress, that she was not to engage in vulgar display, that she was to show in her dress that she was honored and protected by men; in short, her dress was to reinforce the appearance of idleness and helplessness.

The language of fashion provided subtle nuances for compe-

90

Northern artists after the Civil War reflected their contempt for southerners even in depictions of children. Readers of *Harper's* and similar publications often saw illustrations of southerners — black and white, adults and children — as intellectually and socially retarded, ill-mannered, and ill-clothed.

tition among women to establish dominance both over other women and over men. As adolescent women prepared for marriage to attractive and powerful individuals, they scrutinized their own clothing and that of others on every occasion, checking each outfit against standards of appropriateness, changing costumes to appear always in "the right thing." One young woman wore her "eternal tissue silk" and a black silk cape on a social visit, her "pink calico dress and black silk cape" during a morning at home, an "embroidered dress and black lace cape" for church services, and upon returning from church and expecting a gentleman caller, donned yet another outfit. She kept two seamstresses busy, and augmented their work with purchases of fashionable garments. Even by the standards of that society, she "took an inordinate interest in her own wardrobe as a sign of her emerging place in the world and an asset in her ability to attract the attention of a desirable man."[13]

Clothing was an obsession with more mature married women as well, especially if they moved — or aspired to move — in fashionable circles. They too changed outfits frequently, giving lavish attention to turning themselves out in appropriate garments and to using clothing to enhance their images and status. During the course of a day, a southern woman might wear "a morning dress, a dinner dress, an evening dress for teas, and a ball gown." For a quiet morning at home, she might throw on her "robe de chambre," or to attend a ball in the evening, she might wear richly embroidered or brocaded robes. Moreover, women who devoted their lives to their wardrobes and toilettes derided women who exercised different values or lived in different social and economic circumstances. A fashionable lady who visited Hopewell, North Carolina, found the local women bereft of tasteful concern for fashion, and commented on the appearance of the ladies attending church, "I had expected to see some attempt at Taste or Fashion, a few city airs and graces — but no such thing — I think I may venture to say there were not a bonnets [sic] which differed in shape and color in the whole congregation. . . ."[14]

In the hierarchy of the South, mistresses of slaveholding households considered themselves superior to poorer white women and considered the clothing worn by them to be unfashionable and therefore inferior. Fox-Genovese describes a rich southern woman who, while in Texas during the Civil War,

accepted the hospitality of a yeoman family. While she expressed gratitude for their kindness and generosity, she was dismayed that the women of the household had "not a scrap of ribbon or lace or any kind of adornment in the house. I never saw a woman before without a ribbon."[15]

Earlier the Puritans had enacted sumptuary laws, perhaps more celebrated by those who violated them than by those who adhered to their standards of dress; in a similar effort to restrict fine clothing to the upper classes, some southern lawmakers had enacted laws governing slave clothing. In both instances, the laws reflected the long-established association of clothing with class. In the aftermath of the Civil War, whites who snobbishly pinned their self-esteem to fashion unhappily watched freed black women wear the veils and carry the parasols that had been the emblems of white privilege, and saw black men don the top hats, frock coats, and well-cobbled boots that in the past had symbolized power.

91

Distinctions in clothing persisted in advertising imagery.

Broncobuster, Cheyenne, Wyoming, Frontier Days, c. 1905

Western Frontier

When President Kennedy proposed the New Frontier in 1960, he conjured in the imaginations of Americans visions of pioneer bravery and accomplishment, of homesteaders' struggles that resulted in riches, of contests between right (cowboy) and wrong (bad guy) in which right triumphed with the easy quick draw of a deadly six-shooter. Americans thrilled to the dream, even if the evoked visions were taken more from Hollywood's primer of American history than from the real-life stories of struggle, loss, death, failure, hopelessness, and despair that haunted the lives of people who pushed the American frontier westward.

From the earliest times of New World colonization, the concept and physical actuality of a frontier exerted influence on the lives of men, women, and children, urging them to forge across the mountains and into the wilderness, spurring them to test themselves against nature and to win the contest with their axes, guns, and cunning. The white population had moved steadily westward, reaching into the Western Reserve; explorers had hacked and paddled their way through wilderness to the Pacific Ocean; and by the second half of the nineteenth century the magnitude and power of the westward migration forced social and economic change throughout the whole country, touching all segments of the population.

During these years, largely as a consequence of the westward movement, major themes in the story of American clothing, gestating since the sixteenth century, emerged: male and female roles were codified and linked to styles of clothing; ethnic influences and cross-cultural exchanges begat articles of and attitudes about clothing; class distinction and conspicuous consumption impelled both the market and the personal display of clothing; and, with the acceptance of norms for clothing, personal costuming had the power to express distinction or eccentricity, and to declare outwardly the individual's inner condition. The large stage for human drama provided by western migration offered no set script or readily identifying costume for its mythic heroes and villains. As the lore of the West grew, a colorful collection of individuals — often associated with unique styles of clothing — set the costumes for later enactments of mountain men, gunslingers, tainted ladies, intrepid lawmen, and other archetypical characters that vivify western mythology and history.

Conformity and convention, too, contributed to the codification of western — and American — dress. From the beginning of the westward movement, clothing signaled class membership and defined or emphasized the separate and unequal roles of men and women. People migrating westward tried often to dress in the fashions of the East, thereby connoting a degree of leisure and a level of financial security that few homesteaders and ranchers actually found in the tough realities of life in the West. Similarly, they dressed in styles that reiterated and strengthened social attitudes about acceptable behavior for men and women, and the nature of the nuclear family.

Such societal constraints, or conservative influences, however, did not prevent the birth of the prototypes for sportswear, that most American aspect of American clothing. The work clothing of westerners — especially those articles we now identify as "western dress" — were once associated with ranching, farming, mining, and trapping. Levi's and the Stetson hat, two of the most identifiable products contributing to the development of American sportswear, developed to meet the needs of men involved in grunt-and-sweat outdoor labor. These and other items — including cowboy boots, the neckerchief, the fringed jacket or decorated vest, and fringed gauntlet-style gloves — gained popularity among hardworking people; today, however, they are universally worn as sportswear.

In settling their first frontier, the eastern seaboard, the Europeans had pressed the Indians to the west, often removing them from their ancestral and sacred lands against their will, and thus, by destroying delicate balances of power and position that existed among the Indian tribes, inciting territorial wars among the Indians themselves and Indian efforts to preserve their

94

WESTARD BOUND.

lands and ways of life. As the whites pushed into the western area of the territory that would become the United States, they hunted buffalo — a mainstay of Indian life — and by using rifles depleted herds quickly.

Indians and whites encountered one another on the overland trails and in the wilderness, continuing the saga of sharing and of conflict that began with the first colonists on the eastern seaboard. Letters and journals from the overland trip refer often to encounters with the Indians, to the clothing the Native Americans wore, and to the articles of clothing they sought from the travelers. These documents provide glimpses of near-naked Indians adorned with paint and tattoos, of betrousered but shirtless Indians, blankets around their shoulders, of fabulous clothing, and of scruffy, insubstantial garments. There are descriptions of Indians wearing feathers and fur on their heads, beads around their necks, and brass rings on their wrists and arms and in their ears, of Indians in moccasins and leather leggings, and of others in fringed leather garments or cloaks of fur, often with the tails of wolves, bears, or raccoons hanging on them.

95

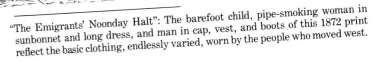

"The Emigrants' Noonday Halt": The barefoot child, pipe-smoking woman in sunbonnet and long dress, and man in cap, vest, and boots of this 1872 print reflect the basic clothing, endlessly varied, worn by the people who moved west.

Lewis and Clark

Thomas Jefferson — usually cast by historians as the quintessential eighteenth-century man — opened the nineteenth century, actually and symbolically, by launching the Lewis and Clark expedition (1804–6). In sponsoring the expedition, which began in Jefferson's restless and rational mind as a means for advancing his personal intellectual interests alongside his political beliefs, Jefferson championed essential nineteenth-century ideals of democracy and westward expansion; specifically, he set in motion the exploration of the vast lands beyond the Mississippi.

Jefferson was keenly interested in Native Americans, and compiled a dictionary of Indian languages. At Monticello, his home in Virginia, he treasured the Indian artifacts, tools, and garments that Lewis and Clark collected. Captain Meriwether Lewis, Jefferson's kinsman and personal secretary, and Army Lieutenant William Clark, an accomplished Indian fighter, proved brilliant choices to accomplish Jefferson's mission. They were sympathetic to his imagination and to his desire for knowledge; they readily adopted his intense interest in Indian life and took to heart his request for observations of Indian "food, clothing, & domestic accommodations." In the uncodified spelling of the time that characterizes their journals, Lewis and Clark prepared for their travels by setting to paper the questions that would inform their observations and brilliant descriptions of Indian dress:

"Meriwether Lewis, Esq."

What garments do their dress usially Consist, in both Sexes? What are the Shapes & Materials of those garments? In what manner are they Worn? What orniments do they use to decorate their person? do they use paints of Various Colours on the surface of their Skins, and what the most usial Colours thus used? do they tattoe (or scarify) their bodys and on what parts? do they imprint with the aids of a sharp pointed instrument and some colouring matter any figures on their Skins and what are the part of the body on which they are usially imprinted. Which are the usial figures?*

Because Lewis and Clark kept those questions before them as they wrote their journals, the accounts provide vital information about Native Americans at the beginning of the nineteenth century. They chronicle the respective styles of clothing and social organization characteristic of the Indians encountered, instancing the use of clothing in bartering with the Indians, acknowledging the adoption of materials and styles of Indian clothing as the white easterners' garb failed the test of the wilderness, and mirroring their own transformation from Virginia gentlemen, clothed in the upper-class eastern male uniform, to nineteenth-century American adventurers in buckskin and moccasins, practicing the wisdom and wiles of the Indians to conquer the western wilderness.

In preparation for their journey, Lewis and Clark anticipated the Native Americans' fascination with the clothing of white men, and included attractive items in their supply of goods to use in bartering with the Indians: red flannel cloth, "hanckercheifs," silk, scarlet cloth, red tape, silk ribbon, beads, calico ruffled shirts, and blankets. To clothe themselves and their men (32 soldiers and 10 civilians) on the journey, they purchased 45 flannel shirts, 31 coats, 15 pairs of blue wool overalls, 36 pairs of stockings, 20 frocks, 30 shirts, and 20 pairs of shoes. In addition, they requisitioned from the Army the basic male clothing of the period: coats, overalls, stockings, frocks, linen shirts, and shoes. This inventory demonstrates that Lewis and Clark intended to dress themselves and their men as if they were on duty in a distant, inconvenient, but

Indian drawing of cavalry sent to destroy them

* Frank Bergon, ed., *The Journals of Lewis and Clark* (New York: Penguin, 1989), p. 21.

96

nonetheless well-regulated military outpost. With this wardrobe, they would be protected from the elements by their serviceable, sturdy clothing, they would uphold military standards of dress, and they would be prepared to cope with rugged terrain and hardship.

But the intrepid adventurers faced ordeals and tests far more frightening, threatening, and unpredictable than might be found at the most primitive of the established outposts. Starting from St. Louis on May 14, 1804, Lewis and Clark, their military and civilian troop, and a large pet Newfoundland dog traveled with difficulty up the Missouri. They wintered among the Mandan Sioux Indians in what later became North Dakota before venturing west across what is now Montana to the Continental Divide. With the help of French-Canadian interpreter Toussaint Charbonneau, and especially his wife, the Snake Indian Sacajawea, who also served as guide and interpreter, the expedition survived an arduous journey westward, reaching the Pacific Ocean in November 1805.

Lewis and Clark spent that second winter with the Chinook Indians, exchanging colored ribbons and other materials the Indians desired for food; they bought a hat "made of Splits and Strong grass, which is made in the fashion which was common in the U States two years ago." The explorers were amused to find that the Indians on the West Coast had traded with New England seamen, wore prized fragments of the sailors' clothing, and enthusiastically echoed sailor talk, directing one another to "haul lead" and calling their disfavored "sumpitch."

Throughout their amazing journey, beset by danger and shadowed by fear, Lewis and Clark moved steadily onward, recording (among other things) information on Indian dress. In adapting to survive in the wilderness, they learned from the Indians to tan leather — a commodity easily gathered from the great herds of elk, deer, and buffalo — and to make clothing and moccasins that both protected them and enabled them to move easily over difficult terrain and through dense vegetation. When Lewis and Clark returned to the white man's world, they wore the leather clothing of the "savages." Thus, the expedition mixed the clothing of two cultures, and exemplified what would become routine appropriation of clothing styles and articles between the two groups occupying the same vast landmass.

After the expedition, William Clark served as U.S. Superintendent of Indian Affairs, negotiating a series of treaties with Native American tribes. George Catlin, a Philadelphia lawyer-turned-artist, joined Clark in St. Louis and accompanied him on visits to the Indians of the West. Catlin's prints, though completed years after the Lewis and Clark expedition, illustrate many of the explorers' observations, and remain a visual record of Native Americans in the early nineteenth century.

While Jefferson sought to know and win the loyalty of the Indians, later Americans of European descent saw the Native Americans as impediments to the quick expansion and wealth that they sought. The respect Lewis and Clark showed for Indian culture, their admiration for Indian skills and ways of life, and their own bravery and diplomacy in dealing with the Indians they encountered were not to be reflected in the official policy regarding Native Americans by the time Andrew Jackson, himself a military hero and Indian fighter, was elected president, and by the time Americans moved westward in great numbers, seeking for themselves and their progeny the wealth and freedom promised by the vast land.

By the end of the century, Native Americans would be slaughtered, their wealth and holdings plundered, and their culture, prey to the appetites of a growing capitalist economy and to bigotry born of religious narrow-mindedness, diminished by government policy justifying its effects as "acculturation."

These same sources also describe what the Indians saw: long trains of huge covered wagons, usually pulled by oxen; men, women, and children moving across vast lands with a rattling, rolling assortment of household goods. The Indians soon identified and wanted many of the items carried by the pioneers — knives, axes, cooking utensils, and clothing. Some also wanted rifles and liquor, often with drastic consequences for both Indians and whites.

Word of Indian interest in such goods spread among whites planning the overland journey, and soon the settlers carried with them household articles and garments specifically for barter. "Anybody preparing to come to this country," one woman wrote, "should make up some calico shirts to trade to the Indians in case of necessity. You will have to hire them to pilot you across rivers. . . . My folks were about stripped of shirts, trousers, jackets and 'wampuses.' "[1]

One pioneer wrote of an ancient Indian who stood in the middle of a trail and waved a battered cavalry sword until he halted an entire wagon train. The Indian then placed a blanket beside the road and commenced bartering by insisting that clothing and utensils be thrown onto the blanket in exchange for his buffalo skins. Other migrants encountered Indians who wanted to trade buffalo robes for horse bridles, clothing, and food. In such encounters, a cotton shirt might be worth a piece of buffalo hide, or a calico apron might secure a much-needed pair of Indian-made moccasins.

The pioneers began their westward trek in clothing they had worn in the East, some of it suitable but most of it ridiculous and cumbersome for the arduous journey. Women's hoopskirts, though fashionable in the East despite their impracticality, proved especially unsuitable for pioneer life. They took up precious space in covered wagons and inhibited the physical movement of the wearer; worse for some women, they readily caught prairie wind and inverted to disclose the wearer's petticoats and drawers.

Those women who ventured from the East in hoops and fancy silks, or who continued to wear fashionable and impractical clothing on the trails, risked being mistaken for prostitutes. Regardless of vanity or interest in fashion at the onset of the journey, most women soon learned that clothing was an integral part of survival, that they should outfit themselves in sturdy and practical clothing, and that they should buy boots if they could afford them. Fashion be damned, they found that smaller-sized men's shoes would do very well, and those who could pay the price happily donned heavy, protective footwear.

In time, trading posts, hostelries, and supply centers dotted the established trails. Such ranches* offered supplies and clothing suitable for the trail and for settlement in the western lands.

The sunbonnet — which came to symbolize female pioneers — was a practical and inexpensive way of protecting the head and shading the eyes from the relentless sunshine of the prairies. Its protective capabilities soon overrode considerations of fashion, age, and class. The richer girls bowed to their mothers' insistence that they protect their complexions with sunbonnets and their hands and forearms with long mitts, and joined the toiling children of poorer circumstances under cotton sunbonnets.

While most female pioneers clothed themselves to meet the rigors of overland travel and hard work in their new lives, some clung to vestiges of femininity in dress, wearing bows and laces to reinforce their identity with feminine — and therefore, *domestic* — values. In a grueling situation, where everyone had to work, women able to wear clothing that connoted frailty and dependence symbolized the values of hearth, home, and motherhood, and emphasized the distinctions between male and female roles in society.

Males on the western frontier were better able to adapt their eastern clothing to meet the mud, sun, storms, cold, and winds of the West. Those who set out from the East in the standard working-class male garb of the day — trousers and suspenders over pullover shirts, with vests and caps — soon bought sturdy boots, tucking their trousers into the tops and donning broad-brimmed hats. Prior to the Civil War, most men wore clothing made by women; during the Civil War, however, men learned to like the factory-produced uniforms, and thereafter bought clothes when they could afford them. The surplus clothing of the Civil War armies appeared on the later-nineteenth-century frontiersmen: heavy coats and trousers, double-breasted pullover shirts, boots, and individually crimped hats contributed to the standard clothing of men in the West.

Affluent Americans were scarce in the first waves of westward pioneers in covered wagons. With the extension of rail-

---

* As described by Colonel James Meline, a *ranche*, in the nomenclature of the time, was "not a dwelling, nor a farmhouse, nor a store, nor a tavern, but all of these, and more. It is connected with a large corral, and capable of sustaining an Indian siege. You can procure entertainment at them . . . and they keep for sale liquors, canned fruit, knives, playing cards, saddlery, and *goggles* — both blue and green." The goggles, as Meline explained, were a prime necessity. "You will find them on sale at every ranche on the plains, north and south. The prevalent heat, dust, and glare make them almost indispensable." (Dee Brown, *The Gentle Tamers: Women of the Wild West* [New York: G. P. Putnam's Sons, 1958], p. 151)

98

"Trading on the Plains —
A Seductive Offer" (1871)

below

"Pilgrims of the Plains" (1871)

roads, however, speculators and investors — in dark suits and white linen as well as dressy hats and low boots that marked them as men free from the rigors of harsh outdoor work — went west in search of fortune.

Women worked continually to mend and wash clothing, an unending task that further differentiated sex roles on the trails. Even so, diarists report seeing clothing beside the trails that was so worn that it had simply fallen from the backs of owners. When a member of the traveling community died on the trail, family members and friends often resorted to treatment of the dead that would have been unthinkable in the East: undressed corpses, wrapped in whatever cloth was available, were submitted to the earth, their rude graves marked with crosses and covered with stones to discourage foraging animals. Their clothing, however, was saved for the living.

Keeping clothing in order presented a serious problem to women on the overland trail, where laundering was next to impossible. The travelers stopped only briefly, usually overnight, not long enough for laundered clothes to be dried, and wet clothing could hardly be carried in the wagons. Even on rare occasions when the wagon trains camped for a day or so, women struggled to find and heat enough water to launder a family's dirty clothes, causing one diarist to complain, "This gypsy life is anything but agreeable. It is impossible to keep anything clean."[2] Another woman, able to launder clothes only three times during the six-month journey from New York to Oregon, remembered one of the laundering places along the Oregon Trail, Soda Springs, where, "some of the women improved the opportunity offered by plenty of hot water here at the springs to wash a few things."[3]

Once the journey was completed, and homesteads or ranches established, life for the men and women who settled the West was only slightly better than it had been on the trails. They had houses, of sorts, ranging from versions of the Indian tepee and sod huts to quickly built houses of rough timber. For food, which was neither fancy nor plentiful, they rationed meager stores, trapped and shot game, and prayed that the seeds they brought from the East would yield a harvest sufficient for a year's meals

100

"Western Sketches — Arkansas Pilgrims in Camp" (1874)

Oscar Wilde's American Wardrobe

On the other side of the Atlantic, Oscar Wilde's flamboyant "aesthetic" costume elicited parallel comments from the staid London community. When he came to America to lecture in 1882, Wilde attracted large crowds as much interested in seeing the large, effete Britisher in his velvet knickers suits, soft collars, and flowing bow ties as in hearing his poetic colloquy on the aesthetic way of life. When Wilde decided to visit the American West, he changed neither his style of dress nor his philosophical attitudes. Sitting on the train, looking out of the windows for hours at a time, Wilde saw cowboys in tall hats, chaps, boots, and carrying revolvers; he saw women in calico dresses, muslin aprons, and sunbonnets; he saw Indians in blankets, articles of western clothing, feathers, and paint; he saw barefoot children; and he saw cavalrymen dressed in the dashing style of General Custer.

By the time Wilde dropped languidly from the train in Leadville, Colorado, he wore a high-crowned, large-brimmed cowboy hat. At the time of Wilde's visit, Leadville had a population estimated at about 30,000; no one was certain, however, because Leadville was a stopover of varying duration for itinerant miners, cowboys, and prostitutes; it was a town of boarding houses and campsites. No one cared much what happened in Leadville, a town noted for lawlessness, drunkenness, whorehouses, and half-crazy miners who came to town to drink, gamble, and enjoy the company of friendly women.

Leadville miners and gents-of-the-bottle took their leisure around the train depot, and enjoyed following easterners down the streets, mimicking their walks and ways, perceived to be fancy and foolish. Among the many Leadville legends, visitors remembered the bootblack who trained his dog to urinate on the boots of fancy foreign gentlemen.

Leadville hardly seemed a compatible place for Oscar Wilde. But within a few days, he had visited the mines and made friends among the miners, he had outdrunk several of the best drinkers in town, and he had won both respect and friendship among a group hardly likely to embrace his concepts of aestheticism. He had also adopted the miner's style of dress and now wore corduroy trousers, which he tucked into high boots, a knotted neckerchief instead of a bow tie, and a full shirt with a western vest. This western outfit, he proclaimed, was the best possible style for men.

Cowboy Clothing

Over years of hardship, experimentation with clothing, and adaptation of available materials and styles to the needs of the frontier, a distinctly western style of American clothing evolved.

The standard cowboy costume, or western style of clothing for men, derived from the influences of frontier conditions — weather, requirements of work, availability of materials — and from a style of dress developed as early as the sixteenth century by the vaqueros of New Spain, who wore large hats for protection against the elements, bandannas, wool or cotton shirts, leather jackets (*chaquetas*), and pants (*sotas*) that laced tightly up the sides. The costume of these early laborers-on-horseback persisted over the years and, with modification, was worn by nineteenth- and early-twentieth-century men in Mexico and the southwestern territory of the United States.

The American western style of clothing mingled various separate garments from the vaqueros and standard male clothing of the eastern seaboard: shirt, jacket or vest, boots, trousers, chaps, spurs, gloves, neckerchief, and hat all took on a distinctly "cowboy" flavor.

The early western work shirt, identical to that worn in the East, was a woolen pullover, often with a double row of buttons. In time, however, westerners wore wool or cotton pullover shirts of muted colors. The earliest western jackets were made of leather and were similar to those worn by the vaqueros; later, however, cowboys wore vaquero-type short jackets made of denim with corduroy collars. The popularity of vests may have derived as much from their association with eastern business clothes as with their convenience.

Boots, unknown to the barefoot vaqueros, traveled west with the pioneers. The standard style, reaching to just below the knee, was worn on the trails, on ranches, and on the great plains. The later "Hollywood boot" — low, highly embossed,

"World's Champion All-Around Cowboy"

The top rodeo stars wear

BLUE BELL

Wranglers

the authentic Western jeans

floridly decorated and bejeweled — was obviously unknown in the working West and would hardly have seemed suitable to the pioneers and cowboys themselves.

Chaps (the term *chaps* is thought to be derived from the Spanish *chaparajos*, or "undressed sheepskin"), another result of vaquero tradition, were protective leather leggings worn over trousers. A popular item of cowboy clothing, chaps were actually skeleton overalls, originally crafted in the American West from very stiff and tight cowhide, and called "shotguns." Later "batwings" had side openings and resembled a double skirt clipped at the sides to give more freedom. Often leather chaps had white buckskin fringes. Cowboys experimented with chaps and sometimes adapted fur rather than leather to the garment so that bear, wolf, pony, sheep, or angora pelts swathed the cowpunchers' legs.

Like farmers, cowboys wore neckerchiefs not merely for looks but with good reason, for they could be tied across the nose and mouth to protect against dust stirred by driving herds. For the most part, neckerchiefs were usually the plain red bandannas still worn today, and recently extremely popular among young people.

Gloves, like neckerchiefs, offered more than decoration; they protected the hands against rope burns and other hazards. Western gloves, usually buckskin with large gauntlet wrists, might be ornately decorated with a spread eagle, Texas star, or silver conchas.

War paint, though usually associated with Indians (or, more recently, with football players), is not technically clothing, but the cowboy learned that soot grease smeared under the eyes served as protection against snow glare in the wintry plains regions.

as well as seeds for the next growing season. Along with their physical difficulties, those early pioneers, homesteaders, ranchers, and miners experienced hardships ranging in emotional detail and significance from the depths of human agony to slapstick comedy, and their ingenuity took them from terrible deprivation to goofy making-do.

Making do with the clothing they had brought with them was not easy. One pioneer summarized the situation when he said, "After we had been here a short time, we carried our whole wardrobe on our backs and our feet stuck out."[4] Everyone was poor; those who had woolen coats or sturdy shoes from the East were among the fortunate pioneers.

For the most part, hard-working women had little choice but to wear the same basic outfit throughout the year: a gingham or calico dress, a sunbonnet, and a muslin apron. Homesteading and ranching men, too, wore simple overalls, cotton work shirts, and caps or broad-brimmed hats. When socks were not available in the winter, men wrapped their feet in rags, and even found it necessary sometimes to wrap gunny sacks around their boots to prevent their feet from freezing in the cold weather. As spring thawing brought mud to ranches, farms, and the streets of villages, men wore their trousers tucked inside the tops of their boots, as they had often worn them on the journey westward.

Sturdy leather boots and shoes — waterproofed by blackening with soot from the inside of stove lids — were a valuable possession for both men and women. Those who had the treasured shoes and boots saved them by going barefoot as much as possible. Men, women, and children often carried their shoes, walking barefoot to the door of the church, grange, or host's house, and putting them on at the last minute, managing thereby both to preserve the shoes and to meet the requirements of civilized social intercourse. In summer, adults wore shoes only for church services or high social occasions; children, however, went barefoot to church and to school when weather permitted. In many instances by necessity more than preference children remained barefoot all year, and stayed home from school when the risk of freezing feet was too great.

When people could afford to purchase boots, they bought them large to allow for the inevitable shrinkage caused by wetness. Most could not afford boots, however, and wore moccasins, which they bought cheaply or made out of animal skins or heavy cloth. They tacked leather uppers to wooden soles to make shoes that, despite their loud clatter on uncovered floors, kept feet warm and dry. When they could afford to buy neither footwear nor the materials for making something at home, people wrapped their

feet in rags and walked where they had to go.

Shoes were not the only cherished items of clothing. The people who settled the West wore to extinction old coats and shawls brought from the East, and carefully meted out the use of "good" clothing. Even good clothing was simple, and often made of muslin, calico, or gingham. "For some years," wrote one woman, "a new calico dress was good enough for the best . . . the leaders of fashion favoring long dresses. Low necks and short sleeves were never seen then. Those who could afford a hat treasured it for the Fourth of July."[5]

Another typical letter writer of the period, relating her own great desire to see Oregon's beautiful scenery, wild animals, and Indians, cautioned those who followed her not to be "worried or frightened at trifles" but to "put up with storm and cloud as well as calm and sunshine. . . ."[6] As an example of her maintaining such perspective, she dressed herself up for the Fourth of July festivities in clothing that would hardly have been fashionable in

Cowboy/rancher

103

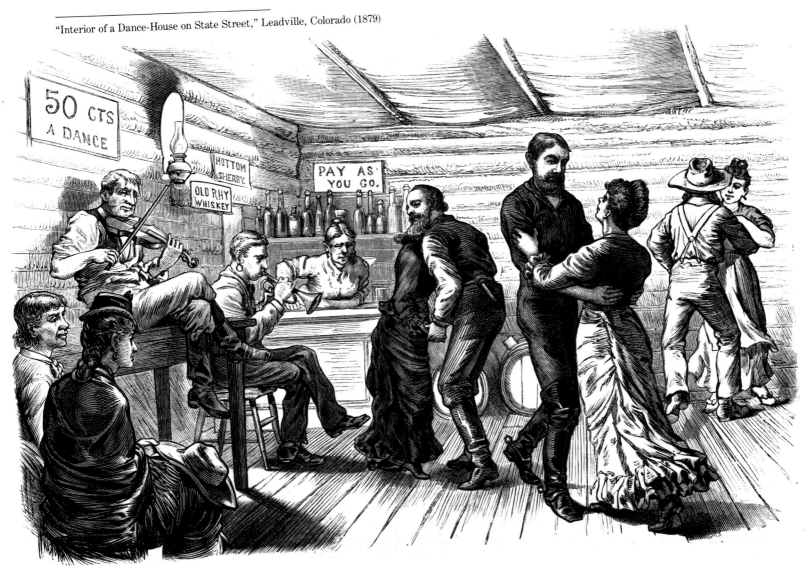

the East: a red calico frock made during the wagon trip, a pair of "macasins" made of black buffalo hide and decorated with silk, and a hat of braided bulrushes, trimmed with red, white, and pink paper streamers.

Once settled, practicality and economy largely determined what men, women, and children wore. But even on the frontier, in the most difficult circumstances and most rustic social situations, people used clothing to convey their sense of worth, their position in society, and their values. Fantasies of fashions for the leisured classes, adapted in shades and shapes possible on the frontier, made life a little easier in a world dominated by hard work, meager supplies, and scant wardrobes of made-over, hand-me-down, made-do, and much patched and washed clothing.

Everyone worked on the frontier, including children, who were assets to a family precisely because they could begin to

work early at strenuous tasks, giving long hours to the needs of the homestead, earning their keep, and contributing to the welfare of the family. Most of the emigrants to the new lands needed new clothing to replenish wardrobes worn out on the trail, and faced constructing it from available materials. One woman surmised that there was only one bolt of calico in the whole of Oregon by the time she and her family arrived.

That was all the cloth we had for dresses at that time. That was sold for fifty cents a yard. It was very poor quality of calico. The women and girls that came here were very destitute. The next summer . . . my oldest sister and I gathered a barrel of cranberries and I sent them to Oregon City and got a little piece of blue drilling that made us a covering. And that was about all; it could hardly be considered dresses, but it was so we were covered. We did not have any ruffles, I think.[7]

In addition to helping with farm or ranch work, women cooked, bore and cared for children, and had also to provide the materials for clothing, cutting and sewing those materials into the articles to be worn by each family member, and keeping the clothes for the family clean and in repair. Hours, often late-night lamplit hours when the heavier chores had been dispatched, were devoted to sewing: new skirts, aprons, sunbonnets, shirts, and trousers were cut and stitched; socks and sweaters were knitted and darned, using the wools and other materials home-produced by the family.

The frontier family typically produced yarns and wools, a long and difficult process that began with breeding and keeping a herd of sheep large enough to supply the needed wool. The sheep, protected from weather and predators and tended through lambing, were shorn each year, either by a family member or an itinerant shearer. Children washed the new wool, often in a nearby river or creek; they picked the burrs and twigs from it and dried the valuable wool, then rolled the fibers into yard-long units in preparation for carding. These rolls were spun into thread and tied into skeins for dyeing with substances extracted from roots, barks, herbs, and berries. A few families could afford to buy madder for red dye or longwood for black.

Only the most affluent frontier families could afford ready-made fabrics and clothing, both of which were costly, difficult to locate, and likely to be subjected to the vagaries of uncertain mail systems. Paper patterns, a luxury that opened doors to dreams of high fashion and a more leisurely style of life, were collected, shared, and passed around among the families in a region. Homemade clothing, whether of the fancy variety from paper patterns or the cruder garments cut from scraps of salvaged fabric, sufficed for most families, and saw continuing life as hand-me-down clothing. Children's clothing, tucked in or let out, patched and repaired, passed from oldest to youngest before joining worn-out adult clothing on the quilting frame or in the rag bin. After the canvas from the overland wagons was used in clothing, the emigrant families on the plains seized grain sacks as well as the bed linens that had traveled west with them, summoning these fabrics to new existence as shirts, aprons, trousers, and dresses. A woman from one such pioneer family recalled the people in her community joked that Kansans could not afford to wear underwear. This, she teased, was patently untrue. The clotheslines of the homesteads were full of undergarments advertising I. M. Yost's flour, irrefutable evidence of clean underwear and prosperity in frontier Kansas.

105

"Making a Tenderfoot Dance"

William S. Hart,
movie version
of cowboy

"The Slave of Gold" (1882), from the *National Police Gazette: New York*

The Alamo

Each frontier family learned and exercised new skill and constant ingenuity to keep itself clothed in the heat of summer and the cold of winter. The pioneers learned from the Indians to make clothing from buffalo skins and to produce moccasins and strong leather leggings similar to those long worn by the Indians of the plains.

Homemade trousers for men, among those who could not afford ready-made garments, remained a problem and tested the innovation of the women who made them. Trousers made at home, frequently by women with limited skills in tailoring, were often ill-fitting and made of odd pieces of material. In one instance, a family, having come west with a large supply of grain sacks imprinted with their name, found that they could not readily cultivate grain crops. When they changed plans for their farm, the frugal wife claimed the surplus sacks and cut and reshaped them into trousers for the men of the family. The neighbors were amused to see these men with their family names imprinted in large red letters on the seat of their new trousers. They, it was joked among the neighbors, would not be lost on the prairies.

Men's trousers were made of duck or other heavy material, including that from grain sacks, which could be purchased for fifty cents each. Typically, men wore hickory, blue, or checkered shirts, along with a heavy over-garment, or "wampus."

Those families with sheep were able to weave linsey-woolsey for garments for both men and women. A man's homespun suit was expected to last a year. Few pioneer men had more than one suit of clothes, and most would have had to lie abed while their wives mended their trousers.

Men commonly attended church or other important social functions in unmatching overalls and jackets, in clothing faded by washing and by the sun and patched with contrasting materials. Men of standing, no less than the humbler and poorer farmers, wore modest clothing made of what was available on the prairies. As an example, Dr. M. H. Clark, a member of the Nebraska legislature in 1855, wore the buckskin attire of the hunter and frontiersman and, as was the custom of the time and place, carried a revolver or two.

Wrote a member of the first Kansas state legislature in 1861: "So I roused myself out of dreamland, dumped into my saddle bags a pair of blue woolen shirts, saddled the cayuse, and hiked to Topeka, across the boundless prairie, dressed in my only suit of clothes, which served for weekdays and Sundays alike."[8]

People on the prairies made straw hats by braiding strands of straw, then sewing the braids together as best they could. Hats were also fashioned from the skins of buffalo, wolf, and other animals who fell before the rifles of the frontiersmen. Animal skins and meat sustained the settlers throughout the newly settled land. The carefully preserved skins provided heavy leather garments such as coats, hats, and shoes, and they served as warm bed coverings during the winter months. The plentiful and easily killed buffalo's tough hide served the pioneers especially well.

The buffalo was indeed their savior. Buffalo robes shut out the terrific cold of the western winters. The bedding that seemed so ample in the wooded, hilly Ohio country seemed pitifully scant in the little log cabin on the windswept prairie. Coats and caps and mittens and leggings were made of this leather, and here the shoemakers' skill in handling leather stood them in good stead.[9]

The tasks involved in cleaning clothing equaled in complexity and rigor those of providing garments for family members. Households on the prairies rarely had either boiler or wringer, the implements used in most eastern homes for laundering. Frontier women washed clothes in iron kettles, boiling them over open fires, using scarce water and homemade soap. With brushes and washboards, they beat and scrubbed dirt from clothing, then spread the wet garments along fences or over shrubs to dry.

107

Doris Day, in the title role of *Calamity Jane*, was costumed in buckskins, a Civil War cap, neckerchief, and boots — the clothing usually worn by men in the West.

No single family's experience on the frontier can accurately summarize the role of clothing, but the Bosts, an Alsatian family that settled in Minnesota in the 1860s, provide an overview of frontier concerns about clothing. The young wife and mother, Sophie, wrote regularly to her husband's parents in Europe. Her letters, reflecting both the hardships and promises of frontier life, also evidence acculturation and ethnic diversity, attitudes about men and women, and interest in consumerism and conspicuous consumption. While grateful for the tranquility she and her family found in the "Far West," Sophie reported on the serious and growing conflict between North and South, as well as the day-to-day concerns of a pioneer: a mare's sickness, her husband's use of scarce money to buy life insurance to protect her and their family, the plight of neighbors struggling to feed and clothe themselves, her disrespect for a bachelor who did not clothe himself properly, and her tribulations with a lazy hired girl. Her letters also chronicle her perception of class distinctions on the frontier, as she writes of her husband's visiting friend who criticized her for spending too much money on clothing for herself and her family, supposing him unable to realize that clothing reflected self-respect. While his low-caste neighbors might go about in rags, might even have the clothing rot off their backs, she mused, "he wasn't able to understand how our neighbors and we ourselves should be less uncouth. But he is surrounded by Irishmen and low-class people, whereas we have Americans from the East who are well fed, educated, and ambitious to make as good an appearance as anyone anywhere."[10]

Not only did she, emphasizing the God-given role of women, intend to insist that her children have good manners and to feed them well, but Sophie wrote that, when buying materials for making their clothes, "I try to find pretty fabrics and to make them as tastefully as I can and . . . I keep the holes mended."[11]

Throughout her long correspondence with her in-laws, Sophie Bost discussed clothing in its many frontier aspects. In addition to her determination to maintain an acceptable level of living, and to reflect it in her family's clothing, she was fascinated by the new machines that greatly facilitated the making and keeping of clothing. When she saw advertisements touting the invention and availability of sewing machines, she wrote:

108

"To the Black Hills, or Bust," *Harper's Weekly* (1876)

Cowboys ready for action, Larned, Kansas

It's wonderful what progress civilization makes! As for me, my head is full of those pretty sewing machines that are being bought by so many families and are so delightful to have! Near here some people have been able to get these little fairies for between $10 and $60; a sewing table I saw the other day cost $25 and was in perfect condition. The stitches it makes are so strong, so pretty, and so quick to make! . . .

"And besides," she continued, "there are washing machines, machines to wring out the laundry. . . . Pretty soon we'll be able to get along without any hired girl. Speed the day!"[12]

Other women settling the West signaled their real or dreamed-of social standing by displaying the fashions of the East, often to the high amusement or open outrage of other westerners. At various times, women in the West wore hoopskirts, bustles, and Mother Hubbards. Perhaps no single item of women's clothing created as much interest and hilarity as the hoopskirt. It, among all of the eastern fashions, was most drastically unsuited to the environment and activities of the frontier West.

The Wichita, Kansas, *Eagle* of April 15, 1880, described a windstorm that "sat down on its hind legs and howled and screeched and snorted," plaguing the women of the community, whose dresses had to be "weighted down with bar lead and trace-chains as their skirts are their only protection from rude gazes in the dust, which rills up the eyes of the men so that they can't see a rod farther than a blind mule."[13]

The billowing skirt, a would-be kite in prairie winds, engaged the unlikely but nonetheless creative efforts of George Armstrong Custer, who is credited with devising a system for managing the hoopskirt. When George and Elizabeth Custer were stationed at Fort Riley after the Civil War, Elizabeth's dresses were all fashionably "five yards around and gathered as full as could be into the waist band."[14] The modishly attired Elizabeth was much adored by her dashing husband, himself costumed in cavalier-style hat, beard, flowing mustache, long hair, and with sashes and fringes on his uniform. When Elizabeth wanted to bathe, George carried her across the muddy grounds of the fort to the bathing facilities. When Elizabeth first walked alone across the parade ground, however, her skirt caught the wind, billowed and lifted over her head. George, according to legend, cut lead bars into strips and ordered Elizabeth to sew them into the hems of her frocks immediately. Other women on the post, admiring Elizabeth's ability to wear fashionable gowns and still walk the parade grounds, followed her example, making lead bars a standard requirement for the hems of hooped skirts on the plains.

Elizabeth Custer and other Army wives, often attempting to keep up with eastern fashions, learned quickly that out-of-date clothing was their fate on the outposts of the frontier. Elizabeth asked anyone returning to the States to bring back special items of clothing or cosmetics. She explained that "shoes ordered by mail were usually sent separately because of postal regulations concerning bulk. We often waited a long time for the second shoe to arrive."[15]

Other Army wives learned that millinery could not be ordered by mail. A woman at an Army post in New Mexico ordered a hat, hoping to receive something suitable for riding horseback or driving a carriage. Instead of the "quiet little bonnet" she imagined, she received from New York "a very gaudy, dashing piece of millinery that would have been suitable for the operas, but was altogether out of place on the frontier. The bonnet cost me twenty dollars and the express charges twenty-two."[16]

But neither bonnet nor shoe could generate the problems of the hoopskirt. Worn over metal frames that extended several feet

109

Ranch Woman

R.H.Kellogg
Rushford WY

110

from the wearer's body and weighed several pounds, it measured five or six yards around. The wearer was intended to stroll leisurely through gardens tended by servants, to be served and pampered: she was literally caged within the metal and fabric of the fashionable garment, severely limited in her ability to move, let alone engage in practical exertions such as work. The fashion connoted leisure, required indolence, and was based on the assumption that women should be helpless and dependent.

Mud, no less than wind, presented problems to women in the fashionable and voluminous skirts over metal frames. The wearer of such a skirt could not lift her hems above mud, and she could not always find a gentleman who would assist her in the task. A practical inventor offered the "instant dress elevator." In December 1874, an advertisement in the Leavenworth *Daily Times* promised, "You can raise your skirt while passing a muddy place and then let it fall, or you can keep it raised with the elevator. It keeps the skirt from filth. It can be changed from one dress to another in less than two minutes."[17] The device was available for the price of seventy-five cents.

In addition to the problems of wind and mud, a hoopskirted fashionable lady, corseted and engulfed in yards of fabric, faced a challenge in riding a horse, either sidesaddle or astride. One young woman met the problem directly by simply removing her hoops and riding in her pantaloons.

Hoopskirts, moreover, were menaces in the often small and crowded kitchens of the ranches and homesteads in the West where they simply required too much room. A Wyoming ranch family brought a hired girl out from the East in 1867, only to find that the young woman wore a hoopskirt that impaired her ability to work in their small kitchen. After discussion, anger, and tears, the young woman agreed to remove the hoops during working hours and to hang them on nails driven into the kitchen wall. When the hoops disappeared, the girl accused her employers of stealing or destroying them. The truth surfaced, however, when women in a nearby Indian settlement performed their evening dances while wearing the stolen hoops, over which they draped shawls.

The hoopskirt lost favor among women in the West who soon adopted the by-then fashionable bustle. One Oregon woman commented, "as long as bustles were fashionable, they wore bustles." She added, "They breathed a sigh of relief when bustles were no longer necessary, although, having worn them so long, one might feel shamefully 'nekkid.' "[18]

"Nekkidness" — or immodest revelation of the female body — was not a problem, however, with a style that became popular in the last two decades of the nineteenth century. The utilitarian and shapeless Mother Hubbard, a loose frock widely adopted as a housedress and named for the nursery-rhyme character, caught the fancy of women in the West and duly received its share of jibes and jests. Initially styled ankle-length for girls, full-length for women, it featured a square yoke with buttons or ties down the front. The frock, easily made at home by women of modest sewing skills, was often fashioned from cheap cotton material or from feed sacks. The town leaders of Pendleton, Oregon, claiming that the skirt movement of Mother Hubbards distracted the horses on the streets and created a public nuisance, passed an ordinance in 1885 that outlawed Mother Hubbards unless they were tightly belted at the waist. Posted notices warned all females of possible fine if they wore clothing that might "scare horses, cause accidents, and ruin business."[19]

Not only women, men, and horses responded to the fashions of the day. In another territory of the West, a young eastern girl watching a roundup rode sidesaddle and wore her proper eastern riding habit. "The bodice of my habit," she later recalled, "was buttoned tightly from throat to waist, but from there on it gave play to all the whims of the wind, with the wind blowing will-of-the-wisp gale, my riding skirt inflated like a balloon. The wild-eyed long-horn steers took one look at clothing they had never seen before, milled a minute and then stampeded."[20] In this event, she said, she discovered that her eastern clothing was not popular around the ranch.

In the main, however, western women had neither time nor money to indulge themselves in eastern fashion. They soon learned to fit their own clothing, and that of their families, to the requirements for survival in a difficult land. Strong shoes or boots, protective headgear, long-lasting and practical clothing for men, women, and children quickly became the desired components of a western wardrobe.

Aberration can only abrade against an accepted norm; eccentricity requires centricity. As norms for clothing were established and understood, as people came to expect other people to look — or at least try to look — a particular way, the base was established by which eccentric dress, as well as behavior, might be determined. It remained only for those so impelled to find the vocabulary and shape expression. Strongly expressed individuality enriched western lore.

Annie Blanche Sokalski, a legendary figure in her day, used both dress and behavior to plant the flag of individuality in the West. She owned thirteen dogs, one for each stripe in the American flag, she boasted. She wore a wolfskin outfit, with wolf tails hanging from it to brush the ground; she wore a wolf-fur hat with a bouquet of wolf tails attached. According to legend she was a crack-shot markswoman who could outride most of the United States cavalry. When General William Sherman first saw her riding wildly across the grounds at Fort Kearney, he is reported to have said, "What the devil of a creature is that? Wild woman, Pawnee, Sioux, or what?"[21]

"Montana Girl" (1903)

111

The Stetson Hat

John B. Stetson's hat — the high-crowned, broad-brimmed headgear, influenced by the Mexican sombrero, that helped win the West — was born on a Colorado plain and manufactured in Philadelphia until the factory moved to its present location in Missouri. The Stetson helped win the West in actuality as well as in countless films and the everyday fantasies of American men and women who learned to pinch the crowns and roll the brims of their Stetsons, and to set them at an individually expressive angle on their heads.

Stetson and his brothers, sons of a hatmaker, continued the family tradition in New Jersey. When John B. Stetson contracted consumption, however, he left the business in the East and traveled west in search of healing air and sunshine, a customary treatment for consumption at that time. In Missouri, he joined a group headed for Pike's Peak.

On the trail, Stetson and his companions were besieged by the summer storms of the Colorado plains. Ill-equipped for the fierce western weather and the sudden pelting rainstorms, the men huddled in tents hastily assembled from roughly stitched together animal skins. Although the uncured-skin canopies kept the rain off the men, they putrefied.

After listening to his companions grumble about the stench of their rotting tents, Stetson boasted that he could make a light waterproof material that would be easy to transport, long-lasting, and pleasant to use. He could, he said, make tents of *felt*. When challenged, the hatmaker's son contrived a crude setup for making the material, removing the fur from a collection of pelts and using a makeshift hunter's bow to keep the fur airborne as he blew a fine mist of water from his mouth to wet the surface evenly. The individual fine strands of fur — most with microscopic barbs or hooks — grasped one another, forming a mat that Stetson dipped into boiling water in order to shrink and cause a tightening of the fibers. Then he shaped and stretched and smoothed the felt mat by hand, creating soft blankets, which he stitched together to make a tent.

Stetson, delighted by his friends' expressions of amazement and appreciation, experimented further with his felt-making setup, making a large hat, a floppy sombrero-like object that incited joking until, by chance, a passing cattle driver admired it and offered to buy it. The first "Stetson" thus sold on a Colorado plain, the prototype for the hat millions would later love.

But at that time Stetson gave scarcely a thought to the hat he had made and sold, and he continued his westward journey, spending a season on Pike's Peak. There, observing the miners, Stetson determined not to undertake the grueling work of extracting ore from the earth; rather, he conjectured, he would make his fortune by supplying the miners with a commodity that they would find necessary.

The "Boss of the Plains," or "BOP," as the favorite Stetson hat came to be known, was, however, not designed until after Stetson had returned east, settled in Philadelphia, produced some sample hats that resembled the European style then worn in the United States, and lost money when they did not gain favor. After a period of experimenting with variations on the then-popular style of men's hats, Stetson turned out a wide-brimmed, high-crowned, soft felt hat — a hat that resembled his half-joke creation on the Colorado plains, and which he teasingly called "Boss of the Plains."

Stetson, a gifted salesman, sent samples to retailers around the country, who appreciated the well-crafted, large, simple hats that could be shaped and worn to express a number of attitudes, from menacing power to stern sobriety to rakish abandon. The "ten-gallon hat," as it was soon fondly named by its wearers, touched both a macho and a romantic chord in the men who bought it. It was a favorite of the Texas cattle barons, as well as down-and-out wandering cowboys, sinister gunslingers, heroic lawmen, and women in saloons and on ranches. In short order, the Stetson signaled success, power, and individuality; it was as celebrated in western lore as sourdough bread, tumbleweed, and the freedom of big skies and expanses of earth.

Ronald Reagan, in the role of a U.S. marshal, sported a slightly tilted Stetson; as President of the United States, he was often photographed in western attire, including a Stetson, at his California ranch.

Lyndon Johnson, wearing his Stetson hat, posed with his horse Silver Jay in 1959. Both man and horse are decked out in western style, reflecting LBJ's deep identification with western history and the strengths and values of the American frontier.

THE LAST CHANCE MINE
1882

BLUE EYES
MINE

CHAPTER 11

Levi's

As news of the discovery of gold in California in 1848 beckoned to opportunists and adventurers, the gold rush was on. Many men, their imaginations enlivened by dreams of quick fortune, set out to find gold, expecting to mine the rich ore from the earth or pan it from rivers and streams.

A family of Bavarian émigrés, the Strauss brothers, saw the opportunities afforded by the gold rush. As dry-goods and wholesaling businessmen in New York, they reasoned that the miners would need items that their business could supply, so they sent a brother, young Levi, to San Francisco to peddle wares to the miners.

With large quantities of heavy canvas intended for miners' tents, Levi Strauss made the long journey to California but found little market for the canvas. In the region's mild climate, the miners slept unprotected under the gentle night skies. According to legend, a crusty miner scoffed at Levi's tent canvas and advised him to sell something the miners needed — *pants*. He told Levi that trousers then available to the miners quickly wore out in the mines, and observed that the flimsy pants were made of material thinner than the tent canvas.

Apparently Levi quickly accepted the miner's advice, took a bolt of his material to a tailor, and had some sturdy pants stitched up. These tough trousers were almost identical to the straight-leg Levi's still worn today, but differed in that they had no belt loops or back pockets. Still, they hugged the hips and were almost indestructible.

As miners found Levi's pants to be just what they needed, word spread; soon miners bought pants that they called merely Levi's. As demand for the durable trousers grew, Levi Strauss realized he had a product with an almost endless market. He asked his brothers to send huge bolts of a tough French cotton material from Nîmes — or *de Nîmes*, later shortened and Anglicized to *denim* — which he dyed indigo, cut, and sewed into Levi's.

Levi Strauss hired tailors to meet the growing demand. From the early 1860s onward, Strauss changed designs only slightly, modifying details as customers desired. A Nevada tailor, Jacob Davis, instigated the most significant change when he wrote to Levi to tell him of his new rivet fastener for pants pockets. Wrote the semiliterate Davis, recognizing that he had a valuable invention, "The secratt of them Pants is the Rivits that I put in those Pockots. . . . I wish to make you a Proposition that you should take out the Pantent in my name as I am the inventor of it." Levi, concurring that Davis had a good idea, filed for a joint patent, which was granted May 10, 1873, as number 139,121, and described as "Fastening Pocket Openings . . . to prevent the pocket giving way at the corners."*

The copper rivets were originally planted at every seam intersection on the Levi's, including that at the base of the fly. Miners, however, did not always wear underwear; when those men thus lightly dressed squatted before the campfire at night, the rivets at the base of the fly produced hot distress and heated protest. Levi, ever mindful of customer comfort and satisfaction, deleted the offending rivet and continued to sell his rugged pants to miners.

In 1873, Levi originated the arcuate, or orange-stitched double arc on the back pockets, a design that became the longest used trademark of any American apparel. In 1886, Levi added

115

_____

* Elaine Ratner, "Levi's," *Dress* 1 (1975): 1–5.

_____

Men like these, photographed in 1882,
wore Levi's durable pants as they mined for gold.

the equally distinguishing leather patch on the back of the waist-band, a symbol that later appeared on Levi's denim jackets.

Levi's jeans, and its competitors' imitations, have become a basic ingredient in western dress, along with the Stetson hat and cowboy boots. In recent years, fashion designer Bill Blass has lauded Levi's as the work of an American genius. Jimmy Carter was photographed wearing jeans in the family peanut fields, Ronald Reagan in jeans as he enjoyed chores at his ranch.

Youthful revolutionaries of the 1960s, rejecting what they considered dehumanizing materialism, wore jeans in order to identify themselves with poor and working people. Within a decade, however, the designer-manufacturer-retailer-advertiser cartel created a fad for "designer jeans," an expensive version of the popular work pants. These upscale blue denim pants, though based on those first fashioned by Levi Strauss, conspicuously announced priceyness with the signatures of contemporary designers. Levi's jeans, a little more than a century after their appearance as protective and cheap clothing for hard work, thus furnished the image for displaying leisure and wealth at once.

PANTS,
BLANKET LINED AND UNLINED

Back   Front

VESTS.
BLANKET LINED AND UNLINED

Back   Front

far left

Levi Strauss, in his later years

left

Levi Strauss and Company, with addresses in New York and San Francisco, began issuing catalogs in the 1870s describing their sturdy "patent riveted clothing."

below

Miner/prospector in Colorado

right

During the period 1875–96, Levi Strauss made work pants, originally of strong brown cotton duck, with copper rivets reinforcing the seams.

117

Cripple Creek Mine, Colorado, 1893

Cripple Creek - 1893

The Attiwill family, of Lynn, Massachusetts, exemplified the styles considered appropriate for young and old, male and female in the late nineteenth century.

CHAPTER 12

Conspicuous Consumption and Self-Consciousness

Romantic dreams of self-worth, whether measured by wealth or recognition derived from heroism, cunning, or mere survival, impelled nineteenth-century Americans across the continent, until the geographic frontier dissolved at the edge of the Pacific Ocean. By the end of the century, self-worth itself had replaced the frontier in the public imagination, and clothing was recognized currency on the social market where people measured themselves against their fellow beings.

Clothing had never been an inconsequential matter in the quest for the rewards of the frontier. Both the make-do rags and crude homemade garments of the poor and the best that taste, money, and circumstances could provide symbolized the relative standing and worth of individuals and families in the outposts of civilization, as from the first meeting of Native Americans and European invaders clothing had revealed for members of each culture position in the community, identity, and cultural heritage. But now the symbolic potency of clothing was no longer a matter of happenstance or cultural determinism. In a maturing country where both technology and increasing wealth allowed more people to exercise choice in costuming themselves, clothing carried some of the properties of language itself, and with it the potential for self-conscious communication.

In the last decade of the century, both scholars and laymen turned attention to the meaning and significance of dress and, in the public interest their writings stirred, identified a frontier of human expression that would continue throughout the twentieth century. Cultural conflicts based on religious and moral conviction centered often and conveniently on the issue of body adornment, whether clothing or cosmetics. Popular writers in the 1890s, perhaps playing upon white prejudice against the nearly defeated Indians, amused their readers with imperious explications of the similarities between the "paint and feathers" of savages and the use of cosmetics by the "civilized."[1]

As typically treated in the widely circulated periodicals of the day, the fashionable woman who skillfully painted her face, as well as the successful gentleman who discreetly employed the powers of hair dye, had more in common with "savages" than they supposed. Moreover, since the fashionable lady and the successful gentleman intended to deceive, the Indian, who applied paint ritualistically, had a moral edge. The Indian squaw "lays on the red ocher . . . with a distinct purpose to have it perceived. . . . There is no sham about the matter at all, but the lady who dabs her skin with the puffballs is most conscious of her success when she fancies that her use of it will not be detected."[2] Males using hair dye, especially on the beard, were reminded that the unfeeling finger of time drew each night a telltale line of white between skin and beard, most visible in a corner of the face's field beneath the ear, which a man shaving could not see with an ordinary arrangement of his mirror. In order to protect his fiction of extended youth from the silent eyes of his friends, a man given to coloring his hair and beard would need to apply color daily, a chore so unforgiving as to be itself sufficient punishment for vanity.

Other evidences of vanity appeared in the clothing styles accepted by both male and female members of late-nineteenth-century society. Why, for example, did men who knew that comfortable and loose clothing enabled them to move and work efficiently, choose tight-fitting clothes? And women, the traditional wardens of vanity, sheepishly followed fashion to such extremes as to threaten their health. In a culture purported to tolerate a wide range of opinions, and to permit "marked individuality [that] may bring the flattering credit of genius," neither man nor woman had the courage to dress except according to accepted standards; neither wanted to risk being thought "odd."[3]

A few differences between the sexes obtained, however, in their habits of dress and in their outward manifestations of vanity:

Though men do not wear high heels which impede progress and distort the sinews of the ankle and the foot, a glance into any shoemaker's window reveals that fashionable servility (common to both sexes) which leads them to cramp their toes and provide a continuous harvest for the corn-cutter. Men do not, however, sweep the streets, except with brooms, and no tailor displays patterns of male corsets . . . though some foolish dandies are said to lace. . . . But the frankly unreserved exhibition of "stays" in shops, and the inhuman outlines of the female figure shown in dressmakers' pictorial advertisements (which affect no concealment from the masculine eye) reveal an ignoring of vertebrate anatomy and a defiance of physiological demands which would rouse the Society for the Prevention of Cruelty to Animals to action if detected in the treatment of a colt, a lapdog, or a costermonger's ass.[4]

In 1894, sociologist and economist Thorstein Veblen published his brilliant essay, "Economic Theory of Women's Dress," in which he addressed the meaning of clothing without reference to the prevalent moral and religious assumptions of the times. Examining the role of dress in defining sexual identity in society, he argued that a woman's clothing functioned as a banner of status for her family and, especially, for her husband.

Inaugurating his discussion, Veblen distinguished *dressing* from *clothing* but granted that the two activities overlap and, indeed, sometimes involve identical items of apparel. Nonetheless, the differentiation between dressing and clothing served as a preamble for Veblen's discussion of "dress [as] an economic factor, properly falling within the scope of economic theory . . . an index of the wealth of its wearer — or, to be more precise, of its owner, for the wearer and owner are not necessarily the same person."[5]

This photograph, entitled "Before the Conquest," depicts a rich woman, assisted by her maid, dressing in preparation for an occasion on which she will both display her status — or her husband's wealth — and triumph socially.

To Veblen, *dressing* referred to the basic activity of covering the human body to protect it from the elements or to conform to standards of modesty, and involved almost no other concerns. But *clothing*, seen as a process involving a latitude of choice born of availability of goods and affluence, provided opportunity for individual expression. He explained:

Of these two elements of apparel dress came first in order of development, and it continues to hold the primacy to this day. The element of clothing, the quality of affording comfort, was from the beginning, and to a great extent it continues to be, in some sort an afterthought.

The origin of dress is sought in the principle of adornment.[6]

Referring to the patriarchal grounding of American society, Veblen pointed out that a woman herself had long been considered her husband's chattel, that her clothing belonged legally to her husband, and necessarily and conspicuously functioned as an "index of the wealth of the economic unit which the wearer represents."[7] Moreover, he noted, the dress of women differs from that of men in an essential manner: it is the product of fashion, which by its nature is always changing and, in ideal circumstances, dictating the frequent purchase of today's fashions, which are tomorrow's castoffs.*

Social rank in American society had become identified with success, and success carried with it the reward of affluence. Thus, to display his achievements and his power, a man put forward his fashionable wife. Veblen further reasoned:

The immediate and obvious index of pecuniary strength is the visible ability to spend, to consume unproductively; and many early learned to put in evidence their ability to spend by displaying costly goods that afford no return to their owner, either in comfort or in gain. Almost as early did a differentiation set in, whereby it became the function of woman, in a peculiar degree, to exhibit the pecuniary strength of her social unit by means of a conspicuously unproductive consumption of valuable goods.[8]

123

Of all the valuable goods available, clothing is one of the most visible. Owing to widespread knowledge of the cost of clothing, the expensive article readily communicates a sense of conspicuous and unproductive consumption, or wealth. Noting that the belief lingered that a wife "was herself a pecuniary possession," Veblen held that "almost the sole function of woman in the social system is to put in evidence her economic unit's ability to pay. That is to say, woman's place (according to the ideal scheme of our social system) has come to be that of a means of conspicuously unproductive expenditure." While a woman's expensiveness may also be displayed in behavior associated with breeding and manners that betoken a long history of leisure and, therefore, of wealth, dress "comes pretty near being synonymous with 'display of wasteful expenditure.' "[9]

Other societies, too, read conspicuous consumption as evidence of power and wealth. In instances where conspicuous

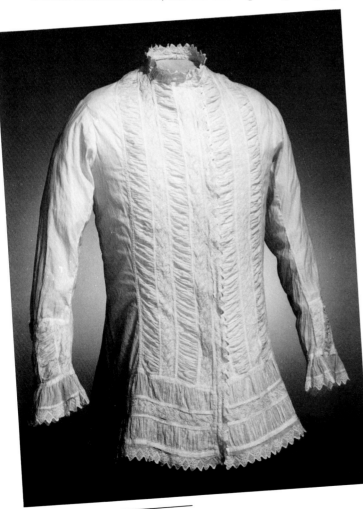

Women's blouse

---

* "Fashion being a goddess; and who can readily comprehend so variable a creature as woman? But though Fashion may be a goddess she is not a deity of caprice, as she is sometimes credited with being; on the contrary, she is a lady of regular habits, preserving certain balances and proportions, one type of clothing succeeding another in regular rotation, and recalling Solomon's dictum, 'There is nothing new under the Sun.' " (O. Fortesque Yonge, "Some Causes of Change in Dress," *Living Age* 223 [1899]: 30)

waste symbolizes status, the purchasers of costly goods may not desire to consume so much as to make manifest their ability to pay. "What is sought," according to Veblen,

is not the de facto *waste, but the appearance of waste. Hence there is a constant effort on the part of the consumer of these goods to obtain them at as good a bargain as may be; and hence also a constant effort on the part of the producers of these goods to lower the cost of their production, and consequently to lower the price. But as fast as the price of the goods declines to such a figure that their consumption is no longer* prima facie *evidence of a considerable ability to pay, the particular goods in question fall out of favor, and consumption is diverted to something which more adequately manifests the wearer's ability to afford wasteful consumption.*"[10]

But, warns Veblen, in late-nineteenth-century American society consumption that heralded power and affluence needed to be contained within an understood canon of good form that precluded ostentation or crude waste suggesting the means for display had been acquired "so recently as not to have permitted that long-continued waste of time and effort required for mastering the most effective methods of display." Recent acquisition of means is only slightly less vulgar, in this system of value and symbols, than ineptitude in conspicuous waste. Given American attitudes that aristocracy of birth is a higher good than mere possession of goods, that the greatness of means possessed is manifested by the volume of display, and that the ability to waste time and goods, "when possessed in a high degree, is evidence of a life (or of more than one life) spent to no useful purpose; which, for purposes of respectability, goes as far as a very considerable unproductive consumption of goods." Thus, concludes Veblen, "The offensiveness of crude taste and vulgar display in matters of dress is, in the last analysis, due to the fact that they argue the absence of ability to afford a reputable amount of waste of time and effort."[11]

In identifying three basic principles of clothing for women — expensiveness, novelty, and ineptitude — Veblen simultaneously summarized the development of American clothing during the nineteenth century and foretold the issues that would shape American clothing during the twentieth century. *Expensiveness*, as thus defined, requires that the effectiveness of clothing must be visibly uneconomical, so that it is apparent that the purchaser is able to spend without consideration of comfort or efficiency. The principle of *novelty* must be readily understood as

evidence of clothing having been worn but for a relatively short time, if possible, and of its inability to withstand any appreciable amount of wear. "Exceptions from this rule," according to Veblen, "are such things of sufficient permanence to become heirlooms, and of such surpassing expensiveness as normally to be possessed only by persons of superior (pecuniary) rank. The possession of an heirloom is to be commended because it argues the practice of waste through more than one generation." Third, *ineptitude*, affording prima facie evidence of incapacitating the wearer for any gainful occupation, "should also make it apparent that [the woman] is permanently unfit for any useful effort, even after the restraint of the apparel is removed."[12]

An aesthetic principle, acknowledges Veblen — that of adornment — has a degree of economic and social importance (although he prefers to think of adornment as a particularizing aspect of novelty), but expensiveness, novelty, and ineptitude are the essential principles of clothing, "and constitute the substantial norm of woman's dress [which] no exigency can permanently set . . . aside so long as the chance of rivalry between persons in respect of wealth remains."[13]

Having linked his theory of dress to capitalism, consumerism, and the role of women in society, Veblen conjectured that much of his reasoning could also be applied to men's clothing and, further, that children should be regarded as "tools" in the hands of women, by whom they are used to further the display of wasteful consumption.

Focusing on late-nineteenth-century developments in women's clothing, Veblen acknowledged the influence of the various reform movements, remarking that "personal comfort [has] lately [become] imperative," a tendency born of "sentimental athleticism (flesh-worship) that has been dominant of late." Nonetheless, he identified the "underlying principle" of the "whole of the difficult and interesting domain of fashion. Fashion does not demand continual flux and change simply because that way of doing is foolish; flux and change and novelty are demanded by the central principle of all dress — conspicuous waste." A desire to adhere to a particular fashion in clothing during its allotted time as the canon of dress will stimulate those who cannot afford conspicuous waste to mimic it by using "facings, edgings, and the many (pseudo) deceptive contrivances that will concur to any one that is at all familiar with the technique of dress." This pretense of a conspicuous consumption — which Veblen characterizes as "pathetic, child-like make-believe" — results in the display of dress that is either crudely expensive or patently inexpensive, supportive of efficiency, and practical in its longevity.[14]

Ideally, a woman, as exponent of a family's financial strength and social status, will not only observe the principles of dress defined by Veblen, but will also put

in evidence the fact (often a fiction) that she leads a useless life. Dress is her chief means of doing so. The ideal of dress, on this hand, is to demonstrate to all observers, and to compel observation of the fact, that the wearer is manifestly incapable of doing anything that is of any use. The modern civilized woman's dress attempts this demonstration of habitual idleness, and succeeds measurably.[15]

Veblen cites the modern skirt as a potent testimony of female idleness. The skirt, he says, and

all the cumbrous and otherwise meaningless drapery which the skirt typifies ... hampers the movements of the wearer and disables her, in great measure, for any useful occupation. So it serves as an advertisement (often disingenuous) that the wearer is backed by sufficient means to be able to afford the idleness, or impaired efficiency, which the skirt implies. The like is true of the high heel, and in less degree of several other features of modern dress.[16]

125

right

Advertisers exploited Americans' desire for a good life, extolling the powers of particular goods — in this case, boys' clothing — to contribute to happiness.

left

In the last half of the nineteenth century, Quaker businessman Daniel Collins Baker dressed himself and his family in styles and fabrics that demonstrated his wealth. Baker, a civic leader in Lynn, Massachusetts, dressed in accordance with standards for affluent and powerful men of the period. Moreover, he dressed his children in clothing suitable for their social station, and as evidence of his own position and prosperity.

GOOD CLOTHING FOR THE LITTLE MEN HELPS TO MAKE HOME HAPPY.

JUNIOR CLOTHING

WE OFFER MANY NEW AND TASTEFUL STYLES IN SMALL BOYS SUITS.

Skirts, corsets, and heels, accepted as standards of dress for women in the late nineteenth century, are compared to what we readily identify as "mutilations" in other societies. While admitting that mutilation is not itself a principle of dress, Veblen nonetheless stresses that "it is scarcely possible to draw the line so as to exclude it from the theory, and it is so closely coincident with that category in point of principle that an outline of the theory would be incomplete without reference to it."[17]

The connection between voluntarily accepted physical incapacity in the name of fashion and the possession of wealth and leisure accounts, according to Veblen, for the failure of the dress-reform movement to shift the principles of women's dress toward "convenience, comfort, or health." It remains, he notes, "the essence of dress that it should (appear to) hamper, incommode, and injure the wearer, for in so doing it proclaims the wearer's pecuniary ability to endure idleness and physical incapacity."[18]

Working women faced considerable disadvantage in a society that required women to appear idle in order to be respectable, for "they have to supply not only the means of living, but also the means of advertising the fiction that they live without any gainful occupation; and they have to do all this while encumbered with garments specially designed to hamper their movements and decrease their industrial efficiency."[19]

Other late-nineteenth-century writers, while perhaps lacking Veblen's brilliance, attempted rational exploration of fashion and of the clothing habits of Americans, often with reference to primitive or "uncivilized" groups, but it was Veblen who parsed the basic grammar of the American language of clothing, and described the ritual role of consumerism in displaying status. Fashion and consumerism in the subsequent years have served to illustrate his tenets, with several variations on the basic theme. Clothing displays status, and clothing also displays disregard for status, an attitude associated with "old money" and therefore mimicked by fashion designers and consumers. Consumerism, display, style, and status have indeed been bold players in mapping the frontiers of the twentieth century.

right

Women's blouses, finely fashioned for the affluent, often combined expensive materials and complicated handwork. The mass producers of "waists" for working women, however, reflected the styles of the day, and emphasized the quality of materials.

far right

Regardless of the style or material of their outerwear, most American women continued to "lace" well into the twentieth century, and many purchased their corsets from mail-order catalogs.

SEARS, ROEBUCK & CO., (Incorporated), Cheapest Supply House on

Ladies' Shirt Waists.—Continued.

Our special Drop Head Sewing Machine may be used as a handsome writing or parlor table when not in use. Retails at $60.00. If interested see our price quoted in this book.

No. 2836. For a fancy Persian pattern, made of soft finish cambric, full plaited front, handsome laundered collar and cuffs, yoke back; this is, indeed, something very handsome and a novelty. We guarantee that your local merchant will pay at least $6.00 per dozen to any wholesale house for these goods; sizes, 32 to 42. Our price, each...............$0.45
By mail, 10 cents extra.

No. 2836.

No. 2837. Ladies' Laundered Waist made of fast colored Percale with the latest effects, medium or dark colors, full Bishop sleeves, standard collar and cuffs, extraordinary value, full plaited front, yoke back. Each waist supplied with the necessary buttons all in their proper places, handsomely stitched throughout. This waist we guarantee to be sold at wholesale in large lots on this market at $7.50 per dozen; sizes 32 to 44. Our price, each......................$0.50
By mail, 10 cents extra.

No. 2837½. Ladies' Laundered Waists, made of Long Island fast color percale, newest drab and tan colors with small figures and stripes. full front, pointed yoke back, large Bishop sleeves, very latest style, Esther collar and cuffs, hand made button holes in the front and cuffs, all supplied with nickel plated buttons. This is something entirely new, in style and in finish, and we think it is one of the prettiest garments brought out this season. Sizes, 32 to 44. Our Price..........................$0.73
By mail, 10 cents extra.

No. 2838. Laundered Waists, made of Simpson's high grade cambric, positively fast colors; black, blue, or red ground with hair line stripe; soft front, stiff collar and cuffs, pointed yoke back, and the latest style sleeves, dressmaker made, nicely finished.............$0.75

No. 2837½.

No. 2839. Ladies' Laundered Waist made from Garner's Celebrated Fast Color Percale, acknowledged to be the best fabric, made in the latest Dresden and Oriental patterns, gathered front, double yoke, fullness below yoke, Dresdemona collar and cuffs, and Marlborough sleeves, the latest London craze, the nobbiest and best made garment in the market. Size 32 to 42. Our price............$1.15
By mail, 10 cents extra.
No. 2840. Ladies' very fine cambric waist in light blue or pink, beautiful shades with full front, English laundered collar and cuffs, all double stitched, pointed yoke with fullness below the yoke, full Marlborough sleeves. For young ladies there is no handsomer waist made than this and something we guarantee will not be sold over any retail counter for less than $2.00. Sizes 32 to 42. Our price............$1.15
By mail, 10 cents extra.

No. 2842. Ladies' Laundered Waist, made of Potomac Mills' best percale in elegant new choice patterns, full front, pointed yoke back with fulness below yoke, Elmira collars and cuff, extra large sleeves. They come in fine new shades of pink and white, green and white, or blue and white with a black stripe. This is a facsimile of an imported waist that cannot be landed in this country for less than $15.00 to $18.00 per dozen. The Elmira collar and cuff is a two-button front and considered strictly up-to-date. Sizes, 32 to 42. We offer this handsome Waist at the phenomenal low price, each.....$0.95
By mail, 10c extra.

No. 5841.

No. 2839.

No. 2843.

We don't want you t[o] save you money and th[e] customers investigate o[ur]

We believe we can serve you better than any other concern, and we only ask a chance to prove what goods we can sell at prices you never dreamed of.

OUR BIG BUILDING IS A BUSY BEEHIVE. 450 EMPLOYES ARE WORKING ON THE T[RADE] DAILY. $5,000,000.00 WORTH OF MERCHANDISE WILL PASS THROUGH OU[R]

We sell a splendid Piano for $125 and ship it subject to examination and trial. Our terms are as fair as those of any dealer and we save you enough money to buy another piano.

No. 2841. Extra fine Cambric Laundered Waists, with detachable collar and attached cuffs. A very sensible garment. Made of Spring Brook Cambric, fast colors, white ground, with blue, pink or black pin stripe and dot, with gathered front, double pointed yoke back, dress-maker made. Each...$1.25

BANNER·BRAND

No. 2842.

No. 2843. Ladies' Laundered White Cambric Waists, extra fine quality, gathered front, double yoke back, with faultless standard collars and cuffs, extra large sleeves, handsomely made...................$1.15

your order to us unless you think we can
will treat you right. We prefer that new
ability before ordering.

NDS OF ORDERS THAT COME TO U
NDS IN THE YEAR 1896.

Corset Department.

Average weight of a Corset is 15 ounces.

This is a progressive age, when you can order one or a dozen corsets direct from the factory. You may say direct, for we are simply your servant awaiting your pleasure. We control a large corset factory subject to the orders of our patrons. Of course we receive thousands of orders for corsets every day, more than any jobbing house who sell to local merchants on long time credit. You can easily understand the advantage of buying all the goods you can of us—the more you save. It will pay to anticipate your wants and make a freight package, thus reducing the charges on each item to next to nothing. If you do not, you are liable to want something at once and go to your local dealer who will charge you a great deal more than you would pay us for double the quantity.

You can save so much money by buying your corsets direct from us, that you cannot afford to pay the retail dealer his price.

In ordering corsets always give size. Take the size from the waist; never from the bust. Deduct about 2 inches from the waist measure for size of corset. No corsets come in extra sizes unless so quoted. Regular sizes, 18 to 30.

Any of these goods sent C. O. D., subject to examination, on receipt of $1.00, balance and express charges payable at express office. 3 per cent. discount for cash in full with order.

Every corset we sell is absolutely guaranteed fully equal in material, fit and durability to corsets retailed at double the money. We sell one corset at the same price as we do a dozen to introduce the department

No 21546.

No. 21546. Exposition, perfectly shaped and a fine fitting corset, equal to any retailed at 80 cents; made of heavy jean, stripped with sateen, wide zone, double busk, two side steels. Colors: white, drab, cream or gold..$0.40

No. 21547. Best quality jeans corset, striped with sateen, bone bust, two side steels, 6-hook clasp, embroidered at top and bottom; in shape, appearances and durability equal to any $1.00 corset; unquestionably the best corset ever produced for the money we ask. Colors: white, drab or black.........$0.50

No. 21547.

No. 21549. This corset is moddeled after the finest French shapes and will fit any lady of average proportion; it is made with soft busts and stayed with unbreakable French wire. Colors: black or drab. Size, 18 to 30.................$0.75

No. 21549.

No. 21550.

No. 21550. French Coutel Corset; extra long waisted; sateen stripped; fitted with unbreakable French wire; trimmed with handsome silk embroidery and heavily flossed, and produces an elegant appearance equaled only by corsets costing double the money. Colors: White, drab or black............$0.95
Extra size in black only; sizes 31 to 36...........$1.25

No. 21551.

No. 21551. High Grade Special Corset, in every way equal to the best imported corset that retails for $2.50; made of the best quality improved sateen, long waisted, high back, extra heavy clasp, elegantly embroidered and silk trimmed. Colors: white, drab or black; sizes 18 to 30. ....$1.25

No. 21552. The Very Latest Improved French Corset, very highest grade workmanship and material; made of finest Zanella cloth, extra long waisted, medium size bust and hips, cross boned, high back, beautifully embroidered and finished in every way equal to any corset retailing for $2.65 each; colors, drab or black; size, 18 to 30...........$1.89

No. 21552.

No. 21554. Comfort and elegance; a summer corset made of improved netting; stripped with satin; reinforced front steels, two side steels, and extra heavy back wire; six hook clasp; as perfectly fitting as any of the highest price corsets. Colors: white or drab; size, 18 to 30...............$0.45
No. 21555. A well made summer corset, with double busk; two side steels; wide zone; in white only; size, 18 to 30. Price..............$0.39

No. 21554.

No. 21556. Nursing Corset. The most sensible convenient and comfortable nursing corset made; well staid on the sides, but very pliable over the sensitive parts of the body; the opening permits the use of nipple without the least inconvenience; made of fine jean. Colors: White or drab; size, 18 to 30. ....$0.90

No. 21556.

Dr. Warner's Coraline Corsets.

No. 21557.

No. 21557. Made in medium length waists. Adapted to ladies of average figure. This corset has been before the public for fifteen years, has the largest sale and gives the best value and best service of any dollar corset ever manufactured. Made in two thicknesses of fine corset jean, heavily boned with coraline in a manner that prevents the corset from losing its shape, and makes it absolutely unbreakable. The hip is extra stayed with clock spring side steels. Colors: drab or black. Each..........$0.90
Extra large sizes, 31 to 36, 25 cents extra.

Warner's 333 Corset.

Boned with Coraline

No. 21557. Extra long waist, medium form. A very popular corset; made of heavy jean, with three boned strips of fine sateen. Beautifully shaped, and a very comfortable, easy fitting corset. Colors: drab or black.
Each...............$0.90

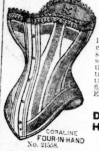

CORALINE 333

No. 21557.

Dr. Warner's Four-in-Hand Corset.

Boned with Coraline.

No. 21558. High Hip. For ladies with large hips whose corsets break down at the sides, should order this corset; it is worth four times the price to anyone so troubled. It is very easy fitting and adds grace to the figure; comes in drab only.
Each...............$0.90

CORALINE
FOUR-IN-HAND
No. 21558.

Dr. Warner's Health Corset.

Boned with Coraline.

No. 21559. Made in two lengths, medium and long waist; adapted to ladies deficient in bust fullness, and those desiring bust support. For both slim and stout figures. The special features of this corset are the Coraline busts, which are light and flexible, and give to any lady an elegant figure, and assure a well fitting dress. This corset, with constant improvements, has been before the public for seventeen years, and has been worn by over six millions of ladies, a success never attained by any other corset. Colors: white, drab or black. Each...$1.15

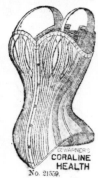

CORALINE
HEALTH
No. 21559.

Dr. Warner's Abdominal Corset.

Boned with Coraline.

No. 21560. Adapted to ladies with either full or slender figure desiring a corset long below the waist, to give abdominal support. Made with extension steels, side lacings and elastic gores on each side. Colors: drab or black. Each. $1.49
Extra large size, 31 to 36 inches. Each.. $1.75

Dr WARNER'S
ABDOMINAL
No. 21560.

No. 21561. Young Ladies' Corset; suitable for girls 13 to 17 years of age; made of good jean; nicely corded; with shoulder straps. Colors: white or drab; sizes, 18 to 26 waist measure.................$0.42

No 21561.

SEE OUR BOOT AND SHOE DEPARTMENT. MANAGER PROUD OF IT. OUR PRICES TELL THE REST

127

Part III

The Twentieth Century

CHAPTER 13

Overview
The Twentieth Century

Americans turned and shaped the nineteenth century on the wheel of their splendid obsession to conquer the geographic frontier. By the time Progressivism impelled Teddy Roosevelt into the White House in 1904, the American West had been won and the frontier closed. New challenges, obsessions, conquests, and hurdles lay in store for Americans on the twentieth century's frontiers of changing attitudes about personality, sexuality, morality, and society, and of changing values regarding success, happiness, and power.

The United States entered the First World War on the side of the Allied powers, intending to help "make the world safe for democracy" by applying democratic procedures to international affairs and guaranteeing all nations, large and small alike, a new freedom from aggression. But that crusade born of Progressivism's optimism failed to produce the millennium, and the resulting disillusionment contributed to the politically conservative reaction of the 1920s and to the abandoned pleasure-seeking associated with the Jazz Age.

As the twenties roared to a close in 1929, the stock market crashed, an event that, in turn, set off the Great Depression, which lasted until the beginning of World War II. People in every segment of American life were financially battered by the crash, the rapidly increasing prosperity of the early decades ended, and dreams died. All Americans — white and black, male and female, rich and poor, urban and rural dwellers — were touched by unemployment, bankruptcy, or loss of savings. Even the men and women who were employed — usually at decreased wages — breathed air poisoned by despair. Americans helplessly watched breadlines lengthen, growing numbers of homeless and unemployed people build shabby shacks of salvaged lumber and cardboard, and ill-clad people eat what they could scavenge. In some degree, all Americans of this period dressed in whatever they could recover from the debris of a decaying social order.

Americans of the Depression saw little indication that either their government or the businessmen who controlled the wealth of the country could alter economic conditions or improve their plight. Businessmen had led the country to prosperity and themselves to great wealth during the boom years of the twenties; now they were unable to stem the country's economic hemorrhage. As the public learned of corrupt practices in the business world, including banks giving illegal advantage to "preferred" customers, they lost confidence in the efficacy of the corporate system. The Hoover administration, insisting that the economy was basically sound, floundered amid policies and projects that pulled employers and employees alike first one way and then another, and which did little to help the people in the most dire straits. The country was locked in terrible stagnation; the people felt helpless.

Hollywood, improving sound and introducing Technicolor, produced a series of escapist movies that Americans eagerly watched. In their stylish costumes as well as the romantic roles they enacted in movies, romantic duos such as Fred Astaire and Ginger Rogers, Katharine Hepburn and Cary Grant, and Claudette Colbert and Clark Gable symbolized life perfected and dreams come true. Untouched by the Depression, they wore elegant and expensive clothing; they fell in love, and after suitable adventures that allowed them to court while surpassing amusing obstacles to their mating, they married and lived happily ever after. Lack of money, a temporary condition in their romantic farces, never caused more than temporary anguish; and, miraculously, luck always came through for them.

131

Woodrow Wilson maintained a dignified and professorial style in his clothing, dressing like most American men who understood themselves to be pillars of probity and rectitude. Wilson's idealism, however, could not prevent the growth of slums created by urbanization and industrialization, or the continuing mistreatment of Native Americans, nor could it ease the immigrant's struggle to enter mainstream economic and social life in the United States.

By the beginning of the twentieth century, Native Americans had been driven from most of the land that had been theirs before European settlement of the New World and before the settlers' westward movement and conquest of the frontier during the nineteenth century. In this photograph from 1900, the chief of the Meskawaki Indians and his council wear both traditional costume and shirts and jackets adopted from the wardrobe of the whites.

At the turn of the century, many Americans lived on farms, where hard work and frugal ways did not guarantee good housing, food, or clothing. To save wear on expensive shoes, children went barefoot as much as possible. Their clothing was often homemade. As it began to fray, Sunday-best clothing of both men and women became work clothing. Men in the fields wore old hats and frayed dress trousers with suspenders. Overalls were cheap, sturdy, and readily available from mail-order houses, but not all men could afford to purchase separate wardrobes for work and for dress-up occasions. Women generally wore homemade cotton dresses, adding an ample apron when working in the fields or kitchen.

In addition to depicting couples representing an ideal and elegant world untouched by economic despair, and the ribald fun of those with no pretense to lose, Hollywood created a carefree image of youth, promoting such stars as Shirley Temple, Judy Garland, and Mickey Rooney. As much as the couples suspended dancing in a beam of light, or those glimpsed smirking at convention, the child stars of Hollywood were the vessels of American dreams, for unlike most children of the Depression, they wore sparkling clothes, lived in secure circumstances, and showed spunk against plot-thickening portents and perils.

In a time when Americans felt helpless, and unable to control their lives or to expect just treatment from life, films featured resourceful stereotypical cowboys, like John Wayne or Gary Cooper, who often single-handedly overcame adversity and meted out justice. Their quiet strength and brave devotion to right living established a view of masculinity that most Americans believed had been born on the western frontier of the country, and not on a Hollywood soundstage. The aw-shucks deep-voice mumble and the pigeon-toed walk of men accustomed to surpassing the tribulations of range life came to epitomize the male quality; western-movie costumes began to set the style by which American men could advertise their tough and honest manliness.

Hollywood cowboy costumes, however, differed markedly from the clothing worn by the men who had actually settled the West. Mail-order catalogs supplied rootin'-tootin' costumes at reasonable prices for drugstore cowboys. An American boy or man could turn himself into a western hero with the aid of a Sears catalog. He could purchase and devise his persona from a wide selection of western hats and colorful bandannas, denim jeans and short jackets with corduroy collars, fancily stitched western shirts with pointed tab pockets, and boots with spurs. Saddles, pistols, and gun belts could also be obtained through the United States postal service.

By the end of the thirties, America was emerging from the deep poverty of the Depression. New products, the fruits of technology, were on the market: sunglasses, nylon, and tampons, among others, found favor with purchasers. Many families were able to buy leisure clothing, items that would have been prohibitively luxurious a few years earlier, as Americans turned to special styles of clothing to support their leisure activities. Retailers were quick to advertise and supply casual clothes that were marketed as especially appropriate for summertime activities.

Those who exchanged civilian clothing for World War II government issue found many articles of clothing designed for war-

Early in the twentieth century, capitalistic frontiers attracted such men as John B. Meyerberg (*center*), a Swiss immigrant who invented the process for evaporating milk. He, E. A. Stuart (*left*), and T. E. Yerza (*right*) founded the Carnation Milk Company. In 1900, these men dressed in the fashion of the day for businessmen, wearing derby hats or soft fedoras, dark suits with jackets that buttoned high on the chest, and shirts with either soft or hard collars. Meyerberg's son was dressed like many young boys in the first decade of the century. He wore a soft cap with a short bill, a short-trouser suit, and a wide-collared shirt.

The pursuit of riches and social status — as well as the clothing that symbolized success — was a frontier of no geographic limitation; many would be called by their ambition to riches, but few would be chosen to captain the great fortunes of the nineteenth century.

133

time uses — khaki pants, for example — to be comfortable, serviceable, and attractive. The signature clothing of war leaders like generals Dwight D. Eisenhower, George Patton, and Douglas MacArthur caught the fancy of civilians and armed services personnel alike. The Eisenhower jacket, a version of the officer's short mess — or dress — jacket, which had been a standard part of military uniform for centuries, was now worn by both men and women. With its useful pockets and comfortable fit, the jacket could be adapted easily to outdoor activities; it was a natural cousin to both the light canvas windbreaker of bird walks and golf links and to the silken brilliance of the team jackets of both playing field and urban street-gang skirmishes of the period immediately following World War II. Military uniforms, designed

At the turn of the century older working men wore clothing familiar to them, often including homemade shirts donned with unmatched vests, trousers, and jackets. Younger men who could afford to dress in the latest fashion chose factory-made clothing and protected such finery with overalls if necessary. In Iowa, young Frank Robinson, in tie and white shirt, helped "Oldman" Garst, who ran a ten-cent dray in the early years of the century.

134

to withstand harsh treatment and to protect the body during extensive physical activity, shared features with traditional American clothing for workers. These same comfortable and practical qualities would later be appropriated by the sportswear industry.

Less popular as clothing to emulate, Patton's boots and jodhpurs, along with his pearl-handled pistols, and MacArthur's crumpled officer's hat, pilot's sunglasses, and corncob pipe added drama to public relations photographs and color to heroic egos. Clothing necessarily provides the palette for such self-expression, self-promotion, or public self-definition. As the cult of personality, the flowering of a media-based society, swayed popular American culture in the last half of the century, articles of clothing, as well as signature styling of wardrobes, would become a primary consideration for ambitious military leaders, politicos, and entertainment stars.

The Second World War, like the earlier great western migration, brought about the need for women to do "men's work," and thus changed clothing styles for both men and women radically. In unprecedented numbers, women entered the civilian job ranks, performing jobs that had been previously considered suitable only for men. Rosie the Riveter, and other women who worked in factories to produce war goods, appropriated and adapted menswear.

The decade of the 1950s, epitomized by the presidency of the popular and patriarchal Dwight D. Eisenhower, fostered conservative clothing that reflected strongly defined gender roles. As American fashion designers gained international stature during the period, and as fashion magazines exercised powerful influence over American taste, many of the American styles of dress found favor in other countries as well.

During the fifties, widespread economic growth and resulting affluence supported the American appetite for consumer goods. Clothing, photographed or seductively rendered, was advertised to appeal to people who dreamed of being physically attractive. The fashion illustrations of the era — whether photographs or drawings — were greatly stylized, with elongated lines and unnatural shadows. Regardless of their bodies or the realities of the costumes depicted, consumers willingly suspended disbelief and imagined themselves assuming the identity of the figure created to sell clothing. Both advertising and publishing benefited from consumer interest in products during the fifties.

Two opposing camps expressed the mood and texture of the fifties. Extreme conservative values — both political and social — found expression for a while in Senator Joseph McCar-

thy's self-aggrandizing media strut at the same time that beatniks, influenced by French existentialism and the burgeoning art world, rejected the prevailing values of the period.

In the 1960s, political and social changes that would revolutionize American life were set in motion by groups outside of traditional centers of power. Blacks in the civil rights movement, students alienated by the complacency of their elders, and women rebelling against the "feminine mystique" exerted pressure on Congress to pass a series of civil rights acts outlawing formal racial segregation and racial discrimination by employers. The social changes arising from the activities of African-Americans, women, and young people would bring about profound changes in American attitudes about family and religion, sex and morality, and about youth and age.

The social revolution of the sixties and seventies gained new freedom and power for minorities. But the liberals' politicization of issues related to gender, sexuality, reproduction, and race also served opponents. The right-wing Reagan administration rode to power in part on "moral-majority" backlash themes euphemized in terms like *family values* and *patriotism*.

The 1980s, marked by a resurgence of materialism and personal ambition (often most applauded when most blatantly at the expense of social and ethical concerns), rewarded fashion designers-manufacturers-retailers-advertisers who concocted opportunities for conspicuous waste. A willing market was easily seduced, and bought — at prices many could ill afford — costumes to support their fantasies of wealth, fame, and well-being.

Throughout the twentieth century, hypocrisy and freedom have both found expression in clothing as men and women have been torn between older, more codified moral values and the opportunities and challenges that issued from science, psychology, technology, and education. Against the continually changing backdrop of conservative and liberal values, American clothing of the twentieth century has been designed and tested on the new frontiers of sexual revolution, sports, technology and travel, communication and consumerism, demographic and ethnic diversity, class definition, and the new aristocracy — the superstars spawned by sports, entertainment, and communications industries. Each of these frontiers — no less than the western frontiers of previous centuries — symbolized human hope for a better life, for fame and wealth, and for power; and Americans in the twentieth century, no less than their westward-moving forebears, have dressed to meet the requirements of the unexplored territories they have set out to conquer.

135

The many-faceted and energetic Theodore Roosevelt characterized the spirit of the new century. On April 10, 1899, in a speech before the Hamilton Club in Chicago, he proclaimed, "I wish to preach, not the doctrine of ignoble ease, but the doctrine of the strenuous life."

In 1885, as a young man ardent to experience the American wilderness as a sportsman and explorer, Roosevelt donned buckskins, a style of clothing worn by Native Americans and adopted by frontiersmen to meet the conditions of the wilderness. Speaking before Congress, December 3, 1907, Roosevelt, recalling his experiences in the American wilderness, warned, "To waste, to destroy our natural resources, to skin and exhaust the land instead of using it so as to increase its usefulness, will result in undermining in the days of our children the very prosperity which we ought by right to hand down to them amplified and developed." Throughout the century, Americans have been divided between those who would wisely husband the wilderness and those who would plunder it for quick profit.

left

In 1898, the uniformed Colonel Roosevelt —
pince-nez clipped securely in place — symbolized
America's growing international presence.
The wealth of the country, two world wars,
and several military peace-keeping ventures,
along with increased international travel,
trade, and technology, would make the United
States a major world power during most of
the twentieth century.

below

President Roosevelt — wearing a plaid knickers
suit, oxfords, and his trademark pince-nez —
poses with an ax over his shoulder. Roosevelt,
an outdoorsman as well as statesman, early
recognized the importance of government
protection of the wilderness. In his personal style
of clothing, Roosevelt indulged his fondness
for the clothing of sports, military life, and the
outdoors; and thus, at the beginning of the
new century, he forecast twentieth-century
American life and clothing.

near right

The dress-reform efforts of nineteenth-century feminists resulted in few visible changes in clothing for American women. While several of the model gowns developed by the reformists did not require unhealthfully constricting undergarments, many women continued to "lace." Reformists did, however, persuade many women to raise their hems to just barely clear the ground, a feature that somewhat lessened the probability of skirts sweeping filth from the floor, street, or chicken yard. Further, a raised hem — even if it scarcely cleared the ground — allowed its wearer to avoid tripping should she not be able to free her hands to lift her skirts when walking or climbing stairs.

At the beginning of the twentieth century, still without the right to vote and with limited possibilities for owning property, most women wore long, dark, and cumbersome clothing. While rich women wore finer materials and more embellishment, rich and poor alike conformed to the day's standards of modest womanly attire.

far right

In 1912 suffragettes and male supporters gathered at Long Beach, New York, to bring their cause to the consciousness of America. These middle-class women wore decorative hats and neatly tailored frocks of light material. The men wore light summer suits or light-colored pants with blazers, in addition to the straw boater favored for summer weather.

Suffragetts at Long Beach, N.Y. 1912. © by Ambrose Fowler New York

Technological advances in the early part of the century — including electricity that powered lighting, telephones, telegraphs, radios, and phonographs, as well as sewing machines and irons in an increasing number of American homes — did not alter the lives of all citizens. Independent craftsmen, like this shoemaker photographed in 1903, continued to ply skills used in an earlier time and to wear the clothing of a preceding era.

Many workers, learning trades related to industrialized manufacturing, worked among others of similar interests and social position. Some factory workers wore work clothing similar to that of the man in the back row, right, of this picture. Others protected their clothing with sturdy aprons, or displayed the vests and ties associated with an affluent gentleman's clothing of the period.

141

By the end of the first decade of the century, men working in factories generally wore overalls.

above

Women who worked in offices turned out in businesslike attire. The Gibson girl look — the latest in fashion for working women — included fancy hats pinned to copious upswept hair, high-necked blouses with long sleeves, and neat skirts that were hemmed just short of floor-length.

left above

In 1909, women workers posed outside the Oshkosh B'Gosh factory, displaying a variety of costumes considered appropriate for working women of the period, including muffs, hats, knit Monmouth caps, greatcoats, dusters, smocks, skirts, and blouses. Hems rested slightly above the tops of high shoes, no longer sweeping dirty streets or putting the wearer at risk of being mangled by heavy factory machinery.

left below

Women workers continued to hold jobs in factories, a trend that had begun in the previous century. In this Carnation Milk Company plant in Mount Vernon, Washington, aproned women work in hygienic conditions, soldering milk cans.

144

left

Black American women had few opportunities for employment save as field laborers in rural regions or as domestic servants in cities and suburbs. In the main, they lived in poverty, and their clothing reflected their circumstances.

These Virginia sisters, photographed in 1910, wore a then-fashionable style — matching plaid tailored suits with long jackets and skirts reaching above or just below the ankle. During this same era, middle-class white students in the eastern women's colleges would have appeared in similar styles, but probably better-fitting and made of better materials.

above

Prostitution thrived in American cities, providing much-needed wages to women who were unable to get other forms of work. In many cases, houses of prostitution existed in urban slums or ghettos, the "girls" — who had limited possibilities for other employment — recruited from underclass populations, often African-Americans or recent immigrants. In one such brothel, Madame Sparber and her girls catered to military personnel in Kansas.

Americans fell in love with the automobile as soon as it was available. In 1903, an intrepid driver maneuvered his VIII Tonneau
through a stream. Both driver and passengers wear ordinary clothing; later, special dusters and hats for motoring
would be developed as the automobile became America's most sought-after consumer item and most potent symbol of status.

By 1910, dusters, caps, gauntlets, goggles, and sometimes even boots for men were necessary for efficient handling of the automobile. Women wore dusters and thick veils that held their hats in place against the wind and protected their hair from the dust of the road.

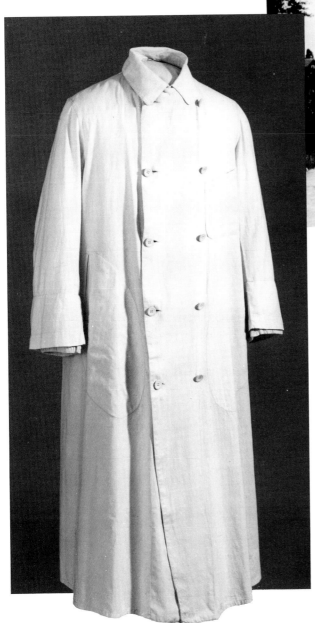

Dusters resembled a combination of greatcoat and worker's smock. Double- or single-breasted, generally with large pockets, they were made of durable material that protected clothing worn underneath from the dust of the road.

When women took up driving — at first considered to be both too dangerous and to require too much mechanical know-how for "the fair sex" — they secured their hats with scarves, veils, and hoods but protected their clothing with outergarments similar to those worn by men. Women drivers, too, donned gauntlets and goggles or sunglasses. Some undertook long-distance excursions. The sign on the car in this photograph reads: "Four Ladies in a Haynes from Chicago to New York."

Edgar Bergen and W. C. Fields

Mary Pickford

Technological advances also brought a boom in entertainment. While Florenz Ziegfeld's *Follies* and other confections provided by vaudeville and Broadway entertained many Americans, it was movies — made possible by the newly harnessed and still-miraculous electricity — that caught the popular imagination. Still without sound, "stars" rose over Hollywood, and set benchmarks for perfect masculinity and femininity.

As the movies reeled before audiences a stock of simplistic characters enacting dreams of allure, heroism, and happiness ever after, Americans began to adopt the behavioral and clothing styles exhibited by their film favorites. "Costuming" was no longer confined to theatrical productions, as moviegoers seized the emblems of glamour, adventure, and happiness, and treated clothing as a means of self-realization, self-identification, and self-aggrandizement.

above

Sports also influenced American clothing in the early decades of the twentieth century and, like movies, would continue to generate new garments and new styles to the present day. Sports champions, like movie stars, attracted fans who wanted to be as much like their heroes as possible.

As more Americans had more leisure time and more money, they began to engage in sports activities of all sorts. Golf courses were built in many sections of the country, and attracted casually clad players. In time, special clothing for golf and other sports would be popularized throughout America and wield influence on dress for all ages and for all activities in every segment of society.

left

Douglas Fairbanks, Sr. (*right*), and Douglas Fairbanks, Jr., as well as other well-known people, helped popularize special clothing for golf.

150

Miss Swim

EVANS
L·A·
©

left

During the first decade of the twentieth century, bathing-suit design began to change. Some daring beauty queens donned outfits then considered risqué. A woman could bare her shoulders at a dinner party and still be a respectable member of society; women exposing their shoulders on the beach, however, were thought to be inappropriately — shockingly — displaying sexual wares.

But bathing suits, whether considered decent or indecent, reflected the era's vision of feminine beauty. In 1904, "Miss Swim" brazenly displayed her hourglass figure, along with tokens of innocence — schoolgirl lace-up shoes, parasol, and bows at shoulder, knee, and ankle.

above

By 1918, bathing beauties in shortened suits — legs visible above rolled socks and stockings, and fanciful caps protecting their hair — cavorted on American beaches.

By the mid-twenties, Americans enjoyed the image of playful leisure — a beach, a sporty convertible automobile, and handsome young men and women in bathing suits that revealed their bodies.

152

In the period following World War I, women's clothing changed dramatically. Women of fashion often wore clothing with soft lines that differed from previous fashions by following the natural contours of the female body. Skirts hung just above the ankles. Fur pieces and buttons, as well as draping and gathering, were combined to create complicated and difficult-to-care-for dresses.

right

During the First World War, many blacks had left the South to find work and greater freedom in northern industrial cities. Once there, they encountered labor unions that opposed black membership, lower pay than that received by whites for the same work, and ghettos that formed around substandard, crowded housing. The race riots that broke out in the major cities of the United States in the early years of the century demonstrated that black Americans, despite the post–Civil War constitutional amendments guaranteeing citizenship and the right to vote, had not gained equal opportunities for education and employment and remained the objects of widespread prejudice and injustice.

"Aunt Letty," photographed around 1920 in New Bern, North Carolina, dressed in the clothing of an earlier period and of poor rural people. She earned her living by selling vegetables door-to-door. Instead of a fancy hat, she carried a basket of green groceries on her head.

AUNT LETTY.
NEW BERN, N.C.

M.E.WHITEHURST & CO.

153

left

The post–World War I era spawned both the unprecedented freedom of the Jazz Age and a widespread reaction against changes in gender roles, sexual expression, and liberalism. The most virulent reactionaries found membership in the Ku Klux Klan. Klansmen, like clergymen, chose uniforms that identified themselves and their beliefs. Here the two meet in a 1923 Homestead, Florida, funeral for a klansman.

above

In the twenties, labor unions tried to organize American workers. The men who attended this union meeting in town all wore hats or caps and scuffed, worn shoes, and worked in old "good" clothes — that is, in suit pants and shirts that were once "Sunday" clothes — or in special work clothes of denim or other strong materials.

In 1925, four men, each a symbol of influence and prosperity in
America, visited the White House (*left to right*): Andrew Carnegie,
head of the companies that formed the United States Steel Company;
William Jennings Bryan, a famous lawyer; J. J. Hill, railway president
and one of the country's foremost real estate developers; and
John Mitchell, president of the United Mine Workers of America,
and a great power in the labor movement.

Of the four in this group portrait of American power, only Mitchell —
the labor leader — shows a light-colored vest and a patterned tie.
All wear dignified, somber dark suits and high lace-up shoes.
Andrew Carnegie clasps his tall hat.

The young
Franklin Delano
Roosevelt
exhibited in
speech, manner,
and clothing
the vigor that
would later lift
the country
from the
depths of the
Depression.

Eleanor Roosevelt

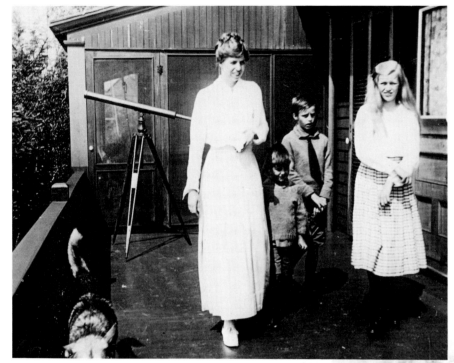

The First Lady, Eleanor Roosevelt, from the same patrician background that produced her husband, identified with Americans born to less fortunate circumstances. Over her years in public service — both during FDR's life and after — Eleanor Roosevelt bought her clothes off the rack, a symbol of her empathy with the personal, economic, and political plight of her fellow citizens. During the decades of Eleanor Roosevelt's public life, she dressed simply, neither displaying wealth nor calling attention to herself through her clothing.

She overcame shyness, and a feeling of inferiority born of her lack of physical beauty. But, in presence and dress, she set an example of personal pride without vanity. "No one can make you feel inferior without your consent," she wrote in *This Is My Story* (1937).

Entertainment industries boomed in the thirties, as Americans sought relief in fantasy from the desperate conditions of the time. Jazz of the twenties spawned thirties swing, a "big band" music that fostered dancing.

Ann Lawinick holds up her partner, Jack Ritof, in a 1930s dance marathon. The partners wear casual clothing of the day.

LUNCHEONETTE SERVICE at the RINGSIDE OR IN THE FOUNTAIN ROOM

In the fantasy films of the 1930s featuring glamorous couples such as Fred Astaire
and Ginger Rogers, expensive and fashionable clothing reinforced the images
of the characters as rich, carefree, and sophisticated — all states of being desirable
to Americans who suffered from the economic woes of the day.

In *It Happened One Night* (1934), Claudette Colbert dressed the part of a spoiled rich woman; Clark Gable, the part of the tough but gentle he-man, a working stiff wise in the ways of the world. In each other, the characters confronted the differences of another class. Americans identified with their movie heroes. Following the release of *It Happened One Night*, in which Colbert saw Gable's bare chest, the sale of men's undershirts decreased noticeably.

left

Judy Garland and Mickey Rooney, often playing characters younger than their own actual years, personified idealized pubescent young Americans. Rooney — awkward, earnest, and bashful — portrayed the male child becoming aware of girls, while Garland, her own physical maturity obscured to the best of the wardrobe department's ability, depicted the girl next door, at once wholesome and appealing.

162

Shirley Temple, in her good-child manners and adorable-little-girl outfits, portrayed the perfect child in films. The child star appealed to adults who faced hardship, hard work, and little hope of an improved economic or social situation.

164

left

Aviation, since its inception at the beginning of the century, had grown as an American industry. Charles Lindbergh's solo flight across the Atlantic — and dashing good looks — contributed to the interest that flying came to attract in the United States.

Female pilots could adapt the special clothing of their male counterparts, or they could purchase outfits for women pilots, including leather jackets, sturdy trousers, helmets, and boots.

above and right

With the growth in air travel, women were hired as stewardesses. The first women in these jobs were nurses, who were expected to care for airsick passengers or to aid in rescue work in case of crashes. Simple, tailored uniforms, influenced by military garb, identified the airline stewardess; in flight, she donned an apron or smock and served food and beverages to passengers.

left

World War II ended the Depression, transformed the role of the United States in world affairs, and changed patterns of American life forever. As President Roosevelt marshaled American forces to join the Allies in the fight against the Axis forces in Europe and the Japanese in the Pacific, some Americans donned overalls and worked their Victory gardens; some worked in plants producing weapons and other products needed to fight the war; and many young men and women entered the armed services.

President Roosevelt in cape, Yalta, 1945.

above

Military clothing of the Second World War emphasized durability and comfort, features that G.I.s and civilians appreciated and which stimulated a nationwide Army-surplus clothing business. Greatcoats, trench coats, and Eisenhower jackets became standard items in American wardrobes.

General Douglas MacArthur dressed in an individualistic manner, turning the military uniform into a manifestation of personal style and statement. The corncob pipe and crumpled hat became MacArthur trademarks.

168

Women at work during World War II

right

During the Second World War, women in unprecedented numbers worked outside the home. Whether in the office or engaged in volunteer work to help sell war bonds, they wore practical tailored clothing. Plaids, tweeds, and flannels were popular for their warmth and practicality.

far right

Large numbers of American women went to work in factories during World War II. This special "factory bonnet" — combining tough materials with feminine styling — was designed by Lilly Dache to meet the specifications of safety engineers.
Made of tough plastic mesh, and featuring a protective broad brim, the hat contains the worker's hair and protects her eyes.

170

left

As the war ended, American G.I.s longed for civilian clothing. In 1945, anticipating discharge from the military, this Army private tried on sweaters in a New York department store.

above

Advertisers addressed the needs of returning G.I.s for business suits, and for the success and security that they symbolized.

Returning G.I.s and their families coveted the material things that were available and that symbolized the good life in America: split-level houses, new cars, and attractive clothes.

In the early fifties, American women wore wide-skirted dresses made from soft materials. Softly pleated or deeply gathered skirts, combined with a small-print fabric in muted colors, produced a feminine style.

172

During the 1950s, a time when society placed high valuation on femininity and issued a correspondingly rigid code of dress for females, several styles of pants found favor among younger women. Designers and retailers tried to combine the convenience and comfort of trousers with a socially acceptable feminine design.

Some women wore the shortened trousers with slim legs associated with Italian resorts, known as capri pants. Many of these pants were influenced by sailor suits; some were made of brightly colored materials. Most were worn with casual overblouses.

right

Bermuda shorts, a favorite form of pants for both men and women during the fifties, varied in style. This combination of Bermuda shorts and vest was worn with a blouse made of men's shirting.

far left

President John Fitzgerald Kennedy and his wife, Jackie, caught the public imagination in part by projecting youthful vigor and love of both casual and formal occasions. Whether wearing leisure clothing on the beach, or decked out in elegant formal garb, the Kennedys' use of clothing emphasized their handsomeness, energy, and glamour.

left

Men often wore their Bermuda shorts with casual shirts and high-top socks.

175

In the sixties and seventies, large numbers of young people united in opposition to the Vietnam War, in support of blacks and women against discrimination that limited their opportunities for social and economic equality, and in reaction against the values in society that fostered these injustices. Rejecting white middle-class mores — including consumerism, accepted patterns of sexual behavior, and permutations of hypocrisy — many young Americans disdained formal education and effected a subculture.

Hippies and teenyboppers, young people who established lives counter to the culture appreciated by their elders, influenced the life and style of the era. While there was no official uniform for rebellious youth, blue jeans and other garments associated with working people, as well as dashikis, caftans, and similar garments with alternative ethnic identity, were popular styles for broadcasting disenchantment with the establishment and identification with the downtrodden. These young people display variations on the counterculture dress code.

Uniformed and club-brandishing military police in this photograph from the
1960s protect the Pentagon from young men and women protesting
American involvement in the war in Vietnam. Most of the antiwar demonstrators
wear versions of their own uniform — shirts, sweaters, and jeans. In this confrontation,
a few of the young protestors wear military-surplus garments, thereby mocking
the power-signifying uniforms of both the military and the police.

Common Threads

During the 1960s, the antimaterialism of dissenting Americans notwithstanding, conspicuous consumption continued to drive the clothing market. American fashion designers enjoyed new fame and fortune, appealing to the affluent in other countries as well. Learning from the trend-setting behavior of rock stars who gained fame and fortune by attracting attention to themselves, fashion designers competed openly for easily identifiable signature styles that would attract attention to their lives and work.

In an effort to reach the mass market, some designers offered a new emphasis on geometry, resulting in hard-edged clothing, often in bright colors.

By the sixties and seventies, many women regarded pantsuits as indispensable, and wore them at home and at work.

The counterculture — or antimaterialist and anti-consumerism — clothing of protesting youth, both male and female, often consisted of T-shirts, love beads, and patched — even artfully so — jeans.

The miniskirt, which found popularity especially among the young, was individualized by a variety of materials, patterns, and accessories.

At the Woodstock Music and Art Fair, held near Bethel, New York, fans jumped from a tree sculpture into a deep pile of hay. Many in the throng of music fans wanted to escape from the materialism of the middle class and to regain the innocence of childhood. Their full-length and cutoff blue jeans, worn with sneakers and T-shirts, resembled the outfits worn by children at play.

181

Women in the 1970s, like these in Washington, D.C., marched in support of the Equal Rights Amendment (which failed again) and in protest against social and economic limitations based on gender. The feminist movement of the late twentieth century, like those of earlier times, incited dress reform for many women.

183

During the 1970s, most men continued to dress in traditional business suits. While the need for reform of men's clothing is less apparent than that for women's, men's fashion designers in recent decades, as well as strongly individualistic men willing to experiment with personal styles of clothing, have initiated changes in the basic business suit by using eye-catching materials or adding an oversize tie.

Leisure suits, often made of synthetic materials, gained brief favor with men during the 1970s. The outfit, which did not require a tie or include a tightly buttoned vest, may have failed because it became identified with lower-class lifestyles and was seen as neither hip nor cool but as the protective coloration of the willing drone.

right

President Jimmy Carter, dressed casually in cardigan and slacks, spoke to the nation from the White House. Carter appeared often in jeans and work shirts, also emblematic of his identification with "ordinary" Americans.

below

Denim was almost universally worn during the 1970s, and outfits for both men and women ranged from traditional Levi's designs to the elaborate concoctions of fashion designers.

184

186

During Gay and Lesbian Pride Weekend 1989 in New York's Central Park, a trio of dancers
celebrated the modern gay rights movement. The estimated five thousand participants wore the casual
costume of young people — blue jeans, T-shirts, and Bermuda shorts — and not the drag or transvestite
styles that homophobic society stereotypically associates with "queers."

Nancy Reagan, wife of President Ronald Reagan and an eager arbiter of taste and social decorum, came to symbolize the materialism and conspicuous consumption of the 1980s, as well as the prevailing high fashions of the day. Mrs. Reagan's elegant attire attracted media attention, as did her failure to pay income taxes on costly frocks "borrowed" from fashion designers eager to have their products displayed by the First Lady.

188

CHAPTER 14

Clothing for the Ages

Americans scorn "mutton dressed as lamb" and know that a mother wearing her teenage daughter's sexy miniskirt risks being perceived as foolish, and that a father donning his jock son's stud outfit may merely advertise his midlife crisis of self-doubts. Until recently, age influenced the styles, materials, and quantity of clothing worn by people. With increasing emphasis on health and longevity, however, older men and women have recently appropriated the sports outfits of younger people; and with the simultaneous extension of adult privileges into childhood and of youthful pursuit of pleasure into the later decades of adulthood, distinctions in clothing have begun to blur measurably, as have the pleasures and privileges that once characterized the ages of human beings.

Just as clothing has served to identify the young and the old, so clothing in America has reflected the social position and value placed on both children and the elderly. The best-beloved child-as-baby-doll wears impractical finery; the child valued for his contribution to the labor force wears what he can find, often the castoffs of adults. Similarly, the elderly venerated for wisdom will not make do with clothing available to the homeless old. At either end of life, human beings depend on others; how we are clothed to embark on life's adventures and how we are clothed as we near death symbolizes our value in society.

Helpless newborn children gurgle or yowl their physical and psychological pleasure and displeasure; sensitive adults may infer from the infant's noises his or her preferences for one form of clothing over another. In the main, adult wisdom has dictated what very young children wear, but today's children, well before school age, are dedicated consumers conditioned by the media to want status and other promised pleasures and powers associated with advertised goods.

Many people end their lives in states of helplessness similar to that of infants; they are often able to do little more than babble or bluster indications of pleasure and pain, of preference or rejection of experience. For those without the desire and wherewithal to acquire their own clothing, someone else's wisdom or common sense will determine what they wear.

In earlier times, human life progressed more or less predictably through stages from birth, to work and procreation, and to death. Relatively recent subdivisions of these simplistic stages of life, and a longer life expectancy, have resulted in changed characterization of the ages of people. Since World War II, Americans have idealized adolescence and young adulthood, seeing the period as one of freedom, fun, and physical beauty, and consequently placing ever greater pressure on themselves to remain younger, to look younger, to act younger, with the result that failure to hide aging — whether with clothing, makeup, or cosmetic surgery — according to contemporary standards of fashion, is akin to a willful exhibition of bad manners.

The fear of aging that permeates contemporary American society is doubly ironic given, first, the longer life expectancy, and, second, the fact that the concept of childhood is a relatively recent invention among human beings. Until the time of the Enlightenment, children were regarded as small adults — as soon as they could function without care, they worked. Society made no special provision for their needs, their special developmental patterns and problems, or any special rights that they should be accorded by convention and law.

Prior to the nineteenth century, children in affluent circumstances were expected to join adult society — to be seen but not heard — when they no longer needed the continual care of their mothers or nannies; children in poorer families were expected to

189

In this illustration of an 1881 North End, Boston, kindergarten class, children are shown in smocks or overalls, high shoes, and long stockings.

190

work and to contribute to the livelihood of the family. Indeed, until fairly recently, children were an important part of the work force, whether in industry or on the family farm. So long as children joined adults, in work or leisure, they were dressed in the same styles as those worn by adults, and were viewed as "small adults."

Similarly, elderly people no longer able to work maintained their status as adults, and often assumed a special role in family chores or in the rearing of children, thus freeing abler-bodied adults for more demanding physical labor. In this scheme, a reflection of extended families, the aged members of society dressed in the clothing that had been fashionable in their most productive mature years, that is, in styles one or two laps behind the fashions worn by their children and grandchildren; and, like children, older people in poorer families were likely to wear hand-me-downs. Before World War II, older American women wore longer skirts, higher shoes, and thicker stockings than

their daughters; their arms were more likely to be modestly covered, and they were more apt to wear dress-protecting aprons or smocks in their houses. When they went out, older women wore hats and gloves, reflecting the contemporary social standards for ladies in public places. Older American men of the same period retained the vests, starched shirt collars, and socks suspended on garters of an earlier era.

From colonial times, both older people and children have been assumed to need warm clothing, and have often worn extra layers, for example, shawls and sweaters for older people, or blankets and special sacks for infants. Infants, from colonial times until the beginning of the twentieth century, were thought to require physical constraint as well as protection from chill. The most severe limitation on natural movement was unquestionably swaddling, an ancient form of child-restraint that was widely practiced well into the eighteenth century and, in lessening degrees, into nineteenth-century America.*

By the beginning of the 1900s, children of the upper classes became the idealized, innocent, and precious fruit of spiritual mothers who represented Goodness on earth, roles — whether natural to the human species or not — that required costuming. In this social theater, dress for children as well as for their mothers was discussed, and finally almost dictated, by popular publications. But while women were urged to clothe themselves in fashionable garb, they were advised to clothe their children in garments good for the child, and coincidentally symbolic of the family's affluence and enlightenment.

Exercise, recognized as beneficial to children as well as to adults, encouraged adoption of styles of clothing associated with physical activity. Photographic studio portraits at the turn of the century often show children in costumes associated with work: the seaman's middy blouse, the worker's smock, or the "peasant" costumes of various countries. But children in poorer families, like the adults in those same families, have traditionally worn what was available to them: homemade clothing, handed-down and remade clothing, or garments bought with precious money or bartered goods.

---

* Swaddling involved wrapping, almost mummylike, a newborn baby in strips of cloth, clinging its arms along its sides, and perhaps steadying its head with a board. Swaddling was said to promote good posture and the growth of strong bones, to improve skin quality, and to protect the fragile infant, but its popularity may have derived equally from the efficiency it offered for child care. Swaddled infants could not harm themselves or household goods while flailing about or exploring their environment; they could be removed from household activities, and — stoutly swaddled — could even be hung on a nail on the wall.

Photographers often supplied both setting and costume for their subjects, thereby helping sitters — or their parents — fulfill their dreams. Sailor suits — along with kilts and military styles — have inspired children's clothing in many decades. Boys at the turn of the century were often photographed in clothing and scenery similar to that seen in this picture.

above

Children of the affluent, in the first quarter of the century as now, were often dressed to display the wealth and station of their families. Clothing that required lavish attention emphasized one's ability to afford leisure, and to hire others to sew and launder.

Copyright-1898.
-by-
Wm.Morrison
26.

The power of poverty over clothing has changed very little, even with the proliferation of ready-made and relatively inexpensive goods. In recent years, adolescents in American inner cities, manipulated by their sports idols in television advertisements, have spent hard-earned or ill-gotten funds on extraordinarily expensive high-top sports shoes and on such extravagant items as shearling lamb and leather coats. These articles of clothing are such potent symbols of status that their owners have, in several instances, been murdered for them.

Before television advertisements persuaded young people to want specific articles of clothing, publications directed earlier

Boys were often dressed in Little Lord Fauntleroy suits at the turn of the century, especially if they were the sons of upper-class — or would-be upper-class — families. This boy may be wearing a fancy costume supplied by the photographer.

American adults in dressing their children. As child-care guides were published in America, along with myriad magazine articles that heaped advice on mothers, both childhood and motherhood were cast by popular writers in an almost mystical aura. The idealization of childhood, motherhood, and femininity bolstered a post–Industrial Revolution society's tendency to consider dress as a material sign of a family's spiritual and economic well-being. Moreover, the idealization of women and children effectively rendered these groups useless, giving them the social niche of toys for, or accoutrements to, successful men.

Within this context, authorities — some representing the medical and educational establishment, others self-appointed — debated the specific qualities required of children's clothing, the role of clothing in gender differentiation, and practices in clothing children which, today, we regard as almost as barbarous as swaddling and binding. Historian Sally Helveston identifies physicians such as Dr. William Dewees and Dr. Job Lewis Smith, who were "pioneers in the fields of obstetrics and pediatrics," as well as "reformers, humanitarians, and educators" such as Lydia Maria Child, Harriet Beecher Stowe, Catherine Beecher, and William A. Alcott, as participants in the widespread discussion of children's clothing.[1]

Other forms of constraint were less obvious than swaddling and binding, and often seem to have stemmed from efforts to dress infants in clothing fitting their special requirements. The conventional clothing of the newborn — "long clothes" — that lasted until the turn of the century, for example, restricted the child's movements as much as they met their stated purpose of protecting him or her from chill. The skirts of these garments extended well beyond the length of the baby, often measuring more than a yard, and exceeding the requirements for mere warmth. Long clothes, expensive to make or acquire and burdensome to launder, enfolded children until they were six or more months old. In order to ensure protection of the infant from drafts, mothers who found inadequate the practice of folding the extra material of the dress under the child — thus enclosing the feet and legs in a sack — took no chances and pinned closed the bottom of the long clothes.

The age at which children should wear short clothes was the subject of considerable speculation, with passions running high and sanctimony resounding through all the opinions aired. Sarah Josepha Hale, editor of *Godey's Lady's Book*, style-setter for the nineteenth-century American middle class, moral tutor to women, and all-around authority on the good life, advised:

The age at which this becomes advisable is somewhat a matter of opinion and circumstance, some mothers adopting the abbreviation as early as four months, others keeping the graceful sweep of long drapery twice that time. The season, too, must be consulted. It is not advisable to expose the little creature to the chance of taking cold in the severity of winter, or the inclemency of fall and spring. But somewhere between the ages of four and eight months the newcomer seems to crave a freer use of limb than the swaddling clothes will permit; and the disposition to creep about the carpet which now becomes developed, is also impeded by them.[2]

Mrs. Hale also urged mothers to remake long clothes as the infant grew, shortening the skirts and loosening the waists, to permit increasing freedom of action for the growing child. The accepted and varied forms of constriction of infant bodies in clothing may have pinched growing children psychologically as well as physically, but straight pins, which were used widely for fastening infants' clothing, punctured them, sometimes seriously. A doctor of the day commented: "Children are frequently much injured by the points of pins being accidentally directed inward in handling them, or by their own movements. I have witnessed several instances of very unpleasant consequences

Poor children — especially those needed for labor in fields and factories — wore anything that was available to them, generally hand-me-downs from older siblings, or made-over adult clothing. These cotton pickers, photographed in the early decades of the century in the rural South, worked barefoot to save their shoes (if, indeed, they had shoes) for Sunday wear.

Poor American children were not only ill-clad, they worked in textile and clothing industries to produce garments for those who could afford them. This ten-year-old mill worker steals a break from her job to look out the window. Textile workers of all ages, even wearing rolled-up sleeves and shortened skirts, were in danger of having their clothing catch in power-driven machinery.

Poor children in the cities during the first decades of the century also wore secondhand clothing.

from this source; and the instances of slight but painful punctures and scratches from pins used in the dress of infants are very common."[3]

Until the availability of the safety pin toward the end of the nineteenth century, both straight pins and needles were used for fastening clothing, as well as benign tapes and strings. Cautious mothers and nannies used the time-consuming method of needle and thread to temporarily stitch closings. Small flat buttons made of synthetic materials appeared on the market early in the twentieth century, and were immediately adopted for both children's and adult's clothing.

The practice of "hardening" — widely applied in the seventeenth century and persisting into the 1900s — was based on the widespread belief that a child would be physically stronger if subjected to air and cold in order to overcome the incremental changes in weather and season. To toughen children, infants were allowed to remain for long periods in soiled diapers; older children were dressed lightly, often going barefoot in near-freezing weather. In the eighteenth and early nineteenth centuries, wrangling over how much clothing a child should wear, as well as what garments and designs were suitable for him or her, was tacit acknowledgement that clothing was linked to health and well-being.

During the nineteenth century, clothing for infants changed little; long clothes were the uniform of infants. Until the beginning of the twentieth century, when new clothing appeared for infants — the so-called "creeping" or "crawling" garments, which were usually made of gingham rather than the solid white materials that had characterized infants' clothing prior to that time — well-tended babies wore binders, undershirts and petticoats, diapers, socks, a loose outer garment, and perhaps an apron. The apron-like creeping garment, which buttoned down the back, allowed children to crawl, an exercise that was by the early 1900s regarded as beneficial to their development, and not just an inconvenient-to-adults activity that preceded walking. The abbreviated garments, in addition to being easy to launder, also permitted more efficient changing of diapers. Rompers, a one-piece overall suit, appeared slightly later, and allowed even greater movement for the infant.

Dress for older children, too, attracted the attention of authorities concerned with the nature of human development and the appropriate treatment of children. Prior to the nineteenth century, corseting, or "straightlacing," was practiced on both girls and boys; and children were often corseted as soon as they began to walk, a measure intended to promote good posture. Along with the evils of corseting and straightlacing, boys were likely to suffer tight jackets with stiff stocks and heavy cravats around the neck. Moreover, children of both sexes wore tight boots that effectively bound their feet, an effort to ensure the small feet then thought to be fashionable.

Gender differentiation in children's clothing mirrors society's attitudes about the sexes in all periods of history. Until the twentieth century, girls were encumbered by the emblems of femininity: corsets, petticoats, pantaloons, bonnets, shawls, stockings, jewelry, parasols, handbags, and complicated outer garments, all of which restricted their activity. Presumed to be more physically delicate than boys, girls, it was assumed, required more clothing to protect them from the elements. It was likewise understood that, as a reflection of modesty, the more clothes a girl wore, the better. During a time in which femininity was equated with inability to perform work, and with ineffable delicacy, richer women and girls displayed their greater femi-

195

196

Photographed in 1909 with an array of toys, this boy wears the typical children's clothing of the time: long short pants over heavy dark stockings, high leather shoes, a loose overblouse, and a short-billed cap.

ninity by wearing layers of physically incapacitating clothing, a clear indication that they were under the care of father or husband. The attitudes that shaped the clothing of adult females also determined the clothing of little girls.

Similarly, the same concerns that impelled dress reformers to rail against the corseting of women, tight-fitting shoes, and crinolines that made stair-climbing perilous and work around a kitchen stove or open fireplace hazardous, fueled concern about the corseting and heavy dressing of girls. Ironically, though girls were deemed frail and in need of protective clothing, their shoulders, necks, and upper chests were often bared, and, overall, their clothing was made of finer and thinner materials than that of boys.

While both male and female infants were dressed in long clothes, generally white, until the beginning of the twentieth century, as children progressed through infancy and the crawling stages, and as they began to walk, both boys and girls wore dresses. Sexual differentiation in clothing — often delayed until puberty — symbolized a child's rite of passage from asexual to sexual being.

Until very recently young boys wore short pants, high stockings and shoes, and a variety of tops or jackets. Over the years, boys have been accorded the privilege of wearing long trousers at increasingly younger ages, and the favored blue jeans are now available for all ages and sizes, including infants.

In 1910, these girls assembled on a schoolyard for physical education. While the teacher wears a long skirt and long-sleeved blouse with a large bow tie at the neck, the girls' dresses are shorter, looser, and more conducive to physical activity. While some of the girls are bare-legged and barefoot, many wear the dark stockings and high shoes considered appropriate for girls of the time.

In the twenties, children's clothing — like that of adults — reflected new freedom in shorter skirts, short sleeves, and styles that encouraged activity.

Teacher I know!

199

This 1931 advertisement featured a boy posed in attitude and clothing to suggest health and brightness. Unlike children of earlier decades, he is free of long heavy stockings, and his shoes, though sturdy, are neither as high nor as heavy as previous footwear. He wears a downsized version of his father's dress shirt and tie, but has not yet been allowed the status of long trousers.

Retired Vice President of the United States Thomas R. Marshall, shown here in Iowa in the 1920s, wore a three-piece business suit typical of those worn by successful men of his era. His hat and cane complete the ensemble of the dignified elder businessman in America before World War II.

In the first decades of the twentieth century, older Americans wore styles reflecting tastes of an earlier time. The women in these pictures wear cotton dresses, probably homemade or purchased from a mail-order store featuring inexpensive and serviceable clothing. The man at left wears a mass-produced suit.

CHAPTER 15

The Roaring Twenties
Dress Reform Redux

The dress-reform movements of the nineteenth century failed. After the moralizing sermons and pamphlets on the unhealthful wickedness of corsets, after zealous demonstrations against the skirts that swept the streets and farmyards of America, and after the careful design and presentation of alternative styles of clothing, little changed. In the first two decades of the twentieth century, women still wore corsets, their skirts still dragged in the filth of the barnyard, and their clothing still prevented them from moving easily. At the beginning of the twentieth century, in brief, women's clothing still identified them as the weaker sex and as the property of men; through clothing, women-as-consumers dressed in conformity with their social roles and to dignify or aggrandize their lords and masters. And women who could afford fashionable dress remained incarcerated in styles and garments that prevented them from walking easily, climbing stairs safely, breathing naturally, or giving any appearance of being able to care for themselves.

A few women, often held up to public ridicule and labeled as eccentrics, were dissatisfied with their role in society and its attendant uniform. They campaigned for the vote, and for equal rights in American society. Clothes, for many of them, symbolized their plight. Anna G. Noyes, speaking for these women as well as for herself in 1907, listed her requirements for a new order of clothing. She wanted a convenient method of putting her dress on and off, so that she should not have to depend upon her husband even for that; a standardized "respectable" length for a skirt; a skirt full enough for comfort in walking or running, yet cut so as to hold its shape, and one designed to be attractive; a method of equally distributing the weight of clothes so as to make them as natural to the body as "skin and bones"; enough

pockets to free her hands from carrying a bag; an overall design based on the natural curves of her body; and no extraneous deformities, either for body or head.

She also wanted to select the coloring in textiles that most suited her own color; to choose textiles for garments, under and outer, because of their inherent physical properties — wool for warmth, linen for coolness, silk for cleanliness; to have touch the skin only those materials that could be readily washed; to buy what would be, in the long run, the least expensive material; to have warm gloves in winter, and not have to be bothered with carrying a muff; to find a becoming hat that fitted and to be able to wear it out without being disdained for failing to honor fashion; to find shoes or sandals that fit; and to eliminate starch, which she considered *dirty* because it was extraneous. She would "eliminate all jewelry, nose rings, earrings, finger rings, arm rings, waist rings, neck rings, cuff buttons, hat pins, breast pins, everything in the jewelry line but a watch, a brooch to secure it, and hair pins." She would also eliminate fur "in this climate, because just as it prevents the body's heat from escaping, it also prevents fresh air from penetrating."[1]

Finally, she wanted to eliminate articles of clothing that required unsafe or unhealthy working conditions for their makers, for, as she said, "I believe that when the new era comes, the whole world will be planning to make less work and more play and song and life for itself, instead of more drudgery and stagnation, crime and death, and we cannot begin too soon to take that attitude."[2] Noting the technological progress of the era — the improvement of textiles through new manufacturing methods, the efficiency of power sewing machines, and the other inventions and processes that were contributing to a general improve-

Goldilocks Rice and Joe Rack, participating in a dance marathon in St. Paul, Minnesota, in 1929.
She wears bobby socks — or turned-down anklets — with her sleeveless cotton dress; he displays wide-legged, striped trousers and a sports jacket of a different pattern and material.

ment in American life — the author in high moral tone observed that changes in fashion should not be equated with improvement in dress. Following fashion, she noted, is a way of displaying wealth, that is, ability to pay for waste.

But even the enlightened Noyes, in attempting to design her ideal costume, succeeded only in devising yet another garment, easily dismissed as the lunatic dress of feminist do-gooders. It was neither attractive nor practical. Like other ardent dress reformers of the period, Noyes articulated the thoughts and feelings of many, but failed to offer a solution to the problem. The dress reformers of the nineteenth century and many women at the beginning of the twentieth century could catalog the problems as Noyes did, but they could neither imagine nor present an appealing solution.

204

A 1924 advertisement for "Radium Home Permanent Wave," featuring a Jazz Age bathing beauty

Nina Wilcox Putnam, though the butt of jokes for her efforts, did model a dress that she considered a solution to women's clothing problems, and one that prefigured the chemise of the twenties. At twenty-four, Putnam believed she had overcome tuberculosis by her own daring. Told that she had only two years to live, she rejected doctors' orders to take to her bed and languish; instead, she moved from her apartment home in New York City to the roof of the building, where she pitched a tent and lived for eighteen months. In those months of solitude and recuperation, which resulted, she believed, from her refusal to conform to the medical wisdom of the day, Putnam thought about conformity, and especially about women's conformity to the fashions of the day, their willingness to wear corsets, outer garments with complicated closings, long skirts, hobbles, and enormous hats held in place by long, sharp hatpins. In her resulting search for a practical and pretty frock, Putnam took up the cause of dress reform with the same zeal and spirit of nonconformity that characterized her fight for health. In 1913, urging "revolt, not reform," she recounted her experience with a garment intended to free women from the tyranny of fashion: "Although this dress is modest and beautiful, and devoid of most of those accessories which have for years been the subject of ridicule by the comic press and the greater part of the masculine population, my wearing of it has been little less than martyrdom, simply because it is radically different from the run of garments worn by women."[3]

Of generous proportions herself, Putnam cut her dress from material fifty-odd inches wide, double in length from shoulder to instep. She folded the material in half, made a slit along the fold large enough to get her head through, and stitched it along the sides — leaving space under the top fold for her arms. She cinched it with a belt, and added embroidery and braid for decoration. When the bottom was hemmed, the simple garment was complete, after about half an hour's work. "What," she asked, "would be simpler or more sensible? There is no fitting, not a button nor hook and eye, no tiresome cutting, no irrelevant ornamentation."[4]

Thus "covered from head to foot without the use of ten to twenty hideous, uncomfortable and unnecessary garments, and sans the vulgarizing shapes of the modern fashions," Putnam's hips and bust were "not accentuated, nor [were] any of [her] movements or natural functions hindered." Putnam went barefoot, sometimes wearing sandals especially designed for "comfort and protection," which cost a dollar per pair.[5]

Her dresses were made of raw silk or brocade, could be easily washed and ironed, and cost as little as two dollars apiece. She did not wear a corset. In outlook and style, Putnam's design somewhat resembled dresses of an earlier German experiment to effect dress reform while providing "beautiful and practical" clothing for women. In its simplicity and convenience, it suggested the styles that would become popular in the twenties.

Putnam said of her outfit, "It is extremely becoming; otherwise, I assure you, I would not wear it." More important to Putnam's way of thinking, however, the garment met the requirements of beauty, comfort, hygiene, and economy. But Putnam's enthusiasm for her dress was not universally shared. "To begin with," she said, "I am told that wearing it is an affectation, that it is a pose, a desire for notoriety. Even my best friends seem to suspect me of this." She was, she says, jeered at on the street and at the opera. Hostile criticism made her self-conscious and uncomfortable even in her country home. She was made to feel "a pariah, a curiosity," and "prim old country ladies" cut her socially because they found her clothes "indecent." She was grimly reminded that it was "not respectable to be so individual"; she was called eccentric by her friends and worse by strangers.[6]

Humiliated and mocked for a year after she made public her "practical and beautiful" frock, Putnam, in 1914, concluded that "dress reform has always proved a failure . . . because dress reform has usually been only the effort of a few scattered individuals to force their personal taste upon the world." Real reform, she speculated, could only come from economic and moral pressure exerted by large numbers of people; but, as hopeful as she was lonely in her cause, Putnam thought she observed the beginning of reform in the "murmur that can be heard to-day among those women who are banded together by the fight they are making for freedom."[7]

While she admitted that dress might be among the least important of the questions before women in the early years of the twentieth century, Putnam saw clothing as symbolic of other freedoms sought by women at a time when they had not yet been granted voting rights, commenting that "the smallest examination into its practical aspects reveals the fact that it affects all their other interests — not as a mere expression of vanity, but as a serious economic factor."[8]

Still a reformer at heart, she recalled that when women took jobs in factories and offices, they encountered unfair conditions — especially in the garment trades. Confronting unfair and unsafe working conditions, some women tried to organize and bring about changes in laws — a means of "legislating vir-

tue into manufacturers," and a hopeless dream, Putnam thought. Dress reform was the way to reform clothing and textile manufacturers. By devising and wearing simple, practical clothing, and by rejecting the dictates of fashion, she wrote, women could change their "insane conception of clothing — [could] strive to make it a normal, useful thing, instead of a hampering, exotic, extravagant thing, which works one group of women to death at miserable wage, because a far smaller group of parasitic women wish to be arrayed like peacocks!"[9]

Life magazine and numerous other popular periodicals of the twenties had fun with the antics and getups of flaming youth. The new styles, universally popular on college campuses in America, lent themselves to easy parody. The cartoonists turned their pens to stereotyping the men's slicked-back hair, bright foppish sweaters and ties, wide-cuffed pants, and affectations such as pipe and ukulele, along with the women's cloche hats, bobbed hair, exposed knees, and low-waisted, flat-chested dresses.

Though exaggerated by cartoonists, the clothing of the twenties — born in speakeasies and on college campuses, and brandished as the uniform of rebellion by the young — completely revolutionized American fashion.

205

Dress, observed Putnam, was "an over-exploited industry whose markets have been stretched abnormally" by the manufacturing and selling of inferior articles, and "by a psychological factor, far more potent even than the law of normal supply and demand" — fashion. According to Putnam, fashion is "a purely hypothetical standard, which is entirely ephemeral and continually altered, artificially," and, moreover, altered for economic reasons. "Year after year," she wrote,

we are made to put the money we begrudge, and that we can ill afford, money we would honestly rather put into other things; money, often, that we have not got, *into that particular twist to skirt or coat or hat which will keep us as ridiculous-looking as our neighbor, while, at the same time, safe from his ridicule; in other words, to save ourselves the discomforts of being out of style. And yet, detesting fashion, as I think the majority of us do in our most secret hearts, we are often hypnotized by it to such an extent that free action is prevented.*[10]

206

Putnam's earnest tone and appeal to reason, however, not only failed to accomplish dress reform but probably invited the ridicule she lamented: it was easier to laugh at her ideas than to consider her prescriptions for social change. But Putnam's desire for practicality and economy in dress, for clothing that would encourage freedom of movement, and for clothing that would not require hours of toil in making and keeping was the same yeast that had worked through the several preceding decades around the turn of the century when women had taken jobs in offices and factories, when they had found the bicycle a convenient and pleasant mode of transportation, and when they had sought higher education for themselves. Concentrating on jobs and new activities, and largely ignoring the social tides of "high fashion," working women had modified or abandoned trailing skirts.

The great revolution in American women's clothing began as these small pragmatic changes accrued; it did not spring from the earnest ideology of Putnam and her nineteenth-century antecedents. Real dress reform was advanced by the massing

Flapper girl, 1922. By 1922, younger American women who rebelled against corsets and wasp waists adopted the flapper fashion. This girl, typical of the period, wears the uniform of her peer group: shortened hems, great coat trimmed with fur and worn rakishly open, unbuckled galoshes, small hat, and simple dress. In the fun and frivolity of the Jazz Age, women revolutionized their clothing. Earlier feminists, who would probably have settled gladly for less dramatic change, became mired in seriousness, which, in turn, translated too often into dull and stern clothing. The flapper's styles, on the other hand, bespoke a hell-for-leather pursuit of pleasure that neither pulpit nor press could hinder.

A FLAPPER GIRL
COPYRIGHT 1922 BY C.W. TURNER

The Flapper

F. Scott Fitzgerald wrote about her in *The Beautiful and Damned* and in *Tales of the Jazz Age*; *Vanity Fair* and *The Smart Set* followed her activities; Billy Sunday railed against her; and many parents shuddered at the mention of her name. She was the flapper, the zany young woman of the twenties who would risk, spend, or destroy anything in her fast-paced chase after pleasure.

Bruce Bliven, writing for the September 9, 1925, *New Republic*, described her as nineteen years old but affecting sophisticated ways intended to suggest greater age. Flapper Jane, as the author called his subject, smoked cigarettes — often brandishing them at the end of a long holder — drank cocktails until she was drunk and suffered hangovers, and enjoyed petting parties. She drove fast. She swaggered. She used slang and cursed in public. She used cosmetics heavily, not to enhance her natural beauty but to achieve an artificially pale mask, dotted by rouged cheeks and cut by poisonously scarlet lips.

And then there were her clothes — "estimated the other day by some statistician to weigh two pounds. Probably a libel; I doubt they come within half a pound of such bulk. Jane isn't wearing much, this summer. If you'd like to know exactly it is: one dress, one step-in, two stockings, two shoes." More horrors followed, as the writer described Jane's clothing, including her step-in — an all-in-one piece of underwear, both light and scant — and her dress, "also brief. It is cut low where it might be high, and vice versa. The skirt comes just an inch below her knees, overlapping by a faint fraction her rolled and twisted stockings. The idea is that when she walks in a bit of a breeze, you shall now and then observe the knee. . . . This is a bit of coyness which hardly fits in with Jane's general character."

Jane bobbed her hair, leaving her "just about no hair at all in the back, and 20 percent more than that in the front. . . . Because of this new style, one can confirm a rumor heard last year: Jane has ears."

Jane reported that the corset is "dead as the dodo's grandfather," and that no amount of advertising can cause it to "do a Lazarus." The petticoat is also a thing for the graveyard, and the brassiere has been abandoned — both superseded by the step-in. While Jane usually wore stockings, "they are not a sine-qua-nothing-doing. In hot weather [she] reserves the right to discard them, just as all the chorus girls did in 1923." But Jane's legs are sunburned, according to the author, so who will notice that she's not wearing stockings?

Jane's dress, according to the article, is

not merely a flapper uniform. [It is] The Style, Summer of 1925, Eastern Seaboard. These things and none other are being worn by all of Jane's sisters and her cousins and her aunts. They are being worn by ladies who are three times Jane's age, and look ten years older; by those twice her age who look a hundred years older. Their use is so universal that in our larger cities the baggage transfer companies one and all declare that they are being forced into bankruptcy. Ladies who used to go away for the summer with six trunks can now pack twenty dainty costumes in a bag.

Admitting that the style of 1925 had gone "quite a long way toward nudity," the author also noted that "last winter's styles weren't so dissimilar, except that they were covered up by fur coats and you got the full effect only indoors."

When asked why women had revolted against earlier styles of clothing and taken wholeheartedly to the flapper costume, Jane informed the author, " 'it's just honesty.' " Rejecting the pedestal of womanhood — "this mysterious-feminine-charm-stuff" — women had chosen independence, including working and voting. In Jane's opinion, " 'There was always a bit of the harem in that cover-up-your-arms-and-legs business, don't you think?' "

Reflecting on his imaginary conversation with Jane, Bliven concluded that

women today are shaking off the shreds and patches of their age-old servitude. "Feminism" has won a victory so nearly complete that we have even forgotten the fierce challenge which once inhered in the very word. Women have highly resolved that they are just as good as men, and intend to be treated so. They don't mean to have any more unwanted children. They don't intend to be debarred from a profession or occupation which they choose to enter. They clearly mean (even though not all of them yet realize it) that in the great game of sexual religion they shall no longer be forced to play the role, simulated or real, of helpless quarry.

Following, or perhaps inspired by, the new freedom in women's clothing, men widened their trouser legs, wore bright colors, donned raccoon coats and porkpie hats; they wore college sweaters and mufflers, promoting a degree of informality that became synonymous with American clothing.

Flaming American youth of the twenties may have brought down the wrath of pulpit, parent, and pedagogue, but Americans of all ages, men and women, benefited from their assertion of freedom in clothing. The real revolution in American clothing occurred in the light of the Jazz Age.

actions of many women who bought, made, and wore clothes; it was not engineered by the mavens of fashion — couturiers, editors of fashion magazines, and retailing geniuses. A revolution in dress occurred, seemingly spontaneously, as American women invested their energies in new forms of work and pleasure, and dressed to fit the requirements of job or play.

Everybody had a stake in the changes that were in the air in the early part of the century; and almost everybody made suggestions, ranted for or against the tidal wave of new styles of clothing and of living. In order to save consumers — especially those with little money to spend on clothing designed to be obsolete as fashion before wearing out — a variety of modes of "standardized dress" were urged upon women, often by somber professors of home economics in state universities. Ethel Ronzone's typical rationale for standardized dress appeared in 1918:

In order to eliminate changes in fashion and to provide for women a type of clothing which will be hygienic, modest, and economic in accordance with our best knowledge of the subject and which will be in harmony with our social attitude, a design was worked out in the Home Economics Department of the University of Missouri under the direction of the author.[11]

Mindful of the benefits of standardized clothing for men — the suit in its several variations — the professor promised beauty, good proportions, and "absolute adaptability to the needs of the body" in her design; she would allow "variations in color and texture of fabric, so long as they do not interfere with health, economical production, our standard of modesty, and our knowledge of what is harmful." Standardization of clothing, she argued, should include dress, underclothing, shoes, stockings, hats, gloves, and coats.[12]

The home economist urged a two-piece dress, the skirt suspended from the shoulders or buttoned to an under waist "in order to be perfectly hygienic" and to rid the wearer of a corset. The skirt, two to two and a half yards around the bottom, depending on the height of the person wearing it, was to be hemmed from four to ten inches above the floor, and was to be both wide and

209

far left

Clothing for both men and women became more casual in the twenties. Mrs. Calvin Coolidge and her son, John, in clothing typical of well-to-do Americans of the period, strolled about Washington.

left

In 1920, two women on a city street sport hats and frocks designed for summer wear. They also rolled down their stockings, exposing a few inches of leg.

By the twenties, American women could order "spring suits in youthful styles" that featured long loose jackets over comfortably cut skirts. Hats fit the head without benefit of the previously necessary, albeit lethal, hatpin. Even these conservative suits marked a radical departure from the heavy clothing worn over corseted bodies in the earlier decades of the century.

In 1923 "smart spring dresses" and "stylish spring suits for women and misses" were available in retail stores, along with "smart flapper dresses of favorite silks." The fashion-minded young woman in almost any part of the United States could do the shimmy in up-to-the-minute styles.

"Lady-Lyke" Foundation Garments

A frock is only as smart as its line in this season of graceful feminine fashions—and that means that some kind of support is necessary. Foundation garments have come back—to mould the figure along smart lines, to hold it firmly, yet allow perfect freedom and grace of movement.

The designers of "Lady-Lyke" foundation garments anticipated the modes and have a garment ready for every figure requirement—they are sized carefully, designed expertly, and fashioned of materials that will hold their shape. As usual, the prices are moderate.

J. C. PENNEY Co., Inc.

See Page One for Nearest Store Address

J.C. Penney Co.

Keep This Catalog for Future Reference

Foundation Garments Are Modish
As Figures Turn More and More to The Feminine Various "Lady-Lyke" Models

Underwear, or foundation garments, had been a major focus of dress-reform efforts in the 1800s. Doctors, educators, and reformers railed against the dangers and evils of "lacing," or corseting, and described the damage done to spine, rib cage, lungs, and other internal organs. "Fashion," however, prevailed; corseting was viewed as a matter of morality—a means of checking the otherwise voluptuous female body, even functioning as a modification of the chastity belt.

The clothing revolution of the twenties included undergarments, of course. As the wasp waist, heavy clothing, and physical inactivity were replaced by a boyish silhouette, light clothing, and physical activities that often included frenetic dancing to jazz music, women chose undergarments that would support both the new styles in clothing and the new lifestyles brought about by the roaring twenties.

211

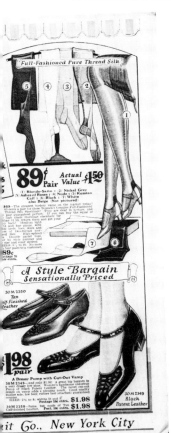

Full-Fashioned Pure Thread Silk

89¢ Pair Actual Value $1.50

A Style Bargain Sensationally Priced

$1.98 pair

it Co., New York City

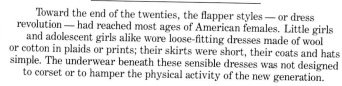

The Economy Centre of Economy Street

J.C. Penney Co.

See Page One for Nearest Store Address

Here Is Apparel for Girls of All Ages

Wool Dresses 4.98

Sizes 2 to 6

Sizes 7 to 14

2 to 6	7 to 10	11 to 16
$4.98	$6.90	$9.90

Dainty Things For Small Folks

98¢ and $1.98

Smart Wash Frocks

98¢ and $1.98

Youthful Hats

$1.49 and $1.98

Toward the end of the twenties, the flapper styles — or dress revolution — had reached most ages of American females. Little girls and adolescent girls alike wore loose-fitting dresses made of wool or cotton in plaids or prints; their skirts were short, their coats and hats simple. The underwear beneath these sensible dresses was not designed to corset or to hamper the physical activity of the new generation.

Hollywood films and fashion magazines spread interest in "lounging pajamas" and other loose-fitting garments with appealingly naughty associations with bedroom and harem. The sophisticated lady, suggested this 1929 J. C. Penney advertisement, would welcome a gift for her leisure hours, perhaps a "satin de chine" robe or "novelty gown," a rayon negligee or pajama ensemble.

GIFTS FOR LEISURE HOURS

short enough to allow freedom of movement. The waist, or blouse, was adapted from "the Russian blouse," and was to be made long enough to obscure the waistline and extend below the hip "to conceal the lines of the uncorseted figure."[13] Belting was optional; and pockets were to be placed at either side.

"Many women," noted the home economist and dress designer, "for patriotic or economic reasons were interested in adopting a standardized dress." They "made the transition to this costume by getting one in the spring to be used as a suit during the spring and summer, so that blouses already on hand might be worn out. In the fall the suit may be converted into an entirely satisfactory dress by the simple process of eliminating the shirt waist."[14]

Women in the first decades of the twentieth century did not adopt standardized dress, nor did they wholeheartedly follow the fashion trends laid before them by the manufacturers and retailers of America. "Have you noticed," asked a writer for the *New Republic*,

how slightly women's clothing has changed in the past five years? Customers, corsetieres, and fabric manufacturers realize it with frantic concern. They are doing their best to turn women back into the former restless search for beauty amid wasp waists, balloon skirts, trains and draperies. So far their herculean efforts have brought forth only minor changes, like the epidemic of monkey-fur trimming and the leering tilt of scarlet hats over the left eye. These trifling victories are of small value to men whose fortunes depend upon women's conscientious following of fickle fashion.[15]

Writing early in the twenties, the author believed that "even a society lady" could wear clothing out, and that American women were buying raglan coats, tweed suits, accordion-pleated skirts, and dark blue and black serge dresses — "almost standardized in their cutting." This new practicality was parent to freedom, and "a woman [could] wear what she like[d] within the broadest range ever yet allowed her."[16]

But the high value working women placed on practicality and freedom threatened the women's-wear industries. Trade periodicals of the time reported that "costumers, corsetieres and fabric manufacturers have made common cause against the almost static condition of their industries." The situation was so dire that (male) representatives of the industries from England, France, and America conferred in Europe — "these impressive men, who thrust their own stout bodies into woollen cylinders

and topped their serious faces with felt domes," these "creators of fairy frocks and petal-dainty hats" that were marketed to women in Europe and America — united in common grievances: customers were not buying clothes merely to display changing fashion; a generation of girls had grown up without corsets and did not seem inclined to squeeze their bodies into them for the sake of someone else's notion of fashion; and specific areas of manufacturing, for example, skirt-bindings, found themselves simply obsolete in a world where skirts no longer swept the ground and required binding. Even the fabric manufacturers wailed alongside the dress manufacturers and the corsetieres; the amount of goods used in dresses was diminishing and, with that trend, their sales and profits. Even the home-sewer had turned to simpler clothing, often laying a folded-over length of cloth on the floor and cutting out a paper-doll-like garment with rounded armholes and simple necks, a basic design — similar to that put forth by Nina Wilcox Putnam — that was becoming "the foundation of a thousand varieties of dresses which later appear with low, broad sashes, jeweled girdles, beadwork, or gorgeous peasant embroidery. Two lengths of wide cloth is all such a dress requires."[17]

Faced with the economic backlash of consumers resistant to goods on the market, the delegates at the European conference took bold action: they offered new designs to the consumer, and they released that startling news to the press. Fashions, they dictated, were to change. "Skirts were to be long; very long. Skirts were to be full; very full. Skirts were to be draped. Waists were to be fitted, to contrast with the billowing below. The hour-glass figure was to return."[18]

Their campaign to create a demand for the new look in women's clothing was furthered by increased advertising throughout the related industries and by energetic presentation of new fashions in shop windows, fashion shows, and articles in women's magazines.

Women by these three channels were to be taught to ask prettily for tight bodices to impede their breath, draperies that must not be crushed, skirts to dribble in the rain, and the weight of yards of fabric. . . .

The campaign was on. Flaring, flaunting, flower-beds of skirts, displayed in shop windows, were to tempt the shopper. Lovely wax figures smiled to prove that tight bodices were not uncomfortable. Charming manikins, at the fashion shows, went mincing down the platform in pointed layers of purple and scarlet chiffon, as quaint as fuchsias.[19]

212

The flapper influence was felt in Colorado by 1928, when the Marion family stood for this picture. While the grandmother (*left*) is dressed in longer skirt and higher shoes, the two younger women wear shorter skirts with dropped waistlines, and one sports a cloche hat and bow-tied shoes, both popular among Americans all over the country.

above

Women had entered the American work force in the nineteenth century, and had adapted their clothing to the needs of office and factory. Telephone operators, such as this one in Colorado, no longer wore crinolines and corsets but instead wore slim skirts and neat blouses to work. Working women, far more than the dress reformists of the nineteenth century, brought about the real revolution in women's dress.

The 1927 graduating high school class in Lafayette, Colorado, while conservatively dressed, showed the influences of the new era: the girls, though wearing the middy blouses and skirts that had long been popular, also wore dresses of loose fit with short hems. And though they wore shoes deemed practical and suitable for young women of an earlier period, they do not appear to be wearing constricting corsets.

Men's suits, 1924. Well before the twentieth century, men's clothing had become standardized, with the suit as the basic uniform. While high, starched collars and tightly buttoned jackets may not have provided the level of discomfort for men that corsets did for women, and while men enjoyed the physical freedoms afforded by pockets and comfortable shoes, their upright, uptight suits and ties, vests and suspenders, union suits and stockings suspended on garters, constricted natural movement. Moreover, men's suits varied little with the season, and summer clothing, even if the woolen union suit were mothballed for the season, caused discomfort in the heat.

As the flappers sought pleasure in their clothing, however, men followed their example and, following examples largely set on American college campuses, accepted a greater degree of informality in their clothing.

By 1922, American men could mail-order suits with softer lines that followed the contours of the body, and with jackets tailored to permit easier movement of the arms and torso. These suits, in worsteds and "cassimeres," remained mostly somber in color — with browns, blacks, and dark grays predominating.

But women continued to buy or make loose, simple, comfortable frocks, as if Nina Wilcox Putnam and her squadron of dress reformers had taught them a thing or two. Whether buying ready-made dresses or the material to make their own clothes at home, women appropriated the new vivid colors, but ignored new styles. All the while, women's magazines, with editorial divisions in bondage to advertising, extolled the virtues and femininity of the new styles; they offered "quaint advice which might have been copied from Godey's Ladies' Book, fifty years ago," warning that the country needed the corset physically, fashionably, and morally. "Being a mother, you must also be a woman of the world," declared one earnest propagandist. "Do you want your daughter to go to a dance unprotected by a corset? If you do not understand, ask your son."[20]

But neither uppity pleading for morality nor all the efforts of the fashion cartel succeeded in stemming the revolution in women's clothing. The growing attitude in the country was summed up by a haughty and experienced saleswoman in a Fifth Avenue shop, who, called upon to account for slow sales of "fashionable" garments, replied, "How can I sell these styles? The flappers won't buy them."[21]

The esteemed *Literary Digest* published a series of letters from readers, under the question "Is the Younger Generation in Peril," which mirrored sentiments on both sides of the moral issue of clothing and related lifestyles of the Jazz Age. Never mind the moral issues, one reader insisted; consider, rather, the power of health and practicality brought about by the flappers' new clothing. Mrs. H. Fletcher Brown, of Wilmington, Delaware, explained that she was "one of the girls" in the previous century's efforts for dress reform, and that she had struggled through all the difficulties of the past styles intended to free women. "Give the girls a chance to speak for themselves," she wrote to the editor, recalling that, when she was a young girl skating, playing tennis, climbing stairs and mountains, boating, and sledding, as well as doing chores in the garden, chicken yard, stables, and house, she wore the modest full ankle-length skirts of the day. She suffered she said, both physical and mental anguish as she stumbled about in "torn braids and hems, and also by reason of wet ankles, due to the length and fullness of the confounded skirt getting underfoot and dipping into all the dirt and water in the world, not to mention time spent in repairs and original manufacture." As a result, she proclaimed, "Skirts can't be too short for me, now that at this age I am climbing in and out of automobiles, and gardening in the mud, and playing golf in all weathers."[22]

Other readers, too, brushed aside moral issues pertaining to clothing and asked the editor and his readers to think of the ease of laundering the simple modern clothes, of the time saved in fitting. As for the corset, one woman wondered "how long any of the men would stand one of them, with bones digging in and garters pulling at every move. No wonder the modern athletic girl wants them off."[23]

One woman, signing herself "Very respectfully, One Girl," expressed outrage that ministers, college presidents and deans, and "even the young men of the country" dared to "sit in judgment upon our manners, morals, and style of dress." She insisted, "It is a question that should be taken to the girls of the country, the real girl; the girl who takes an interest in her studies; in athletics; likes to dance; enjoys life; and likes to have

215

Fashionable men in the twenties might still appear in walking suits, a formal style consisting of top hat, stiff collar and bow tie, a cutaway coat, waistcoat with lapels, and creased trousers. Cane and gloves completed the ensemble.

Knickers, 1928. Influenced by the fashion of both the golf course and the college campus, men in the twenties often wore knickers, or plus fours — a loose sports knicker made four inches longer than the traditional style. Patterned high socks, oxfords, and heavy knit cardigan sweaters added to the relaxed and informal quality of the costume.

friends of the opposite sex." The girl in business, "who earns her own living and is constantly thrown with men of all kinds and descriptions," should determine her mode of dressing, without preachments from males.[24]

Men should not be permitted to tell women how to dress, she asserted; nor should women be under any obligation to protect men's "feelings" — meaning, in the euphemism of the day, sexual arousal presumably caused by a glimpse of female ankle, bare forearm, or clavicle. Rather, she asked,

Why are not men made to control these "feelings" just as women are? Why should the fact that a girl has legs arouse the wrong kind of impulses in a man? Does he think we travel on wheels? We are mere human beings, but we have just as much feelings as men do, and we can be just as emotional, but we have been taught to control these feelings because they are wrong; but men have always let their feelings control them, and now they blame it on women.[25]

216   In 1922, Nina Wilcox Putnam also suggested that men butt out of the debate on women's clothing. "I don't like to drag up a person's past and throw it in his face any better than most women do," she wrote, "but whenever I hear a man crabbing about women's clothes, I cannot resist reminding him that men once wore dresses; not baby dresses, but regular gowns." She cited "the nappy little conquest costume worn by Julius Caesar . . . and the everyday suit he wore . . . [consisting] of a knife-pleated skirt so short that no modern flapper would have dared go him one better." This daring costume, she said, was unsurpassed in fashion until several centuries later, when the French "dragoons adopted horse tails for wear. . . . For several hundreds of years men went around in skirts, quite without self-consciousness," and included a range of styles from Euclid's good-looking "sleeveless chemise gowns . . . that were so heavenly comfortable down to the stunning Russian effect that dear old Henry VII wore one winter."[26]

Continuing her romp through costume history, Putnam characterized the frock coat as "but a poor degenerate descendant of those eloquent costumes which the late senators of Rome or rather senators of late Rome dragged magnificently throughout the mire." Pants — "meaning cloth cylinders extending the entire length of both legs" — according to Putnam, came late to the male wardrobe, but were also used by the Victorians to conceal "the pedal appendages of little girls and the nether limbs of pianos."[27]

Putnam confessed that she had had "a bad attack of dress reform" in her youth, in which she "discovered that women's clothes were ridiculous," often the object of derision in the comic sections of magazines, and the inspiration for jokes. It was the era, she reminded her reader, of the fashionable hobble, which, in retrospect seemed even more barbarous than the "straightforward corset," or "row after row of tiny hooks and eyes outlining the spinal columns of thousands of women," or three-inch heels laced to women's legs by eighteen inches of binding, or "hatpins, which sometimes missed the hair and met the head."[28] Moreover, dresses in the early twentieth century required a wasteful amount of material, were time-consuming and tedious to make, and involved more toil in keeping them clean and mended. There was, in brief, nothing rational or practical or healthful about them.

When Putnam set out to reform dress, she made "a decision [that was] in a woman . . . as radical as a Democratic leader supporting the tariff." She recounted her determination to ignore fashion ("what They wore") and to resist the efforts of society and advertising to seduce her to the dress of the moment. After all, she reasoned, the same social forces that pressed for conformity in clothing worked against naturalness and reason on other fronts as well.[29]

When she determined to clothe herself "in reason," Putnam discarded corsets, "but this forswearing necessitated an entirely new brand of outer dress." Self-mockingly, she continued:

Even though I now considered myself an intellectual, I wanted to look attractive. And one difficulty about accomplishing such a result lay in the fact that there was a good deal of me to look at. I was, as the saying goes, an eyeful, for if I happened to be standing in front of it I completely hid the landscape. And so in order to show myself to the greatest possible advantage, I had to conceal myself as much as possible. And thus it came about that I invented the first chemise-model gown worn in America.[30]

In 1922, Putnam reminded her readers that, in 1914, she had worn the prototype of the flapper uniform. But, she admitted,

---

Hollywood stars, on and off the screen, showed Americans how to look. The styles of the twenties, worn here by Rudolph Valentino and a friend, produced in luxurious materials and worn with theatrical flair, had an aura of sensuality, fun, and energy.

Americans found the image irresistible, and no amount of moralizing from editorial writers or church officials could dim the luster and promise of unending pleasure.

"Like the original of most epoch-making inventions it was a trifle crude." However inexpert her efforts at dress design, Putnam had indeed taken deadly aim at corsets, hooks and eyes, high-heeled shoes. She was, she claimed, "the first of my generation to have a dress slip over the head without any fastening," which became an almost universal aspect of women's fashion by the flapper era.[31]

What Putnam attempted as an expression of rationality, practicality, and conscience met with mockery and scorn. The chemise donned by the flappers in the fun of hell-bent rebellion, however, won the day. Putnam applauded the flapper who, to her way of thinking, was inappropriately disparaged for her nonconformity. The flapper not only had the courage to *do* what others — including Putnam — had merely dreamed of doing, but she got away with it "in spite of clacking tongues and censorious writings." The flapper style of dress, Putnam observed, had spread across the country, and the manufacturing and retailing establishment had bent under the force of public desire: supply had been shaped by demand. As Putnam noted, women had donned the flapper's sensible attire "and Dame Fashion, that unreasonable but extremely powerful dowager, has backed her up, until many of the critical matrons are turning out uncorseted, in low heels, their heads adorned by hats that stay on without hatpins and dresses that drape, hookless, in comfortable semiclassic lines." Moreover, Putnam applauded the hygiene and practicality of the flapper costume. While she deplored the Jazz Age "impatience of social forms," she acknowledged indebtedness to "their impatience of silly irrational clothing." On balance, she pronounced their dress reform to be the "one recent revolution that will have a permanent effect upon society at large."[32]

Though Nina Wilcox Putnam was not alone in being the butt of jokes for attempting dress reform, she did have the last laugh. In the end, however, it was not dress reformers who brought about the revolution: it was the wage-earning and fun-loving younger American women who changed women's clothing; it was the Jazz Age and the flapper, symbols of sexual freedom and abandonment in the pursuit of pleasure, that accomplished what no nineteenth-century dress reformer could have imagined. By the 1920s, American women had discarded corsets and the hourglass figure for underwear that produced a flat-chested boyish silhouette; they bobbed their hair; they raised their skirt hems to their knees; they rolled down their stockings; and they wore makeup, swore, drank, danced, and professed free love.

218

In the twenties, women found new freedom in their clothing, and enjoyed outdoor activities and sports.

CHAPTER 16

Sports

With the western frontier closed, twentieth-century Americans tested their physical endurance, prowess, and luck by means of engaging in sports. From the first days of the century, Americans sought outdoor adventure and play, a tendency encouraged by President Teddy Roosevelt's rough-riding vigor as a sportsman. Automobiles, airplanes, the spread of boy- and girl-scouting programs, the popularity of sports on college campuses, and the celebrity of champions contributed to the American fascination with sports.

Early in the twentieth century, the world of sports established outposts in big business, and as the century developed, American interest in sports revolved around a number of concerns, including health, education, and the media's cult of personality. Sports generated major industries in entertainment, facilities, equipment, and clothing. Most Americans contribute to the success of these industries as they root for teams and gather to watch sporting events in arenas and stadiums or before television sets; as they buy paraphernalia and mementos attractive to sports fans; and as they buy jackets, caps, shoes, and other articles of clothing designed and manufactured for sports.

Sports are seen today as an essential means to good health, physical fitness, and attractiveness. People of all ages who want to feel physically well, live a long time, or have beautiful bodies run zealously, shoot baskets, ride bicycles, join teams, work out, hit balls, balance, jump, bend, stretch; they swim and sail; they ski and skate; they play golf and tennis; and they dress for all of these events, whether to sweat off pounds or stress or to shout their favorite team toward victory.

Participation in sports is nearly ubiquitous and has become a widely understood American metaphor for corporate and social life. Through sports, Americans test grit, courage, cunning, competition, strength, and skill — the values and virtues that, in imagination whetted by romantic fiction and movies, are cred-ited with the winning of the West, national triumph in wars, and dominance of the world economic and technological powers.

America's love affair with sports, with roots in the physical challenges of the frontier, matured in the twentieth century, along with the growth of professional teams and their followers. Teams, with their stress on working together — "teamsmanship" — for the good of the whole rather than for individual gain or glory, parallel corporate structures. Moreover, a good team — like a good company — wins; and winning results from the combined wit, power, skill, cunning, and luck of all the players. The team thus enacts American social and business ideals, and iterates by winning example the importance of competition, fair play, grace in losing, and magnanimity in winning.

The influence of sports is felt in every aspect of American life, from diet and fitness concerns to the language we use in communicating with one another. Sports images and jargon influence the slang related to both sex and business: both businesspeople and sexual predators speak of "scoring," "making points," or "touchdowns." Businesses hit targets or put the ball into the other guy's court; they set goals and win games. Americans deify sports figures — champions — much as they do the heroes who have proved themselves in war, on the frontier, or in times of disaster; sports figures, along with the superstars of entertainment and media fame, serve contemporary Americans as role models, and as mythic beings blessed with superhuman powers.

Advertisers find it beneficial to identify products with sports: a father and son in Munsingwear union suits tussled with a football in 1913, the same year that Arrow shirt men brandished wooden tennis rackets and Eastman Kodak movie film enabled an onlooker at a horse show — where, it should be noted, Whitman chocolates might be eaten — to record jumping events. Moreover, the clothing, or personal style, of popular sports fig-

---

In 1900, the Elmira College basketball team posed with their coach in dark, heavy clothing that does not suggest intense physical activity.

ures is manufactured and sold, often with the signature of the sports hero affixed and with advertising campaigns associating the prowess of the winner with the article of clothing. Tennis stars today appear in clothes covered with the logos of products they endorse; and Jimmy Connors changes shoes on camera several times in each of his matches. Jim Palmer displays more body than brief, thereby advertising underwear.

The monetary value of endorsement contracts to athletes — reported by the media to run to millions of dollars — indicates the value of potential sales through the identification of sports heroes with specific products. When the very popular Earvin "Magic" Johnson announced his retirement from basketball because he had tested positive for HIV, he elicited not only widespread concern for his health but also extensive speculation as to whether he would keep his lucrative contracts to endorse products.

As Americans participated increasingly in sports and vigorous physical activities and as, in the decades since World War II, they became more aware of the benefits of physical fitness, clothing designed especially for sports has been adopted for everyday wear. Articles that once served as the special uniforms of particular athletic pursuits — for example, the polo shirt, football jersey, boxing shorts, baseball cap, tennis shorts, ski parka — now also appear on nonathletes of all ages. President George Bush, whether helling around the Kennebunkport harbor in his cigarette boat or around the golf course in his cart, wears the good ol' boy's baseball cap.

By the end of the nineteenth century, organized sports — especially those that involved teams — were often played in uniforms. In addition to identifying members of opposing teams, uniforms encouraged the development of special designs to meet the needs of the human body engaged in specific sports.

Over the decades of the twentieth century, Americans have discussed the merits, purposes, and qualities of clothing for sports. Since collegiate teams often forged the direction for sports clothing, and more men than women went to college, sports uniforms for women developed somewhat more slowly than those for men. Men's standardized clothing, moreover, could be adapted to sports; clothing worn by women, conversely, thoroughly covered the body in heavy drapery and severely limited physical activity. If, then, women were to play sports, modest and utilitarian dress would have to be devised. As popular publications in the early twentieth century urged women to dress "appropriately" for sports and to participate wholeheartedly in games, many writers tried to link dress for sports to fashion.

222

Early in the century, as women took hold of the new horseless carriages and learned to drive, retailers urged special motoring garments on them. When women stepped into the cockpits of aircraft, they donned suitable costumes for their daring conquest of the skies. The duster and the leather jacket, the tied-on hat, and the helmet with goggles were understood to be necessary for driving and for flying, and both costumes possessed a mystique that generated an aura of chic.

COPYRIGHT 1901
BY D.S. DARK N.Y.

Riding Suit No

But women who decided to tramp, camp, and canoe in the wilderness — as men had for centuries — found no costume immediately available. According to one writer of the period, a woman on a canoe trip needed to plan her clothing carefully to meet the conditions of the forest and should select garments to provide both freedom and protection, including strong and waterproof shoes. "These are among the costumes open to women," she wrote, "short skirts, bloomers, knickerbockers with a knee cuff, bloomers alone, and riding breeches." Further, the writer suggested that "a skirt, to be sufficiently short for the woods, must come just below the knee. A longer skirt is an impediment in getting into and out of a canoe and in climbing over windfalls. . . ."[1]

On balance, however, the outdoorswoman voted "unreservedly for *riding breeches,*" which allowed a woman to get into and out of a canoe quickly and easily, allowed her to climb over rocks "without danger of stepping on her skirt," and allowed her to paddle on her knees "with a freedom which can be obtained in no other garment." Riding breeches freed the waist, yet "they extend down into the stocking and shoe top," giving the wearer "the feeling of being more completely dressed." She observed:

In riding breeches, one can do things with a minimum of effort. . . . On outings with men women are at a sufficiently great disadvantage because of their lesser strength, without having their progress impeded by a skirt which must be dragged over windfalls, disentangled from protruding snags, and constantly pulled out of one's way in ascending rocky hills. . . .[2]

Other women stressed "the regulation bloomer costume [as] the most satisfactory for life in the open," but only if designed to protect modesty. "There is a way," wrote a woman hiker,

by which the wearing of bloomers may be enjoyed by all, both young and older girls. Make a short circular skirt, about ankle length or a trifle shorter, and button it down the front with cloth covered buttons of material that the skirt is made of. . . . When one has reached the country or mountainside where bloomers are suitable, remove the skirt and place it as a cape. . . . When "civilization" is again reached, this cape may be quickly transformed again into a skirt.[3]

Riding breeches, at the beginning of the twentieth century, were often worn as an extension of fashion, and not merely as a utilitarian garment for tramping fields, hiking over rocky terrain, or exploring the wilderness by canoe.

The director of physical training at Wellesley College, Lucille Eaton Hill, surveyed the needs of women for sports clothing and, with help from her departmental colleagues, published a guidebook in 1903. Hill introduced her subject by reminding readers that the dean of the college, in a recent commencement address, had pronounced the "girl of today" more independent in her manners and, happily, freer in her life than college girls of previous generations. "She may ride a horse without an accompanying groom," the dean offered as evidence, and "she may bestride a horse; she may row and run and swim and take part in a hundred athletic exercises without being one whit less a woman." Still, the dean thought, "some things she had better leave to men. Fiercely competitive athletics . . . are not womanly." Hill's book, however, included suggestions for clothing for a range of physical activities, including cross-country walking, swimming, golf, running, field hockey, lawn tennis, bowling, fencing, and riding.[4]

The college woman who strode out across the country, according to Hill and her colleagues, should wear old clothes, and they should be warm but not too tight. "No constriction of any part of the body can be permitted; loose waists, knickerbockers, and short skirts are always desirable." The walker's stockings should be large enough, made of soft material, and free of holes. "Round garters should not be worn," since they might hamper circulation. Whenever possible, the walker was advised to go bare-headed, but any hat worn should be light, plain, and easily held in place against wind and rain. The sweater, if required, should be made of soft woolen yarn.[5]

But, warned the expert, "shoes and boots are the most important items of the costume. These have always been the worst failures in clothes, which," she added, "have been bad enough in every particular." Walking shoes, unlike the fashionable footwear of the day, should protect the wearer's feet, should support the ankles, and should allow easy and painless movement. "Pointed toes are undesirable," she stressed, but allowed that, "if there be a point, it should be directly in front of the great toe."[6]

Wellesley's swimming coach, Edwyn Sandys, insisted that "the greatest difficulty the female pupil has to encounter is found in the costume which that all-powerful factor, custom, has declared she must wear." Women's swimming costumes, judged either for practicality of rationality, were found both "absurd and useless." The coach continued: "No one knows this better than the female professional swimmer who, of course, is businesslike and practical in everything she does. Because she has

223

learned that every unnecessary thread in a costume means an unnecessary drag upon her efforts, she eliminates every possible inch of fabric."[7]

Coach Sandys did not expect the well-bred college woman to adopt the competitive (and, therefore, masculine) attitudes of professional swimmers; but he advised her that she might do well to remember the old saying: " 'Enough is as good as a feast,' " and to eliminate unnecessary yardage in her swimsuit. "Just to satisfy myself upon this point of costume," he said,

*I once wore a close imitation of the usual suit for women. Not until then did I rightly understand what a serious matter a few feet of superfluous cloth might become in water. The suit was amply large, yet pounds of apparently dead weight seemed to be pulling me in every direction. In that gear a swim of one hundred yards was as serious a task as a mile in my own suit. After that experience I no longer wondered why so few women swim really well, but rather that they are able to swim at all."[8]

seen a more healthy and attractive-looking lot of women."[10]

In addition, golf was thought to develop the player's character. The coach confided that

*women play cards, croquet, and other games [and do not always] seem to think it absolutely necessary — shall we say — to adhere strictly to the rules. And in golf? I have played in almost all the large tournaments for seven years and have never yet seen a woman cheat. Not only does it make them more honorable, but it helps them in little ways. They learn to be cheerful losers, generous winners; and these things in themselves help to make them better women."[11]

How should a woman dress to arrive at such an elevated level of sportsmanship and womanliness? According to Griscom, she should first realize that there is no distinct golfing costume, "but I should advise a short skirt, a shirtwaist that does not bind, and a sensible pair of shoes large enough to be absolutely comfort-

The Wellesley guidebook recommended a one-piece, loosely fitting suit of "fine, light woollen stuff, with the skirt as an adjunct, but not as a part of the actual swimming suit." Such a costume would meet all requirements for swimming "while greatly lessening the tax upon one's strength."[9]

Walking and swimming notwithstanding, Wellesley's golf coach Francis C. Griscom, Jr., insisted, "The best game for women is golf." The game kept a woman in the open air "for hours at a time without overtaxing her strength." While tennis is a splendid game, according to the golf coach, "it is too violent for many women . . . the same is true with hockey, basketball, cricket, and most other games which a woman undertakes." But golf, which can be played in most months of the year, makes a woman strong. For proof, offered Griscom, "Let an outsider go to one of our women's tournaments, and say if he or she has ever

able, and with very low heels. Some prefer tennis shoes with no heels at all. One must have rubber or hobnails on the soles to keep them from slipping. It is a great aid in playing not to slip."[12]

Running, too, required special footwear and clothing, and "the use of high-heeled shoes of any description should be absolutely discarded." Instead, advised the running coach, the run-

opposite

At the turn of the century, women golfers might appear in a modified version of the Gibson girl look, or in costumes of their own devising. Regardless of the style of dress, however, they covered their limbs and wore hats and constricting garments when they teed off.

above

In the early years of the twentieth century, people were likely to wear unspecialized clothing for outdoor activities. In 1900, a group of men and women in Des Plaines, Illinois, wore everyday hats, caps, and clothing for their tennis games.

ner should select "a low-cut shoe with a spring heel and felt or light leather sole. At Wellesley," she said, "I have coached the students with the regular spiked shoe in their track work, as it insures greater firmness and surety of footing." She also advised light clothing, with "the underwear free from binding appliances, and round garters and tight belts should not be worn."[13]

The female tennis player, too, should wear loose-fitting clothing. "The waist should not fit too tight, and it should be particularly free at the elbows and shoulders. The skirt should be short and stiff enough not to get in the way of the knees or to bend so much around them as to bind or interfere with the player when she is making a stroke or running to reach the ball." Shoes, advised the coach, should "fit the feet snugly, and not allow them to slip around inside. Many players wear low canvas slippers with rubber soles, and find them more comfortable and less tiring than leather-bound shoes."[14]

Hill's guidebook to sports contained detailed suggestions for dressing for the sports available to college women at the beginning of the century, and emphasized the need for comfortable, sturdy, functional clothing. Sports in colleges, for both men and women, would prove a significant influence on American clothing.

American clothing was influenced by the decade-by-decade growth of college and professional sports, which generated special clothing for participation in specific sports, the widespread desire to emulate the style of sports heroes, and the linking in public perception of sports clothing with a desirable lifestyle. Professional sports boomed in the early decades of the twentieth century: in 1900, the American Baseball League was created, fueling the swelling passion for baseball; soon the Professional Golf Association, the American Professional Football Association (later known as the National Football League), and other organizations formed to promote specific sports.

Public interest in sports swelled around the champions of the period: William "Bill" Larned in tennis, Ty Cobb in baseball, Jim Thorpe in football — and a lot of other sports as well — captured public imagination and helped place sports in the forefront of American life.

By the twenties, baseball had come to draw almost fanatic interest. The Black Baseball League, organized in Chicago in 1920, tried to give the country's black baseball players a chance to play the game. But baseball, strictly segregated until many years later, developed largely through white teams and white stars like Babe Ruth, who, by the standards of the day, was a rich man when, in 1920, the New York Yankees bought him for $125,000 and he hit fifty-four home runs.

During the twenties, radio broadcasts of sporting events whetted listeners' appetites for sports, and soon fans could follow the play-by-play report of their favorite teams in the World Series. Radio broadcasts, along with newspapers and magazines, also brought the feats of individual champions to the American home: Helen Wills and Bill Tilden starred in tennis, Gertrude Ederle swam the English Channel, and Johnny Weissmuller swam one hundred meters in fifty-nine seconds.

Professional sports and professional players became big business, as promoters found huge profits in baseball, boxing, football, tennis, and golf — all of which catered to the spectator's desire for excitement. Crowds flocked to see professional ath-

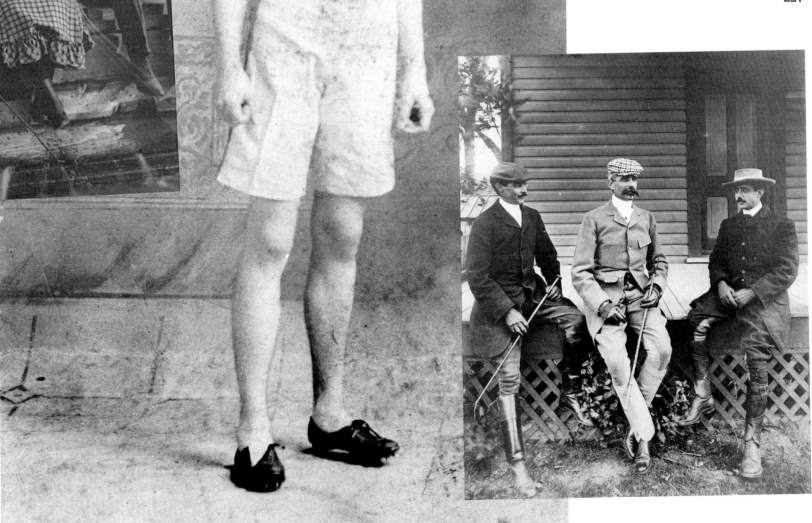

far left

In Colorado, in 1901, these women wore stylish hats and fashionable clothing while their male companions wore business attire for an afternoon of fishing.

left

In 1901 a student athlete from Pennsylvania State University wore shorts and a sleeveless shirt for track competition.

below

The standardization of men's clothing permitted the adaptation of the business suit to outdoor activities.

227

letes, who for the first time in the nation's history achieved the status of heroes.

The growing popularity of golf was transforming the American landscape, as country clubs — once exclusive and rare — sprang up around the country to provide golf courses for the thousands of upper-middle-class men and women who were learning to play the sport. The perceived link between golf and affluence furthered the popularity of clothing associated with the game. In 1930, when Bobby Jones won the United States Open and the Amateur and the British Open, American fans had another champion to applaud and emulate.

The Depression, however, not sports and players, occupied American attention during the first part of the thirties. But when the economic pressures eased, sporting events again attracted great crowds, and sports regained the prominence enjoyed in the previous decade. And sports heroes thrilled their fans: Joe DiMaggio batted and played outfield for the New York Yankees for fifteen years; Joe Louis, the preeminent black athlete of the age, won the world heavyweight championship in boxing; and Don Budge became the first player to capture the tennis grand slam by winning the United States, British, French, and Australian men's singles championships in 1938.

In the sixties and seventies, millions of Americans avidly followed athletes and sports events on television, as huge numbers continued to attend the contests. By the beginning of the eighties, major league baseball attracted almost 40 million people yearly, college football about 35 million, and college basketball about 30 million. As fans bought tickets, sports prospered, but television brought previously unimagined riches to the world of sports.

Today, men and women from that world gain celebrity, endorse products, and influence clothing in the same way that heroes do from the worlds of entertainment, public affairs, and other forms of achievement. Apart from the champion's personal endorsements of garments, and identification of "winning" with articles of clothing worn by sports heroes, the whole phenomenon of sports has altered American — and world — clothing immeasurably.

By 1906, William T. (Mother) Dunn (*left*), star football player for Pennsylvania State University, wore a standardized collegiate football uniform: turtleneck sweater with college letter or insignia, well-padded pants derived from knickers, high woolen socks, and lace-up running shoes. Some early collegiate football players (*right*) wore lace-up vests over the standard pullovers.

230

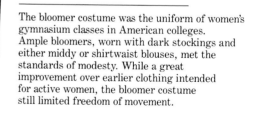

The bloomer costume was the uniform of women's gymnasium classes in American colleges. Ample bloomers, worn with dark stockings and either middy or shirtwaist blouses, met the standards of modesty. While a great improvement over earlier clothing intended for active women, the bloomer costume still limited freedom of movement.

231

above

By the forties, women on college athletic teams customarily wore simple short shirt-waisted dresses over modified bloomers, a costume thought to retain the femininity of skirts but to allow full and fast physical movement in sports.

right

By the fifties, women athletes were likely to wear shorts and shirts for most sports.

232

Women like this one, posing with a golf club in a photographer's studio, c. 1906, could play golf in clothing similar to that which they wore every day.

Some garments — like this golf cape dating from 1899 — were designed specifically for women athletes.

At the turn of the century, men might wear
two-piece woolen bathing suits that covered the chest
and thighs but left the legs and arms free to move. Moreover,
men's suits were designed to fit closer to the body, and to
use less material than women's swimming costumes of the
period. By 1919, men's bathing suits bared even more
arm and more leg (*above left*), making swimming easier.
Wool was heavy, likely to sag when waterlogged, itchy, and
undesirable by today's standards for swimwear materials.
Prior to the development of synthetic fabrics, however,
wool bathing suits were deemed utilitarian.

In 1900, women wore bathing suits with
daringly short sleeves, but also with long
skirts over even longer bloomers.

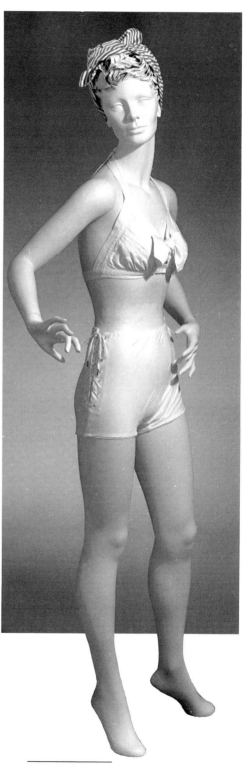

By the late twenties, women's bathing costumes, even when worn with stockings and shoes, reflected a new freedom and new attitudes about modesty.

The twenties brought women the freedom to experiment with new styles. Wearing this beach pajama outfit with matching hat, a woman in the twenties revealed bare arms.

In the early forties, influenced by Hollywood, women often wore two-piece swimsuits, with the intention of displaying rather than hiding sexual allure.

For those hesitant to bare midriff
and use their bathing suits to package
and advertise sexual attractiveness,
there were demure suits that
recalled gingham dresses.

By the sixties, the bikini
had become the accepted female
attire for the beach.

236

CHAPTER 17

Gender and Clothing
Identity, Self, and Society

For much of our history, it has been assumed that clothing served as a secondary sex characteristic; that is, clothing was accepted as a means of identifying gender, exceeded in its reliability only by genital examination. While exceptions to this convention have been remarked, so-called "cross-dressing" has been closeted with taboos and associations of titillating kinkiness, which in turn has provided a language of clothing useful to Hollywood and everyday amateur actors projecting character.

Moviemakers have mirrored the public's understanding that clothing is different for men and for women, and that members of either sex who deviate from the socially established norms for male or female clothing either risk ridicule and ostracism or set the stage for a good joke. Dustin Hoffman as Tootsie and Julie Andrews in *Victor/Victoria* made sexual stereotyping the substance of humor and plot.

Distinguishing between the sexes — and all that such distinction implies and evokes — has been a primary function of clothing, and male and female styles of clothing, in turn, have also served as a base from which to emphasize — even to the point of parodying — sexual distinctions and stereotypes for purposes of reinforcing the social roles that have traditionally been assigned to males and females. The widely recognized codification of clothing that defines gender enables members of the same sex to use garments to compete with one another for distinction as super-feminine or super-masculine. Clothing, almost as much as manners and gestures, makes the he-man and the she-woman. With few exceptions, conformity to these stereotypes precludes a member of either sex from wearing any suggestion of the clothing of the other — save in parody or irony implicitly emphasizing the wearer's gender. A man wearing a brassiere or a woman wearing a codpiece, unless they are rock stars in performance, can expect disparaging remarks on Main Street, USA. Western male attire proves the exception to the rule, however; as one of the most masculine of clothing styles, western fashion grants fancy shirts, gaudily decorated jackets and jeans, and high heels to those who wish to be Marlboro men.

Certain women have appropriated male dress in an effort to gain for themselves the power and professional recognition reserved for men. In doing so, however, they have often been impugned as "unwomanly" and "unnatural." The nineteenth-century French writer George Sand is probably as well known to Americans for wearing men's clothing as for the books she wrote or the intellectual prowess she demonstrated. Calamity Jane, Annie Oakley, and a handful of female figures in the shadows of frontier history survive in popular memory dressed in their buckskins and rough male working attire. A few older residents of Washington, D.C., recall a turn-of-the-century female doctor known for her bravery in the Civil War and her intrepid practice in the slums of the nation's capital city but more widely recognized for her style of dress.

From the beginning of the century, Americans followed avidly the findings of the sexologists. The popularization of psychoanalysis provided a vocabulary for self-examination; sex manuals promised liberation and fulfillment; other studies reported that consenting adults, in whatever privacies they found, engaged in a wondrous variety of sexual acrobatics to achieve sexual pleasure. Americans read Freud, Kinsey, Masters and Johnson, and Dr. Ruth Wertheimer; sexology became a popular subject for home study and for ostensible self-improvement as well as for "analysis" of motivations, repressions, sexual preferences, and expressions of self and others.

Sex — both as human activity and as expression of natural law — has been a major preoccupation of twentieth-century culture. Artists, of both high and popular persuasion, have ex-

237

Marlene Dietrich in top hat, white tie, and tails

plored sexuality in dance, drama, literature, and the plastic arts, and have often extended the boundaries of understanding, or provided sensational vicarious experience. Scientists and social scientists have investigated sex — including varieties and permutations of sexual activities as well as the nature of gender — and their popularized findings have offered instruction to sexual adventurers, and jargon to armchair amateur (and professional) psychobabblers.

While it is unlikely that men and women of the twentieth century have been more fascinated than their predecessors by sexual matters, contemporary Americans openly argue about sexual politics. Both those groups who urge greater sexual freedom and their gainsayers find evidence on which to base their arguments. As the century began, science promised revelations that religion had withheld, making the establishments of the two orders sometimes uneasy with one another. Today, intellectual and political patrons of empiricism and fundamentalism disagree on sexual issues, with the empiricists broadcasting data in support of change and the fundamentalists invoking natural law. Warriors from both camps uniform themselves to show their strength and to battle onward toward victory. Within this context the recent feminist movement and social activism to gain social and medical approbation for homosexuality have brought into question the prevailing definitions of gender and the societal roles to which men and women have been conditioned throughout the greater part of American history. As attitudes about gender have changed, and as women and homosexuals have won political and social freedoms, the rigid distinctions between clothing styles for men and women have blurred.

Clothing now serves to make personal statements regarding gender and sexual politics. For the most part, gender definition through clothing, until recently, depended on trousers, and on who wore them. Until the Second World War, it was assumed that American men wore trousers as the essential ingredient in their standardized uniform, and that only sometimes did well-bred women wear slacks, or, more recently, trousers or pant-suits.

Trousers themselves have a long history in the clothing of the species, beginning probably with men pulling the back hem of robes forward between their legs, and tucking them into their belts in order to work in fields or ride horseback. Ancient sculptures depict men wearing loose trousers, and the Bayeux tapestry shows horsemen, foot soldiers, and others in the eleventh century wearing full trousers to the knee, trousers reaching to the ankles, and tights. In the ensuing centuries, men wore slashed pantaloons and tight hose, varying the size of the pantaloons, richness of ornamentation, and size and prominence of the codpiece used to hold the two segments together.

Trousers as we know them evolved in the nineteenth century, the English dandy Beau Brummell being credited with inventing the tight breeches, buttoned on either side from waist to the middle of the thigh, and held by a strap beneath the instep of the foot, that served as a prototype for today's trousers. At the time of the French Revolution, long pants were identified with the peasants, and distinguished them from the knee-breeches-wearing aristocrats. Both knee breeches and Beau Brummell's style of tight long pants were worn — as were fringed buckskin trousers on the frontier — by American men in the early years of the nineteenth century.

Bifurcation was the topic of essays and popular comment well into the twentieth century, and generally referred to women admitting the existence of legs (or "lower limbs") and, further, displaying them encased in the controversial bloomer costumes, or harem suits. In 1911, that baggy-pant garment appeared in high fashion, adorning stylish ladies at both European and American centers of taste and fad. In that year, too, the Vatican campaigned against "harem trousers," and the Illinois State Legislature debated a ban on both bloomers and the hobble skirt, the former designed to free legs and the latter to enclose them in a tight tube, evidence that the interests of masculine supremacy in Illinois found dilemma in bifurcation.

Gender identification through clothing has been seen especially in conventions related to assigning trousers to male children. Now, however, both male and female babies are likely to be suited up in rompers, overalls, mini-jeans, or other forms of pants.

Dr. Mary Edwards Walker (1832–1919), a graduate of the Syracuse University medical program, volunteered to serve as a surgeon for the Union Army during the Civil War. For three years, however, she was not permitted to practice medicine, but was assigned to the nursing corps. In order to use her medical training fully, Walker determined that she needed to dress in a manner that signified her position. She adapted men's trousers and frock coats, and demanded professional respect.

As a commissioned assistant surgeon — the first woman to hold such a position in the United States — Dr. Walker served heroically throughout the Civil War. Decorated for her services, she nonetheless attracted disparaging remarks and open hostility because she persisted in wearing men's clothing. Congress eventually passed a special decree granting Walker the right to wear trousers.

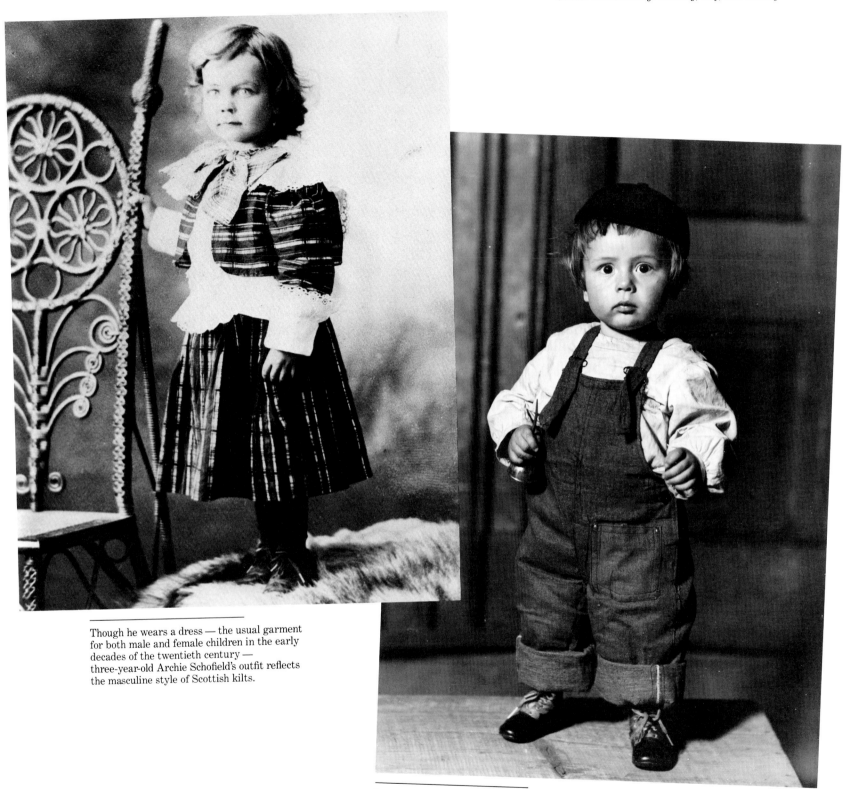

Though he wears a dress — the usual garment for both male and female children in the early decades of the twentieth century — three-year-old Archie Schofield's outfit reflects the masculine style of Scottish kilts.

In 1908 Jules Starbuck of Horton, Kansas, wore his first overalls and carried an oil can — hardly a safe or suitable toy for a toddler — to emphasize the role and costume of little working man.

242

"Slacks girls" operated drill presses
at an Erie, Pennsylvania, war plant.
During World War I, women who worked
in factories often wore long, full knickers —
a variation on the bloomer costume —
with simple blouses, sturdy shoes,
and hair-containing headgear.

left

In 1943, about 85 percent of the employees
who worked in Caterpillar's aluminum
foundry were women. To get the job done,
and to further the war effort that subsumed
the country at that time, women workers
adapted male attire to their need for strong,
safe, and economical clothing.

below

By the 1950s, American women held
numerous jobs that, before World War II,
had been considered to lie exclusively
within the male domain. A Detroit cab
company hired thirty-five women drivers
after the war, and most of them wore
the casual clothes of the "cabbie" rather
than the fashionable frills of the day.

243

PGP-23306

Men wearing women's clothing, if in earnest, incites homophobic hostilities; if jesting, however, a man in woman's clothing provides predictable sight gags. Cary Grant, wearing a woman's negligee in *Bringing Up Baby*, shouted, "I've gone gay!," invoking a term used to refer to homosexuality. The incongruity of this matinee-idol image of masculinity in the frill and frivolity of female costume struck a hilarious note in the film.

Complete with outlandish wig, Grant also appeared in a WAC uniform (*I Was a Male War Bride*), his posture and sagging-at-the-knees stockings emphasizing the incongruity — and therefore humor — of his costume.

247

An estimated 60,000 people watched nearly
10,000 marchers in the fourteenth annual
Gay Pride Parade in Los Angeles in 1984.
This bewigged man, though tarted-up in
female attire that would mark a woman as
whorish, expresses a degree of appreciation
for — and enjoyment of — female clothing.
His high heels, mesh stockings, sequined
dress, elbow-length gloves, feather boa,
and jewelry — all worn over a visibly male
physique — combine the basic ingredients
of outrageous female clothing with both
allure and comedy.

top right

Madonna's incongruous combination of
visible black brassiere and bare skin, along
with macho leather jacket, jeans, and thick
leather belt emphasizes her femaleness, and
satirizes clothing-as-gender-characteristics.
By mixing stereotypical garments,
Madonna is teasing and alluring at once,
as she exploits attitudes about what is
and is not acceptable dress and behavior.

248

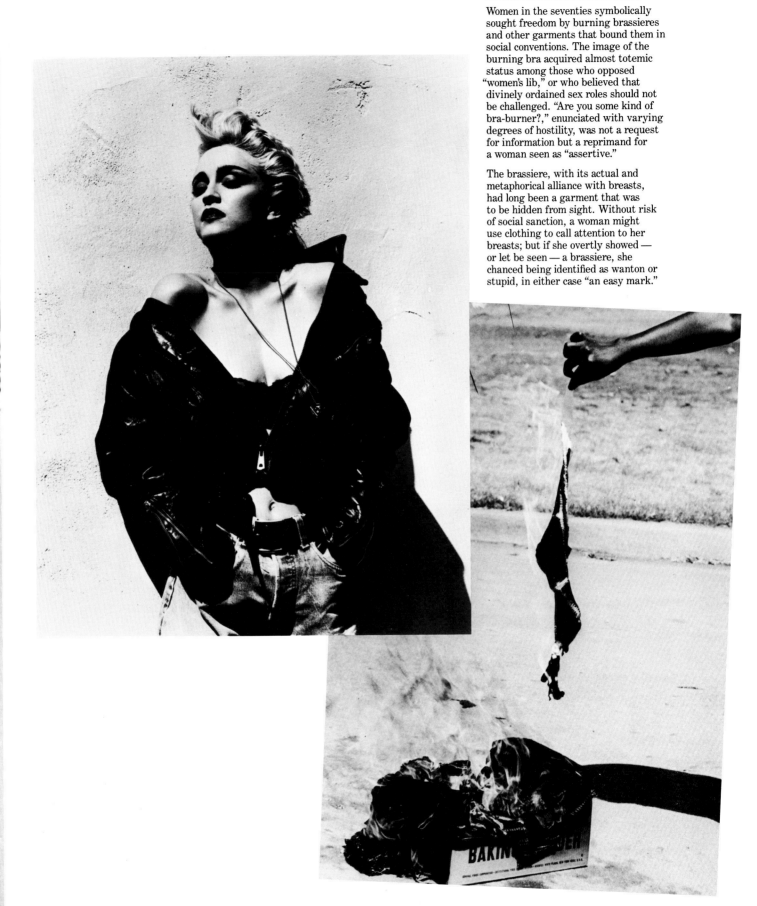

Women in the seventies symbolically sought freedom by burning brassieres and other garments that bound them in social conventions. The image of the burning bra acquired almost totemic status among those who opposed "women's lib," or who believed that divinely ordained sex roles should not be challenged. "Are you some kind of bra-burner?," enunciated with varying degrees of hostility, was not a request for information but a reprimand for a woman seen as "assertive."

The brassiere, with its actual and metaphorical alliance with breasts, had long been a garment that was to be hidden from sight. Without risk of social sanction, a woman might use clothing to call attention to her breasts; but if she overtly showed — or let be seen — a brassiere, she chanced being identified as wanton or stupid, in either case "an easy mark."

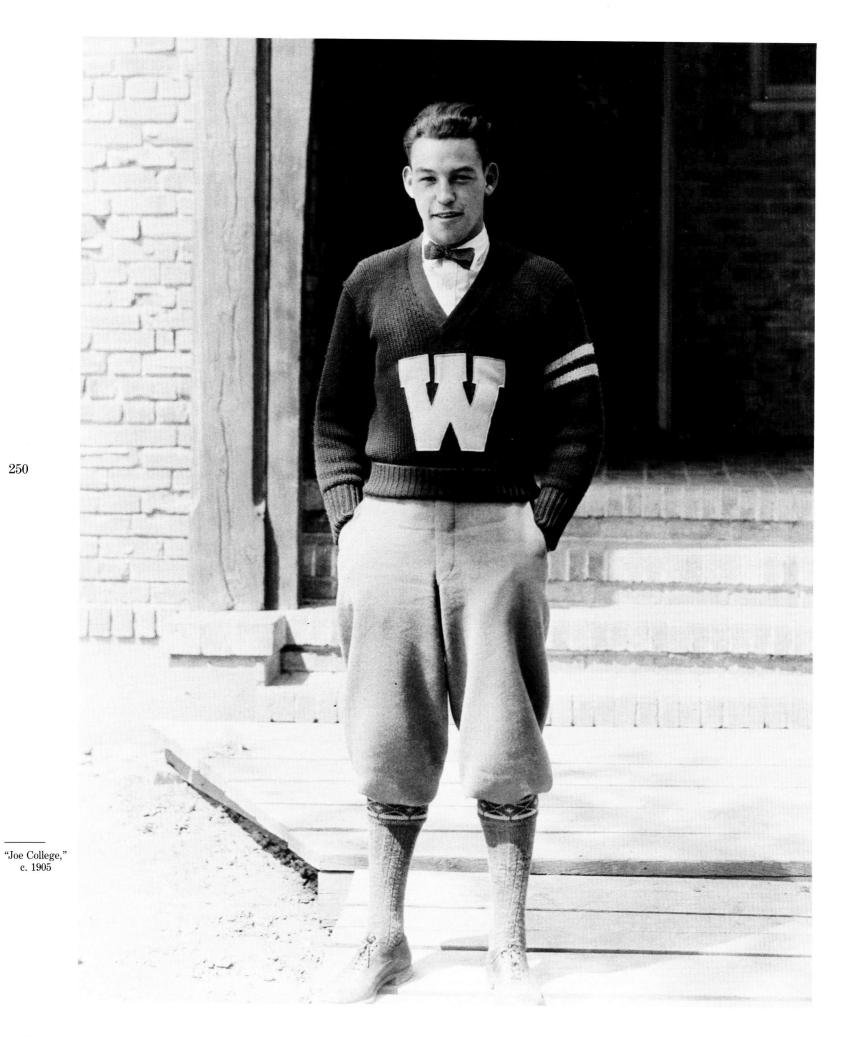

250

CHAPTER 18

College Styles

Church fathers in colonial America established colleges to ensure an educated leadership class by preparing young males for the ministry, law, medicine, and teaching. Such professional grounding was reserved for the affluent, or for those already designated by circumstances of birth and gender for power in the emerging country. In time, however, higher education in the United States opened its doors to the sons of middle-class America, to women, and eventually to nonwhite minority groups; conventional wisdom recognized that a college diploma provided the most dependable means of upward mobility to generations of young Americans. As the privileged young of affluent families were joined on college campuses by the ambitious young from modest backgrounds, institutions of higher education provided a microcosm of American society, its class distinctions, expectations, values, manners, and dress. As in the larger society, clothing reflected class membership, individual aspirations, and peer-group pressures in the form of fads and fashions.

By the late nineteenth century, colleges and universities provided an atmosphere for examination and experimentation with social values and attitudes, as well as with manners and styles of dressing. Clothes became a means for self-identification, for attracting or avoiding attention, for gaining or losing popularity; uniformity of dress defined membership in particular campus groups or cliques. College life included emphasis on sports and physical fitness as well as preparation for responsible or powerful roles in society, promoting attention to clothing dedicated to specific activities or to symbolizing power and status.

The college graduate in America expected to live better, earn more, and have more influence in society than the man or woman with less education. Men preparing to become doctors, ministers, lawyers, and captains of industry dressed to advertise their learning and their present and future claims on status. To wear the newest fashion in clothing or to argue the newest idea under discussion in the classroom broadcast the college student's intention to claim power.

In the nineteenth century American college men dressed in accordance with the understood privileged position that higher education symbolized. They would be leaders; they would prosper; and their attention to dress displayed their fashionable taste and their destined lives as pillars of rectitude.

As women pursued higher education, at first more often in single-sex than in coeducational institutions, their clothing, too, reflected not only the subculture of campus life but their expectations regarding work, marriage, and affluence. While Oberlin College had admitted women in 1837, and the University of Iowa and Cornell University did so shortly after, higher education for women was regarded by many throughout the nineteenth century to be biologically unnatural, as a process that ran counter to women's intellectual ability, and as a form of socialization likely to lead to defeminization. Women, given too much learning, according to the conventional wisdom of the period, might fail as wives and mothers, might aspire to knowledge and experience inappropriate for the weaker and fairer sex. Nonetheless, as women's colleges like Bryn Mawr, Radcliffe, Smith, and Mount Holyoke developed in America, increasing numbers of women turned to education, and to the personal and professional rewards that it promised.

In the United States, higher education has served a number of social functions in addition to development of the intellect: time in college has allowed the adolescent to mature in a protected society; a college education has provided entry to the higher levels of the job market; and, perhaps most important of all, the college diploma has distinguished the upper middle class from the lower middle class in American culture.

As publicly funded institutions of higher education made the privileges of college available to an increasing segment of society, elitism has been defined both by membership in the population of college-educated citizens and by the particular college granting the degree. Thus, as colleges have spawned experiments in fashion, they have also established benchmarks for snobbism in American society.

Colleges, as microcosms of American culture, have emphasized attitudes about masculinity and femininity, an antidote, perhaps, to lingering fears that too much education (whatever that might be) might result in a man's being too sensitive and, therefore, a sissy; or might cause a woman to take on masculine attributes that would make her a misfit in society. Styles of clothing on campuses have, at any given time, tended to mirror precisely society's perception of masculinity and femininity.

The relatively protected environment of the college campus traditionally affords adolescents a situation in which to test personal style, to experiment with behavior, and to test their own tolerance for conformity or need for rebellion.

253

above

The first American women to enter college were regarded often as "unnatural" and were thought to be foolishly seeking to improve their minds, an affront to their ordained roles as wives and mothers. By the end of the nineteenth century women students, cloistered mostly in single-sex institutions, generally wore sedate fashions reflecting the widely held opinion that women were spiritually superior and physically weaker than men, that women's bodies should be protected from the naturally lascivious eyes of men and from the rigors of competitive sports and strenuous physical activity.

left

In the protected society of college campuses, both men and women students adopted new fashions more readily than their parents or other young people their age who joined the work force without benefit of higher education. The willingness of college students to experiment with clothing, to enjoy fads and shifts in fashion, has made the American college campus an important testing ground for clothing. Moreover, since college students often have had money to spend on clothing, they have become an important market for manufacturers and retailers.

254

Women college students were encouraged to study to become teachers, missionaries, and wives of professional men.

Many colleges, supporting the conventional role of women in society, offered special courses in the "womanly arts," such as sewing, cooking, and other skills associated with homemaking. Sewing classes displayed their products, palpable evidence that the feminine attributes and interests of women were not being subverted by unbecoming intellectual rigor or unwomanly engagement in sports.

Typically, graduating classes of women in the late nineteenth century posed in virginal white dresses for photographs, reminding posterity at once of their femininity and of their bridal expectations. Indeed, women were often reminded that "to educate a woman is to educate a family," the slogan that rationalized an otherwise questionable affront to concepts of femininity in America.

In the 1920s, women's fashions on college campuses changed, as did female clothing throughout the country. A quartet in 1920 (*left*) wore demure afternoon dresses. By the middle of that decade, however, a similar group of young women (*above*) combined boy-style caps and college cardigans, pleated skirts, and large-collared blouses with bow-tied scarves.

One informal college uniform for women during the 1930s consisted of cardigans, pleated or gored skirts, and simple blouses (*left*).

Texas State College for Women established dress codes in an effort to erase class distinctions through dress and to promote concepts of appropriate attire for specific activities. The above page from the college's 1935 bulletin shows the different uniforms approved for college students.

In 1946, the largest class up to that time registered for the fall term at Harvard, with 75 percent of those entering being veterans. The scene was repeated throughout the country as G.I.s returned from the Second World War and enrolled in colleges, bringing with them the comfortable and practical khaki pants, well-fitted shirts, and casual jackets of military uniforms, garments that soon gained popularity among both men and women on American campuses.

259

above

During the fifties, American college women donned clothing that emphasized "little girl" qualities: Peter Pan–collared blouses, simple skirts, and sweaters. Penny loafers ascended in popularity, but the familiar anklets previously worn with saddle shoes remained an essential part of the wardrobe. The virginal and wholesome American college "girl" of the fifties — like her older sister, the dedicated housewife and mother — was a stereotype of the female role during that time of "togetherness" and the nuclear family.

College women, urged by magazines such as *Mademoiselle* to adopt particular attitudes and values, as well as styles, purchased the requisite costumes (conveniently advertised in the same magazines) to fit their social roles.

above right

The class blazer, worn with simple dark skirts and sensible shoes — sneakers or loafers — was another favorite outfit for women in American colleges in the late fifties.

In the late fifties, the ballerina shoes and long full skirts of the "new look" dominated college fashion.

opposite

College men, following the standards set by the previous college generation of veterans, enjoyed casual clothing: Bermuda shorts, washable khaki pants, comfortable cotton shirts or sweatshirts, and loafers and sneakers. G.I.s who enrolled in colleges strongly influenced the trend toward casualness. Older than their classmates who had not served in the military forces, G.I.s often scorned the fraternity-driven collegiate social life, preferring more informality in dress and recreation. The casual trend set on college campuses in the late forties and fifties continued, including variations on bits and bobs of military uniforms, until the eighties. During that period, and the university spawning of the Yuppie, college students of both sexes who saw themselves as the future field marshals of capitalism decked themselves out in expensive-looking and boardroom-formal suits and ties.

left

By the sixties, men and women in college wore the fads popular among young people throughout society: women donned hot pants and miniskirts, white boots with heels; men often wore bell-bottomed slacks, denim jeans, T-shirts, and sneakers.

below

261

By 1969, women in the Reserve Officer Training Corps, or ROTC, groups that formed on some college campuses adopted "female" versions of men's uniforms and, untroubled by irony, wore low-heeled pumps and stockings to gun-drill sessions.

The Arrow Shirt Company created images of clean-cut virile men, neatly groomed and stylishly dressed. The advertiser, however, did not tell the customers that the company also counted on being able to convince them that the "modish, mannish" chap would require a different collar for winter's end and spring's beginning.

A $1.50 garment, a shirt manufacturer assured prospective customers (*below*), "will look best on you longer than ordinary shirts, because it is made of better than ordinary color-fast fabrics."

ARROW
COLLARS and SHIRTS

DEVON is a good collar for the summer's end and the autumn's beginning. Modish mannish, comfortable.

2 for 25 cents

THE makers depend upon the good qualities of Arrow Shirts to sell you another of the same label.

$1.50 and more

Send for booklets. CLUETT, PEABODY & COMPANY, 473 River Street, Troy, N. Y.

Cluett
Color-Fast COAT SHIRTS

A Cluett Color-fast Coat Shirt will look best on you longer than ordinary shirts, because it is made of better than ordinary color-fast fabrics. *$1.50 and up*

Send for booklet, "Proper Dress," Cluett, Peabody & Company, 435 River Street, Troy, N. Y.

CHAPTER 19

Consumerism and Communication

For two hundred years, advertising has been an increasingly potent force in the lives of Americans. Manufacturers, as well as retailers, use advertising to reach the public, and to convince the consumer that loyalty to a brand name is rewarded by excellence of materials and workmanship and, most important, by fashionableness. Russell Lynes wrote:

Manufacturers are concerned with markets and markets are made up of people who want to buy and who can afford to. Basic needs for clothing, food, shelter, and transportation make people buy some things, but a complex of desires, ambitions, and emulations makes them buy a great many things that they do not need. The function of much advertising is, of course, to create desire where no basic need exists. . . .[1]

From eighteenth-century shop signs and broadsides to contemporary television and print advertisements, Americans have been informed and influenced by pitches aimed at persuading them to exchange money for goods or services. The methods of persuasion — whether hidden or blatant — seek to involve the prospective purchaser's fantasy, seek to co-opt the customer and transform him or her from observer to collaborator.

The communications-consumer connection works. Few contemporary Americans, even among those living below the official poverty line, select and wear clothing purely on the basis of utilitarian concerns — anticipated life of the garment, quality of workmanship, and function. The contemporary clothing industry — from designer to manufacturer to retailer to advertiser to wearer — is firmly based on the understanding that people will buy and wear garments that they do not need, and that they will buy and wear garments that they expect to abandon rather than to wear out, or fully use.

Consumers select and wear clothing that enables them to conform to images, dreams, and fantasies; as they imagine themselves, so will they dress. The communications industries — whether the advertisers overtly acting to establish the dreams people will seek to materialize by purchasing designated objects, or the entertainment media presenting desirable roles and styles — provide images for the consumer.

Early in the century, advertisers began depicting attractive people using goods, thereby linking in the consumer's mind the image of the model with the item being sold. Advertisements for the Hoover Company, for example, illustrate changing American ideals for women over more than three-quarters of a century.

Robert S. and Helen Merrell Lynd, in *Middletown*, their sociological study of a typical American town, limned the reaches of conspicuous consumption and the fundaments of American consumerism observable at the end of the first quarter of the twentieth century. The same deeply embedded attitudes and values related to clothing that the Lynds exposed just prior to the Depression remain vital to American life after another fifty years of additional advertising-driven purchasing, and despite observable changes in social patterns. Americans, now as then, buy clothing in order to identify themselves to others — to display or hide wealth, to gain or deny status, and to join or reject groups. Throughout the twentieth century, however, the language and presumed power of clothing has been set by the growing communications industries, by films and magazines and television.

Early in their book, the Lynds acknowledged the powerful role of motion pictures, advertising, and other forms of publicity in establishing standards regarding the clothing objects that befit a well-off person in America. The people of Middletown, from all walks of life, they said, went to the movies "with an intensity of emotion that is apparently one of the most potent means of reconditioning habits," and were transported through the powers of imagination "into the intimacies of Fifth Avenue drawing rooms and English country houses, [where they watched] the habitual activities of a different cultural level."

The growth of popular magazines and national advertising involves the utilization through the printed page of the most powerful stimuli to action. In place of the relatively mild, scattered, something-for-nothing, sample-free, I-tell-you-this-is-a-good-article copy seen in Middletown a generation ago, advertising is concentrating increasingly upon a type of copy aiming to make the reader emotionally uneasy, to bludgeon him with the fact that decent people don't live the way he does; *decent people ride on balloon tires, have a second bathroom, and so on. This copy points an accusing finger at the stenographer as she reads her* Motion Picture Magazine *and makes her acutely conscious of her unpolished nails, or of the worn place in the living room rug, and sends the housewife peering anxiously into the mirror to see if* her *wrinkles look like those that made Mrs. X . . . in the ad "old at thirty-five" because she did not have a Leisure Hour electric washer.*[2]

264

Local retail establishments in Middletown held style shows in a calculated effort to

influence the local standard of living. On two successive nights at one of these local shows a thousand people — ten-cent store clerks, tired-looking mothers with children, husbands and wives — watched rouged clerks promenade languorously along the tops of the show cases, displaying the latest hats, furs, dresses, shoes, parasols, bags and other accessories, while a jazz orchestra kept everybody "feeling good."[3]

Style shows, set against the powerful backdrop of movies and magazines, helped persuade women to *buy* rather than *make* clothing. Making clothing for the family had been among the primary chores of housewives of earlier generations, but by the twenties, American women had become consumers; they desired manufactured clothing, and wanted to purchase fashionable ready-made garments from mail-order catalogs or from local retail stores.

According to the Lynds, "As late as 1910 there was practically no advertising of women's dresses in the local newspapers, and goods by the yard was prominently featured." The changes in Middletown's desires for ready-made and fashionable clothing,

The mail-order catalog and rural free delivery allowed early-twentieth-century Americans in every part of the country to select clothing from a variety of manufactured garments.

Levi Strauss directed an advertisement for "His first pair of trousers" to American mothers, suggesting that sturdy copper-riveted overalls had earned customer confidence and, simultaneously, calling attention to the mother's role in her son's ritual passage from infants' clothes to trousers.

according to the Lynds, opened possibilities for the student of cultural change to observe differences in attitudes between men and women, between younger and older people, and among those of different levels of education and class membership. Noting that the family house and yard as well as wardrobe in Middletown had yielded to the automobile as an outward "emblem of conspicuous membership" in a socially competitive society, the Lynds asked,

will the automobile, the new religion of higher education, and other new means to fuller living cut down the money spent on clothing . . . ? What emotional outlet in these days of quickly assembled home sewing is compensating Middletown's women for the pride in needle craftsmanship, in the neat seam, overcast and bound, dear to the housewife of a generation ago?

And they asked, "As the woman becomes less the passive recipient of the man's advances in mating, will her present use of dress appeal diminish?"[4]

They wondered, too, what influence the new twenties styles might have on the future of clothing in Middletown, noting that the trend was toward simple lines and "fewer ruffles and tucks, plainer flounces, straight instead of gored skirts, no fitted bodices and sleeves — and in their place are straight-line one-piece dresses 'as easy to make as a doll's dress,' " fashion's response to the newer freedom and aggressiveness of women.[5]

Middletown working-class families felt the pressure of high school dances and social activities, and often struggled to provide children with the clothing required to maintain social acceptability, or status, in the school community. A working man

and wife, needing both incomes to support their children, spent $250 in 1923 and again in 1924 on their two sons' high school commencement clothes. The Lynds observed, "Just because they are somewhat *déclassé* socially, the compulsion to dress as the crowd does frequently rests as a doubly compelling necessity upon the children of this class." Further, they noted:

The importance of the right dress in this battle of clothes was naively described by a recent Middletown high school graduate who had appeared at one of the Christmas dances in a $90 "rust-colored gown." "I was so pleased that nobody spoke of how nice it looked. You know if your mother makes a dress at home people always come up to you and say, "How nice you look! Isn't it pretty!" and you know they're condescending. I was sorry though that my dress wasn't described in the paper, for you always like that. But it isn't the best dresses that are usually described."[6]

265

The automobile became the most important status symbol for Americans, and advertisers often depicted desirable cars in the presence of well-dressed owners, thus powerfully connecting ownership of these specific automobiles with general prosperity and status.

Appearing frequently in the Middletown papers, descriptions of clothing typically and predictably follow this model:

Many fashionable dresses were worn by the guests, among them being a green crepe built over gold satin which was worn by Miss _____. The blouse was made [with a] basque effect and trimmed with gold lace. A gold headband, gold slippers, and gold hose were worn with this dress. Miss _____, was lovely in a smart frock of flowered pussy-willow taffeta made over white crepe de chine. It was fashioned [in a] tunic effect and caught with turquoise blue ribbons. She wore white hose and black satin slippers and a blue headband. Another attractive gown was that worn by Miss _____, which was of green brocaded chiffon velvet, fashioned with flower trimmings. She wore black satin slippers and matching hose. Miss _____ was stunning in a gown of dark blue chenille, fashioned with dark brown fur trimmings; she wore gold hose and gold slippers.[7]

With the increasing use of central heating in houses, no one could argue that the sole use of clothing was to maintain bodily comfort. Issues of morality, however, persisted regarding women's clothing in Middletown. While it was conventional in the 1920s for men's clothing to cover the body from chin to foot, women and girls could — at peril or discretion, depending on the point of view — shorten their hems, and emphasize their legs by wearing sheer silk stockings; they could bare more of the arms and neck; and they could abandon corsets and petticoats to reveal the natural lines of the female body.

As Americans selected their clothing from ready-made garments, the importance of advertising, films, and other forms of communication increased rapidly. Manufacturers used advertisers to convince the public of its need for specific ready-made garments; the American consumers proved an easy mark, with

266

The Gold Medal flour advertisements of 1908 and 1916 show differing attitudes about women as time passed. In the first, the housewife is encouraged to identify with a long-skirted, aproned woman exhibiting a flour sack and a rolling pin — that is, with a housewife using a product as a part of her regular routine. The second, however, shows a smartly turned-out woman golfer, linking the product with a more active life of "fresh air, good exercise, proper food."

imaginations easily transfixed on articles of clothing attached to status.

During the fifties, after the war years in which consumer goods were scarce, Americans went on a buying spree. Encouraged by credit availability, many families set out to buy their dreams, to fill their houses with appliances and their wardrobes with clothing that showed them to be affluent and fashionable.

Levi Strauss and Company, among others, recognized the expanding market for blue jeans. With the new casualness in dress that followed the Second World War, and with both women and children adopting jeans for leisure wear, special Levi's and other denim jeans were produced and marketed, capitalizing on the western tradition and on their suitability for outdoor wear by women and children as well as by cowboys and workmen.

In 1950, sociologist David Riesman and his colleagues published *The Lonely Crowd*, in which they argued that Americans of the postwar era differed significantly from earlier generations. Typically, according to the authors, the new American was an urbanite and "other-directed," or one who patterned his behavior on that of others. Shaping himself to the values and images learned chiefly through the media, but also from friends and associates, the postwar American was found to be a conformist. And how did he exhibit his conformity? By acquiring the emblems, or things, identified with the model. The "other-directed" person, thus, is the perfect consumer, driven not by conscience or need, but by the desire to appear (if not be) like others.

The basic tenets of *The Lonely Crowd* were illustrated a year later when J. D. Salinger's *Catcher in the Rye* was published. Holden Caulfield, the adolescent narrator of the novel, agonized over the power of "phonys" at his prep school. Caulfield, resisting societal pressures to join the other-directed majority, ignores accepted standards for both dress and language.

For many Americans coming of age since World War II, conformity to society — the process of becoming other-directed — has been tantamount to becoming adult. And the shift from the casual clothing of the adolescent to the grown-up garments of successful men and women has been one evidence of maturation. As the privileges of adulthood — sexual expression, independent consumerism, political activity — have been extended to younger and younger groups of Americans, advertisers have promoted increasingly "adult" styles to that group.

"Training" brassieres are sold to prepubescent girls, along with cosmetics, perfume, and dresses that, several decades ago, would have marked their wearer as a prostitute. The combina-

Advertisers often play upon the consumer's identification of a salable object with a famous person. In this case, the very popular Frank Sinatra is shown wearing a bow tie. The advertisement was intended to persuade women to buy bow ties for husbands, sons, and boyfriends, and to persuade men to buy bow ties in order to approximate Sinatra's appeal to women.

tion of media and peer-group pressure makes it difficult, in some communities, for children not to conform.

Teenage boys, targeted by finely tuned advertising campaigns, are persuaded by their sports heroes that they must wear special — and most likely, costly — garments: pump-up sports shoes, warm-ups, brand-name sweat clothes, or T-shirts emblazoned with the initials or logo of a designer.

Social workers have recently noted that teenage girls join gangs, modeled on those of urban boys, for two purposes: they protect one another against real and imagined dangers, and they work together to shoplift articles that "everybody has." In their culture, possession and display of things determines worth; the girl who fails to conform in manners and dress to the behavioral patterns of her peers — or who is not "other-directed" — will be ostracized, or perhaps harmed.

Consumerism, fueled by the communications industry, is a way of life in America, and as essential as if it were a state religion. Indeed, consumerism, as practiced today, is firmly rooted in a belief in magic. Objects are believed to possess supernatural powers, and ownership of specific objects is believed to bestow upon the owner desired powers or states of being. Thus, "I think, therefore I am" translates in the desperate modern-day search for self-worth to, "I have, therefore I am somebody." Media mentors show us *somebodies* and what they *have*, telling us that the two are intertwined, and that having is a measure of worth.

267

268

a.

Throughout the twentieth century, Hoover vacuum cleaners have been advertised
with women whose clothing emphasized the manufacturer's message.
In 1909 (a), a maid — an older woman in the modest dress of a servant — uses
the machine to clean an affluent home; by inference, the "lady of the house"
is enjoying both leisure and wealth. A younger maid (b), properly aproned, cleans
a stylish house of the twenties, also freeing her wealthier employer for
other activities. The 1964 advertisement (c) features a woman who could be mistress
or servant: the practicality of her dress is offset by her high heels but neither,
in itself, denotes class membership or work status. By 1979 (d) and 1985 (e),
however, attractive women in slacks — liberated, healthy, and apparently in
control of their own environment — seem to identify the vacuum cleaner
as a tool for dispatching household chores and to free time for other activities.

b.

c.

d.

e.

270

Page Four

Bright Cottons!
BADMINTON SUITS
Perfect summer outfits! Smart shortie suit with detachable skirt to match! In smart prints, stripes. 12-20.
1.98

Sporty Beauties!
SLACK SUITS
Smart styles! Two-tone combinations or outfits with stunning plaid shirts! Cottons and rayons! Sizes 12-20.
1.98

Striking Styles!
SWIM SUITS
Ballerina skirts and other favorite styles! Of sleek rayons molded with "Lastex." Lovely colors. 32-40.
Other Striking Styles....2.98
1.98

Favorite For Sports!
COTTON SHIRT
Look smart and be comfortable in this combed cotton shirt with crew neck.
49¢

Sportswear Values!
98¢

Smartly Tailored
WOMEN'S SLACKS
Wear them for long-limbed swaggering grace! Good-looking twill, homespoking, and other smart fabrics! Lovely colors to liven your play days! 12-22.

Your Playtime Pals!
NEW SMARTALLS*
Flattering built-up overalls in nautical styles, bright with braid and buttons! Of sturdy cotton twill that wears so well! 12-20.

FUN FOR SUMMER!
SLACK SUITS
2.98
Striking styles—of fine rayons in brilliant color combinations! Casual in-or-outer tops jacket styles—some in contrasting stripes. With handsomely tailored zipper slacks. 12-20.

GIRLS' BRIGHT PLAY CLOTHES!

SUN SUITS
Flower-bright prints!

SMARTALLS
Sturdy cotton drill, braid trimmed,
49¢

PLAY SUITS
Bright striped pique. Sun-back.

Smart SLACKS
Colorful cotton drill!

SMART STYLES!
SLACK SUITS
For fun-loving lassies! Of bright summer fabrics. Sizes 7 to 14.
98¢

Gay Cottons!
PLAY SUITS
Smart shortie suits! Matching skirts! 8-16.
98¢

GIRLS' SLACKS
Stripes, solids! Cleverly trimmed! 8-16.
79¢

Young Mermaids'
SWIM SUITS
Ballerina styles! Rayons with "Lastex"! 8-16.
OTHERS! 8-16......1.49
SIZES 4-14........98¢
1.98

Hairline Design
SWIM CAP
With adjustable chin strap. Designed to keep hair dry.
25¢

Right With Slacks!
PLAY SHOES
1.98
Smart, lighter saddle tan that goes with all colors! Comfy moccasin-type toes! Leather soles and heels. Sizes 3 to 9.

FOR A FOOT-E

Growing Girls'
Sport Oxfords
2.98
Brown and white glove leather! Leather soles, heels.

Saddle

Spectator
PUMPS
White elasticized su turf tan trim.

Children's
SLACK SHO
Saddle tan wi soles. 12-3.

T-Strap Sandals & Saddle Oxfords
TWO FAVORITES!
White T-straps, leather soles!......1.98
White glove leather, brown trim!......1.69
Sizes 8½ to 11½......1.49

White Tennis
OXFORDS
Sturdy duck with creped soles.
98¢

Children's
OXFORDS
Sanitized*! Canvas! creped soles.
79¢

PENNEY'S
J. C. PENNEY CO., INC.

STACKED WITH BARGAINS! COME-A-RUNNI

Days

The gals take over! This weekend our women run the sto They bought the ki bargains you want don't miss a single Charge It!

KNIT TOP 'N CORDUROY PRINTED PANTS!
any
2 for $3
Ankle length motion corduroy pants in all the latest patterns! Combed cotton knit top with ¾ sleeves with note with the slacks. Many styles! 4-14.

DEEP TONE COTTON RAINCOATS
8.88
For fair or foul weather wear! Detailed with fly front, split shoulder and slash pockets. Fully rayon lined for finishing touch of luxury. Regular shorts, longs.

WOMEN'S WAIST & BIB APRONS Nylons and cottons 2 for $1	**Women's Acetate Tricot Briefs** White, colors. S-M-L. 5 for $1	**MEN'S TIE SELECTION** Prints, stripes, solids. 44c
Women's Cotton Corduroy Slacks Various colors. 1.88	**Women's Rayon Neck Scarfs** Prints and solids. 4 for $1	**COTTON JERSEY WORK GLOVES** Knit wrist. Brown. 4 for $1
COTTON BROAD-CLOTH BRAS Circle stitch cups. 32-40 A, B, C. 2 for $1	**100% COTTON SHEET BLANKET** Big 70"x90". $2	**MEN'S COTTON WORK SOCKS** Nylon reinforced heel, toe. 6 for $1
2-WAY STRETCH GIRDLES Panties, garters, too. S-M-L. 99c	**50-YARD SPOOLS THREAD** White or black. 5 for $1	**BOYS' COTTON BRIEFS, T-SHIRTS** Sizes 6 to 16. 3 for $1
WOMEN'S FANCY HEAD SCARFS Assorted prints. 2 for $1	**20" BOUDOIR LAMPS** Rayon acetate stretch shades. 2 for $8	**BOYS' COTTON CREW SOCKS** White. Stripe tops. 4 for $1

FANTASTIC LUGGAGE VALUE!
$6

BOYS' SHIRTS! WARM COTTON FLANNEL
$1

MEN'S FINE 100% COTTON DRESS HOSE
38¢

SAVE! MEN'S BRIEFS AND T-SHIRTS
2 for $1

VINYL PLASTIC WINDOW SHADE BUY!
$1

SPECIAL ELECTRIC ALARM CLOCKS
3.66

APPLIANCES
9.88

WHITE RAYON TIER CURTAINS
1.88

New Cotton Corduroy Prints
88¢

COTTON DIAPER FLANNEL
5 yards $1

SAVE! VINYL UPHOLSTERED HIGH CHAIR
$12

BOTH PENNEY STORES OPEN EVERY NITE!
DOWNTOWN PENNEY'S OPEN DAILY 9:30 'til 9! PENNEY'S ELMWOOD PLAZA OPEN DAILY 10 'til 9!
BOTH STORES OPEN SATURDAY 9:30 'til 5:30!

DOWNTOWN STORE ONLY!

By the middle of the twentieth century, retailers stressed variety, as well as value and style. They took advantage of seasons and festive occasions, too, to encourage buyers to dress up in new clothes.

opposite

A Maryland couple, dressed in the clothing typical of the fifties, shopped for a television set, the latest thing in home entertainment.

272

far left

In Washington, D.C., a clerk shows a woman a dress in the latest design.

left

In the fifties, women in Lancaster, Kentucky, examine recent styles of cotton dresses in the Lerner's store.

below

In addition to new styles and new products, new materials appealed to the consumer. In 1951, a woman tries on a sweater made of Orlon, a new synthetic fiber manufactured by DuPont.

THE BIG WHEEL IN A TEEN'S LIFE .. THE PERFECT CIRCLE SKIRT

TEENS' 10 to 16

Sanforized Broadcloth Full Circle **$2.98**   Sanforized Multi-stripe Denim **$3.49**   Embossed Cotton Flower Print **$3.98**

BOLD MULTI-PLAID WHIRLAWAY skirt in cool 'n smooth cotton broadcloth. Yards of colorful fabric twirling from a tiny waist. There's a wide patent-like plastic belt to make your waist look little. Side zipper. Washfast, max. fab. shrink. 1%. *Teens' sizes* 10, 12, 14, 16. *State size.* Shpg. wt. 1 lb. 6 oz.
077 K 6170—Multi-color plaid $2.98

MULTI-COLORED STRIPES make a whirling dazzler of this top-quality denim cartwheeler. It's a full circle that's tops in summer eye-appeal. Side zipper. Wash separately, maximum fabric shrinkage 1%. *Teens'* sizes 10, 12, 14, 16. *Please state correct size.* Shipping weight 1 pound 13 ounces.
077 K 6184—Multi-color striped denim. $3.49

COLORFUL FLOWERS bloom on crisp glossy embossed cotton that makes a full circle sweep from the nipped-in waist. Wide patent-like plastic belt. Wide tunnel belt loops. Side zipper. Washable. *Teens'* sizes 10, 12, 14, 16. *State correct size.* Shipping weight 1 pound 7 ounces.
077 K 6173—Floral print on white ground $3.98
Also in Solid Color embossed cotton (sizes above).
077 K 6174—Navy blue full circle. $3.98
077 K 6175—Aqua green full circle. 3.98

See Page 105 for descriptions of the Teens' blouses shown here .. and many other pretty ones, too.

A GLOSSY EMBOSSED COTTON, button front panel, unpressed pleats. Washable. *Teens'* sizes 10, 12, 14, 16. *State correct size.* Shipping weight 1 lb. 6 oz.
077 K 6104—Navy blue. $3.98
077 K 6105—Pink. 3.98
077 K 6106—Mint green. 3.98
B THREE GATHERED TIERS give a billowy sweep to this colorful cotton "squaw" skirt. Washable. *Teens'* sizes 10, 12, 14, 16. *State size.* Shpg. wt. 1 lb. 4 oz.
077 K 6113—Multicolor print. $2.98
C UNPRESSED BOX PLEATS, checked rayon and acetate suiting. Patent-like plastic belt. Crease-resistant. Dry clean. *Teens'* sizes 10, 12, 14, 16. *State correct size.* Shipping weight 1 lb. 9 oz.
077 K 6119—Navy, white check . . .$3.98
077 K 6120—Brown, white check . . 3.98
Also in rayon and acetate gabardine.
077 K 6121—Solid color navy. $3.98

SIZE CHART FOR TEENS' SIZES 10 to 16

Order size . . .	10	12	14	16	
If bust is 30½	32	33½	35	in.
If waist is 24½	25½	26½	27½	in.
If hips are . . .32½	34½	34½	38½	in.
Skirt length . . .28½	29½	30½	31	in.
(including waistband)				
Slack length . . .39½	40	40½	41	in.
(including waistband)				

A $3.98   **B** $2.98   **C** $3.98

106 . . SEARS-ROEBUCK SPORK

...ed BY THE COWBOY

...young miss is flattering her figure
...pered lines of LEVI'S California ranch pants
...g styling from the wide open spaces.
...erfection with the traditional LEVI'S skill,
...vorite fabrics and colors!

wonderful, washable
fine-combed cottons
. . . regular and sheen
gabardines, plain and
striped twills, corduroys
and standard denim,
about $4.95 to $6.95

patterned Dacron®-
wool blends . . .
five fabulous colors,
about $12.95

beautiful all-wool
elastique . . . four lovely
shades, about $19.95

LEVI'S
CALIFORNIA
RANCH PANTS
SANFORIZED

at better stores everywhere, or write

Levi Strauss of California · San Francisco 6 · makers of world-famous LEVI'S®

---

above

Special fashions or fads — like these circle skirts of the early fifties — were marketed to teenagers who were assured that for reasonable prices they could have the "bold multi-plaid whirlaway skirt" or the "multi-colored . . . denim cartwheeler" or the "crisp glossy embossed cotton that makes a full circle sweep from the nipped-in waist."

Special pants "inspired by the cowboy" attracted fashion-conscious women of the fifties. Clothing for children, also with a western influence, was presented "for rugged wear." In the sixties, special white Levi's were directed toward the teenage male and were presented as combining the comfort and practicality of work pants with the "uptown" look of summer white slacks.

Fully clad baseball star Jim Palmer,
familiar as the slightly clothed model in
Jockey's advertisements for men's
underwear, comments on Jockey underwear
for women, here modeled at an underwear
fashion show at Macy's, in New York.
The all-cotton garments, lauded as clean-
cut and comfortable, resemble underwear
designed for men, and thus appeal to a
growing taste for androgynous clothing
that is nonetheless sexy.

CHAPTER 20

Diversity and Uniformity

After more than two centuries of simmering a rich diversity of cultures, an amazing array of conventions in dress pours from the American melting pot. These conventions or styles are uniforms — logical constructs, or grammars, of clothing — that proclaim the wearer's individuality, eccentricity, elected group membership, or involuntary association in a formal organization, such as prison or the armed services. Who escapes uniformity, whether as benign as the busy executive's consistency in taste or as enslaving as the subteenager's gluttonous appropriation of a rock idol's sequined getup?

A uniform is dependent on repetition of an understood degree of sameness, on unvarying qualities or actual physical properties — including specific garments, insignias, or colors — resulting in a distinctive look that identifies its wearer. An individual may construct a uniform — a personal style — that consistently calls attention to his or her uniqueness; or, conversely, an individual donning a uniform determined by others and worn by many will relinquish singularity and gain recognition as a member of a group.

Uniforms worn by men and women in the armed services, the police forces, and certain professions identify their wearers to their peers and to others. A uniform not only announces its wearer's membership in a specific group identified with specific powers and functions in society but, with its stripes and embellishments, also makes clear its wearer's rank within the corps he or she serves.

In a more ironical and less codified vein, often contributing to stereotyping of ethnic groups, clothing worn by people of shared origin or culture has sometimes been so stylized as to be *consistent* within the group, and *expected* by those outside the group.

Unofficial uniforms have provided identity for ethnic groups in America, and have had the power to emphasize distinction and separation. Women who immigrated from Europe in the early twentieth century tended in general to maintain the conservative style of dress of their homelands; their daughters, however, rarely accepted the constraints of their mothers' conventions.

From the initial confrontation of white European invader and Native American, where men from each culture sized the other up and noted the clothing worn, people have worn the uniforms of their groups — uniforms that have allowed them to know and be known as enemy or friend to other groups. Native Americans, subjected to intense governmental efforts to annihilate them altogether, isolated on reservations, and stripped of their heritage in a process of education and acculturation, have felt a particularly intense heat — a melting pot not of their making or choosing.

Players in the drama of America as a melting pot, celebrated in the inscription on the base of the Statue of Liberty and in countless political speeches and editorials throughout the country's history, have worn various costumes. Pictures of immigrants, often lumpy figures in shapeless clothing, linger in the collective imagination, reminding first-, second-, and third-generation Americans of their roots in distant lands and cultures.

Until the recent celebration of ethnicity, and a resulting effort to preserve distinctive culture and costume of origin, groups of new Americans worked hard to melt into or mingle with the prevailing culture — or what they believed it to be. Clothing serves those who would mingle as well as those who would remain distinct, and is — as it has always been — the easily understood, recognizable outward sign of an individual's identity.

279

Apache Indian chiefs

As Native Americans and Hispanics participated in the society of Anglo-Americans, they often adopted the clothing as well as the conventions of people with European roots. For many members of minority groups, conformity to the culture of the majority has been obligatory for access to the privileges of membership in society.

Wearing the conventional costume of their countries of origin, and carrying clothing and household
goods, immigrants came to the United States seeking new opportunities.

Individual identity was a right denied to Africans sold into slavery in the United States. Immigrants against their wills, they were forced to wear the uniforms of slavery and later the uniform of poverty. Black men and women nonetheless preserved aspects of clothing remembered from happier times, perhaps described by older generations to younger, with the sources of those described conventions growing dimmer with each successive decade. Whether as a result of actual efforts to glorify African roots or of imagination and the desire for freedom from middle-class attitudes about dress, recent styles of clothing — or, if not actual styles, *attitudes* about clothing — have originated in or been influenced by urban American black communities, and have often defined hipness.

While the middle-class white male has been especially constrained in the somber costume of affluence and power, the black American male — who has had little hope of power or affluence, and, therefore, no need to "dress for success" — has been free to enjoy and experiment with clothing, and has been free to use clothing artistically for self-realization and expression.

In the main, other groups of Americans have not been legally and socially enslaved but have often been relegated to ghettos and separated from the mainstream of power and income by invisible but strong barriers of prejudice, and they have often been identifiable by their clothing — a uniform of poverty. That uniform of poverty, and some of the lifestyle associated with its circumstances, was adopted by many young people in the sixties as a symbol of rebellion against materialism, and of solidarity with people trapped in poverty.

In the 1980s, the Japanese fashion world offered to the affluent American and European markets a series of chic garments based on the "poverty look." For a mere $250, the purchaser could don a pair of "strappy little black booties" inspired by the worn-out and pieced-together footwear of peasants. Giant-size T-shirt dresses, complete with artfully dyed soil colors, stains, and holes were also available. The "aesthetic of poverty," to a costume historian, suggested "the cold materials, the asymmetric void . . . the exquisite chill and piquant aloneness to which the zen aesthete aspired."[1]

Just as the "poverty look" has been available to middle- and upper-class Americans, so has a "rich look" been pitched to the poor. The sewing machine, in its early years, was put forth by advertisers as the means for cheaply achieving better- and richer-looking, more fashionable, garments. Virtually all advertisement stressing the "more fashion for your dollar" attitude is designed to persuade a consumer that a richer, more trendy

Black musician

283

appearance is possible at low cost. After all, to persuade consumers to buy clothing in order to stay in style is to reinforce the economic potency of the principle of rapid obsolescence — without which neither the fashion nor the communications industry would prosper in twentieth-century America.

Arguably, anyone who belongs to a group — whether based on gender or ethnicity, on social status, or on adherence to or rejection of cultural conventions — is likely to wear clothing that proclaims identity. Socially underpowered individuals — whether ethnic or economic — are urged to conform to the standards of dress (as well as mores, manners, and values) of the empowered group or class. Similarly, members of power groups wear uniforms that make themselves recognizable to each other and to the less fortunate.

284

Copyright 190
E. J. Davison

far left

Black woman, early twentieth century

left

John Harney, nattily dressed for the photographer's studio, was born in Slovakia in 1872, and served as a private guard to Emperor Francis Joseph of Austria-Hungary before immigrating to the United States. He settled in Colorado and died there in 1937.

Boys in a turn-of-the-century midwestern "orphan asylum" wore institutional uniforms — sailor blouses with button-on short pants, long stockings and high-top lace-up shoes — resembling the nautical style worn by middle-class American boys of the period.

Uniforms ensure conformity and, thus, limit individuality. They identify a wearer as a member of a specific group, with or without rights and privileges. School uniforms — as well as those used by scouting and other youth groups — are often based on military styles that, in turn, suggest the wearer's patriotism and compliance with regimentation.

These nautically uniformed orphan boys also display flags and patriotic hats, suggesting that they belong, if not to parents, to a country and to the particular orphanage in which they dwell.

Our Gang (*above*), a group of children featured in movies of the thirties and forties, appeared in stereotypical costumes of gender and race. White boys appeared in neat long or short pants and short-sleeved shirts, a sensible style for physically active youngsters. The black boy, however, wore clothing that marked him as socially inferior — ragged clothes clownishly too large, old-fashioned shoes, and a silly hat — and which branded him as an outsider. The girl wore frilly dresses with bows on the sleeves, a bow in her hair, and feminine sandals — clothing that also limited her membership in the group and her ability to participate in the activities of the majority.

left

A skinhead in Milwaukee discussed his views on racism while displaying his tattoos — bodily adornment advertising his affinity with a poisonous spider.

Using physical posture, haircuts, and facial expressions, as well as military belts and insignias, "skinheads," or Neo-Nazis, transform blue jeans and casual slacks, T-shirts, team jackets, and even traditional shirts and ties into outfits that resemble uniforms. Like the KKK, these white supremacists intend to bully and frighten those who hold different political and social attitudes, and to reinforce their sinister aura with their version of the "Heil Hitler" salute.

290

In the South Bronx, New York, members of a street gang pose in male bikers' costumes, including heavy leather belts and wrist bands, leather jackets and vests, and blue jeans. Hairstyles and beards also foster the outlaw appearance and mystique of the gang. Police maintained that this gang — known as the Ching-a-lings — supported themselves by selling marijuana, while gang members claimed that they protected their neighborhood, and that they — not the police — preserved law and order in the depressed community. Other residents of the area easily recognized the characteristic uniforms of both gang and police.

The women and children associated with the South Bronx motorcycle gang hung out on the steps of their communal house. Living as outcasts, without help from social services or the police, the men, women, and children of the gang wore blue jeans and T-shirts, as well as Native American–style headbands and hairstyles, in order to proclaim their status as social outsiders, or outlaws.

292

Entertainers and other public figures employ conventions — or uniforms — of dress to communicate their special interests and skills. At the Grand Ole Opry in Nashville, Tennessee, dress-up western attire — consisting of shirts with decorated or inset yokes and sleeve cuffs, close-fitting trousers, pockets outlined in stitchery, heeled cowboy boots with square toes, and Stetson-type hats — prevents these musicians from being mistaken for performers of other types of music.

Entertainers Eddie Van Halen and Michael Jackson, like the Grand Ole Opry performers, wear the uniforms of their form of entertainment. Performing together in Dallas, Texas, in 1984, they wore the dress-down and dress-up styles of contemporary popular musicians. Van Halen's costume combined features easily associated with poverty and working people's clothing, and resembled the outfits of many blue-jeaned and T-shirted fans. Jackson's personal style of costly androgynous garments has been widely copied by young followers throughout the world.

CHAPTER 21

Superstars
The New Aristocracy

While we agree to agree that America has never fostered or sanctioned an aristocratic class, our society confers both the power and celebrity associated with a ruling class on a special group of individuals. Their title is not duke or duchess, prince or empress, but *star*. Stardom, unlike hereditary title, is achieved through fame. Stars rise and shine in a galaxy created by the media and worshipped by stargazers. And stars may form from the energies and circumstances of notable accomplishment in the arts, government, entertainment, learning, or other realms of human endeavor. A star may be physically beautiful or ugly, may be decent or rotten, may be law-abiding or scornful of accepted patterns of behavior; a star may amuse or horrify, may appeal or repel, or may help or threaten the well-being of others. The only requirement for stardom is fame, and fame is measured in column inches, sound bites, and photo spreads in popular magazines.

Whatever else stars do in our society, they set fashion and fad; their way of living and dressing becomes a template into which nonstars feel compelled to fit their lives. With the rise of an aristocracy based on fame, figures from the entertainment and media worlds have claimed a disproportionate share of the galaxy of stardom. Others who become pop stars range from Mother Teresa to the latest serial killer, from Stormin' Norman Schwarzkopf to Jane Fonda. In becoming a star, it matters less what an individual does than that he or she does it in the full glare of public attention. Andy Warhol based his career as a pop artist on his ability to exploit familiar imagery to call attention to himself and his lifestyle.

Stargazers stand dazzled and enchanted before the illuminat-

ing aura of public attention; to be famous is to be immortal; to be known and remembered beyond the time and space usually allotted to an individual life is heaven. Warhol would have democratically allotted minutes of fame to everyone, thus stripping fame of its potency. Fame, by definition, must be the fate or achievement of the few among the many; without rarity, fame loses currency.

In the nineteenth century, wealth was thought to be the fate or just reward for natural superiority: to achieve wealth was to achieve divine blessing. The fairly simple materialism of the nineteenth century has given way to a more complicated, post–Industrial Revolution expression: *celebrity*. To achieve — *to be somebody* — in the last decades of the twentieth century is to be *famous*, to be a *celebrity*.

Given this worshipful attitude about celebrity, it is not surprising that the badges — clothing, cars, houses, and other trophies of wealth and power and fame — associated with a particular star incite widespread emulation. Elvis look-alikes have affected more than sideburns and pout; indeed, the King's pelvis-clasping style of pants and billowing shirtsleeves have appeared — with or without an electric guitar and sexy gyrations — on three generations of youths and would-be youths. More than one adolescent American has donned a single glove on an uplifted hand, and imagined himself or herself to be a Michael Jackson clone; more than one American male has stood before his mirror and set his eyeglasses on his nose while he imagined Sylvester Stallone's familiar face; and more than one woman has thought of Jane Fonda as she checked the contour of her jeans, or, dressing for work, has imagined Murphy Brown.

295

At the beginning of his career as a crooner who incited teenage fans (and, in numerous cases, their mothers) to swoon, Frank Sinatra's sex appeal rested in part on his appearance. Youthful and skinny, his boyishness was emphasized by his style of dressing — padded shoulders and large-collared shirts with romantically wide or bow ties, producing a modern version of Beau Brummell's dandyism.

Elvis Presley's appeal, like Sinatra's, was reinforced by his manner of dressing. His leather clothing — alluding to images associated with outlaw bikers and sadists — suggested dangerous nonconformity, and furthered the rock star's reputation as a Pied Piper who exploited youth with seductive suggestions of forbidden pleasure and wild lifestyles.

Elvis also performed in his own version of a romantic or cavalier style (*right*), including wide-sleeved shirts open at the neck and two-toned shoes.

When the President and the King shook hands in the White House, two worlds — as different as their clothing — met. For his supporters, Richard Nixon's business suit and tie provide the norm — a backdrop of standard men's wear — that serves to emphasize the outrageous qualities of Elvis Presley's ornate belt and chains, wide-collared and tieless shirt, and flamboyant suit. For Presley fans, however, his costume identifies him as anticonformist, antibureaucratic, and pro-youth. Presley's clothing, like his music and lifestyle, influenced his fans to heed the mutinous message of rock music, and to find means — in dress or activity — to offer affront to the middle-class ethos that Nixon personified.

By appearing together, each man gained status in the other's camp — or hoped to.

Stars, the aristocracy of twentieth-century American culture, exist in a public court, with attendants of suitable mien. These attending fans — known also as groupies — pay obeisance with public admiration that includes affecting garments of clothing or styles of dress associated specifically with the star. The Marlon Brando wannabees wore their torn T-shirts; would-be Marilyn Monroes added lift to their brassieres, height to their heels, and flair to their skirts; countless riders of the urban range have given their Stetson a Gene Autry tilt, hooked their thumbs in Levi's with a Paul Newman hip-hugging fit; and high school cheerleaders, hanging their sex appeal on Madonna's style, today wear underwear as visible garments.

Those who cluster around the stars, actually or in dreams, are seeking a better life where excitement and glamour, fame and power, ensure more money, more or better sex, and a panoply of other status symbols. In the interim, while the dream waits to hatch under luck's warming touch, the groupies, or star worshipers by any other name, adopt the emblems of the star. They assume that, magically, the status of stardom will follow.

298

Bob Dylan won fame both as a social protestor and musician, and often performed in blue jeans, loose cotton shirt, vest, scarf, and hat — a style combining aspects of clothing associated with the dandy, the cavalier, and the working man. Dylan's style — which has now become a standard mode of dress in mainstream American casual clothing — was first adopted by students and by "hippies," young people who protested the materialism of American life by dropping out of middle-class lifestyles, living in communes, and refusing to dress in the accepted fashions of status-conscious and successful adults.

opposite

Jane Fonda, like Dylan and other entertainers who rejected established lifestyles, protested conditions she considered socially unjust. In 1970, wearing a maxicoat and carrying a beaded Indian handbag, Fonda joined Native American pickets at the federal courthouse in Seattle, Washington, to claim land that the Native Americans believed rightfully belonged to them. While one man carries an Indian-style blanket and Fonda displays the beaded bag, members of the protest group are dressed in clothing similar to that worn by young people throughout the country.

300

Cher, famous as much for her costumes in which brevity rivals substance as for her singing and acting, appears here in a concoction of esoteric materials and exotic images. Combining references to her Native American heritage with extravagantly platformed heels, the celebrity emphasizes both sensuality and lighthearted rebellion. Cher's daring, in fashion as in her outspoken determination to shape her own life, inspires widespread imitation among her followers.

Jane Fonda's appearance in particular styles of clothing — as well as her support of social and political causes — attracted emulators. Her display of leg and leather in this high-boot and miniskirt outfit was replicated by many young Americans who identified with Fonda's beliefs and saw her clothing as symbolic of her values and attitudes.

Madonna, Marilyn Monroe–style sex symbol and popular singer of the eighties and nineties, mocks so-called family values and religious symbols in her dress, as well as in her performances. Here she wears both the Star of David and a crucifix as if they were junk jewelry, consciously combining icons that many people hold sacred with costumes intended to suggest whorishness, wantonness, depravity, and sexual kinkiness.

Would-be Madonnas, material girls who want no preaching from papa, make the local scene, hang out in malls, and buy garments that will further their fantasies of being as famous, daring, and beautiful as their iconoclastic idol.

Two trendsetters of the eighties and nineties, as incongruous as Nixon and Presley save for their shared passion for personal style and appearance, Nancy Reagan and Michael Jackson share the camera at a White House ceremony. Jackson wears his signature one glove, along with satin-striped, ankle-length trousers, a mock-military jacket and baldric, and low-cut white socks with patent leather slippers. Standing beside him, Mrs. Reagan displays a trim and expensive suit, matching high-heeled shoes, a frilly blouse, and gold jewelry.

Both celebrities dress in recognizably feminine styles; each satirizes traditional female clothing styles — he by crossing gender lines in clothing, she by slavish adherence to the clothing styles of class-consciousness.

Like other celebrities, Nancy Reagan and Michael Jackson inspire dress-like, be-like followers.

Epilogue

Throughout the five centuries since an amazing collision of Stone Age Native American and European Renaissance cultures set in motion the forces that would become the United States, American clothing has been styled and worn to reflect concerns for protection, modesty, conformity, display, and expression. It has also served to identify opposing groups in social, gender, and class wars — the unheralded civil warring that has fueled much of our history. And clothing has acquired potent expressive power — whether exercised individually or by groups — serving as psychic armor or camouflage, as pennants of aggression or submission, as tributes to status or creed, and as outward evidence of mind, collective or individual.

A major theme in American clothing was struck in the first encounter between Native Americans and men of the European Renaissance: each ethnocentric group thought the other decidedly weird, given to strange customs and bizarre costumes. Both were right. Neither proved successful in transcending the barriers of culture — that serendipitous nurturing soup of manners, mores, language, and shared history into which human beings are born, and which they accept as normal and right, if not divinely ordained. Each group was formed by its culture; and each group feared, hated, and tried to destroy the other.

In the last five centuries, individuals have occasionally and inexplicably transcended the walls of their cultural jail, and have looked upon members of other groups as versions of themselves, both similar and dissimilar. That perception of shared humanity, however, has been the exception to the culturally resident chauvinism that has conditioned much of our history.

Clothing — almost as much as skin color, hair texture, and language — has identified the "others" and the "outsiders," those whom "we" or "insiders" are obliged to fear, hate, and contain (if not destroy). African-Americans have been ridiculed in cartoon and stereotype for the uniform of poverty imposed upon them. Similarly, as immigrants have come to the United States, articles of clothing associated with each group have been used to stereotype — and thereby dehumanize — them: Italian-, Irish-, Asian-, and Spanish-Americans, and every other group of hyphenated Americans, have been stigmatized and uniformed by vests, baggy trousers, overblouses, exotic hats and caps — all emblems of separation from mainstream society, all markings by which "they" can be spotted in the emotional field of continual social (if not civil) war.

Gender wars, only somewhat more subtle, have also flared and fizzled throughout our history. In general, clothing has symbolized women's lower estate, and has been the instrument by which women have been kept in a gender ghetto. During the history of America, women have accepted or been forced into corsets, binding and immobilizing footwear, hoops and hobbles, and other forms of clothing that have put them at physical risk, limited their abilities to work and play, and effectively turned them into useless objects, the tokens of someone else's status in society. Fashion — as this psychological, social, and economic phenomenon is known — may have been a cruel slave master, but its slaves have been docile, if not eager to submit.

Children and older people — their beings and their roles in society — have been identified by garments and styles. On either end of life's span, people may rely on others to clothe them. Unable to make their own choices in clothing — and thereby to express their own sense of worth — young children and the infirm elderly, like dolls, are costumed by others, and thus their worth to society (or family) is assigned and signified by those who keep them.

Americans today parade through life in varied, colorful, often fanciful clothing. They wear uniforms to identify themselves as members of the police, fire-fighting, or military forces; to set themselves apart in elite groups or clubs; and to claim solidarity — comradeship — with others in the informal but understood uniforms of special interest groups, of those holding and enacting specific values and attitudes.

For every archetypical character in American lore and legend, there is an identifying garment: fur caps for Ben Franklin and Davy Crockett, capes for Marianne Moore and Franklin Delano Roosevelt, Hawaiian shirts for Harry Truman and Hawkeye Pierce, white tie and tails for Fred Astaire and Marlene Dietrich, oversize tramp clothing for Charlie Chaplin and Judy Garland, and western garb for Ronald Reagan and Dolly Parton.

American clothing today, as in the past, mirrors the lives and aspirations, the fantasies and facts, of the men, women, and children who comprise the country. The parade of American clothing, now as in the past, is a pageant of ethnic and class diversity wherein workers and idlers, makers and consumers, men and women, young and old dress in accordance with their chosen, created, or fated roles in our civilization.

Sports heroes, rock stars, entertainers, and public figures

catch attention and become the contemporary trendsetters in matters of dress; they create new looks, new signatures, and continually push the frontiers of clothing into the realm of fantasy. As teenagers and other fans attempt to be like their heroes, they dress like them.

An abundance of uniforms — and not just those associated with fire fighting, policing, and warring — provide those who desire it with the comfort of conformity to group and dress code; conversely, uniforms make excellent targets for those who loathe the creed behind them. The "rich look" and the "poverty look," though worlds apart, identify their wearers, and become uniforms in effect if not by decree. Bag ladies and the ladies who lunch recognize each other and one another, as do men from skid row and men from exclusive clubs.

Certain aspects of clothing are powerful suggestions as to the attitudes, lifestyle, and social purposes of the wearer: a rhinestone-decorated stocking; a fur coat with head, tail, and paws of the original fur-wearer preserved as decorative appendages; a black leather bikini or jock strap; earth shoes clamped over ragg socks; a cowboy hat decorated with a swastika, skull and crossbones, Confederate flag, military insignia, or the tips of peacock feathers. Like fingerprints, clothing identifies its wearer whether the wearer wants to be identified or not.

Different garments, worn by different people, take on different dispositions, different auras, and different meanings. We do not look with the same eyes at identical tennis shoes worn by an elderly nun and a high school jock, or identical baseball caps worn by George Bush and Jennifer Capriati, or identical blue jeans worn by Paul Newman and Bob Dylan. Clothing absorbs, amplifies, and projects colorations of its wearer. In some instances, articles of clothing become signatures — or synonymous emblems — of their owners: Mark Twain, Tom Wolfe, and Garrison Keillor share a predilection for white suits; Michael Jackson catches attention by wearing *one* glove; and none of the astronauts, male or female, looks quite as impressive in street clothing as in the paraphernalia of the spaceship.

Superman knew this. Mild-mannered Clark Kent fooled the world and then stepped into a telephone booth to rip away his mundane covering and reveal himself as faster than a speeding bullet, able to leap tall buildings. He was known by his costume. So was Little Orphan Annie, who — rather like the Virgin as depicted in several centuries of paintings — never changed her dress, never risked going incognito.

Clothing in the United States has changed as styles and fads have come and gone, as fortunes have risen and fallen, and as people have been persuaded to want and to buy specific garments. Today clothing is a potent form of communication. Strong opinions take root as people "read" other people's social status, character, and interests from their clothing. We watch a social-climbing woman identify the designer (and his or her relative social and professional status) of another woman's outfit. We see a rich man glance at another's tie, or shoes, or trousers, or, at a party, move a little closer to a younger and sexily dressed woman. Teenagers befriend or bedevil other teenagers on the basis of the garments and styles of clothing and the logos and labels that they display. Suburban couples in his-and-her logo-crested T-shirts, casual slacks, and duck-emblem belts smile upon the next-door neighbors whose clothes conform to the prevailing style of the community. And we see people look away from tattered and dirty street people, or even cross the street to avoid passing close to them. In each case, in the flash of a synapse, messages have been sent out and received, acceptance and hate fixed, and courses set in human recognition and interaction.

We are fond of clucking conventional wisdom to one another, and saying that there is no such thing as progress, or that the more things seem to change, the more they are actually the same. In the realm of clothing, however, real changes have occurred, and they often reflect or signify profound variations in social patterns as well as deeper values, attitudes, and mores in our culture. Children today wear clothing that encourages them — boys and girls — to move and play without constraint or self-consciousness. Modern women have far more options in dress than their grandmothers — or even their mothers — had. And modern men, though still inclined largely to the business suit, can vary their dress without expectation of ostracization. It is possible today for men and women to wear similar clothes without forsaking femininity or masculinity; or, conversely, it is possible for one sex to appropriate aspects of the dress of the other without being cast from society. It is now acceptable for older citizens to wear clothing associated with youthful sports activities, for teenagers to flaunt sexuality with their clothing, and for men and women in blue jeans and T-shirts to go almost anywhere and do almost anything.

Americans in the last decade of the twentieth century still pursue frontiers of personal, social, and political life, where, with whatever resources are at hand, they dress to play their individual and collective roles. Even the emperor, we are told, has new clothes.

303

Notes

CHAPTER 1
In the Beginning . . .

1. William S. Simmons, *Spirit of the New England Tribes: Indian History and Folklore, 1620–1984* (Hanover, N.H.: University Press of New England, 1986), p. 66.

2. James Axtell, *After Columbus* (New York and Oxford: Oxford University Press, 1988), p. 128.

3. Louis Wright, ed., *The Elizabethans' America* (Cambridge, Mass.: Harvard University Press, 1965), p. 27.

4. Anonymous manuscript 841, Moreau Collection, Bibliothèque Nationale, Paris. Probably not by Cartier but by Jean Poullet, who sailed with him.

5. Wright, *Elizabethans' America*, p. 38.

6. Ibid., p. 42.

7. Ibid., pp. 97–102.

8. Ibid., p. 106.

9. Ibid.

10. Ibid., p. 107.

11. Ibid., p. 110.

12. Ibid., pp. 111, 113–114.

13. Ibid., p. 118. See also Thomas Harriet, *A Brief and True Report of the New Found Land of Virginia*. Introduction by Paul Hulton (New York: Dover Publications, 1972).

14. Wright, *Elizabethans' America*, p. 130.

CHAPTER 2
The Seventeenth Century: *Mixing Cultures*

1. For a discussion of moccasin-making, see Catherine Casse, "The Iroquois Moccasin: Its Utilitarian and Symbolic Functions," *Dress* 10 (1984): 12–24.

2. Louis Wright, ed., *The Elizabethans' America* (Cambridge, Mass.: Harvard University Press, 1965), p. 137.

3. Ibid., p. 142.

4. Ibid.

5. Ibid., p. 165.

6. Ibid., p. 166.

7. Ibid., p. 169.

8. Ibid., p. 173.

9. Ibid., p. 177.

10. Ibid., p. 215.

11. Ibid., p. 216.

12. Ibid.

13. Ibid., p. 217.

14. Ibid.

15. Ibid., p. 218.

16. James Axtell, *After Columbus* (New York and Oxford: Oxford University Press, 1988), p. 106.

17. Elisabeth McClellan, *A History of American Costume, 1607–1870* (Philadelphia: George W. Jacobs and Company, 1904), p. 48.

18. Ibid., p. 85. See also David Freeman Hawke, *Everyday Life in Early America* (New York: Harper and Row, 1988), pp. 111–114.

19. McClellan, *History of American Costume*, p. 85.

20. Alice Morse Earle, *Customs and Fashions in Old New England* (1893; reprint, Rutland, Vt.: Charles E. Tuttle Co., 1971), p. 62.

21. Ibid., p. 317.

22. Ibid., pp. 289, 317.

23. Samuel Eliot Morison et al., *A Concise History of the American Republic*, 2d ed. (New York: Oxford University Press, 1983), p. 26.

24. McClellan, *History of American Costume*, p. 94.

25. Alice Morse Earle, *Child Life in Colonial Days* (1899; reprint, Detroit: Omnigraphics, 1989), p. 304.

26. McClellan, *History of American Costume*, p. 125.

27. William Penn, *Some Fruits of Solitude* (New York: Truslove, Hanson and Comba, 1900), pp. 21–22.

28. McClellan, *History of American Costume*, p. 32.

29. Ibid., p. 35.

CHAPTER 3
Birth of a Country: *The Eighteenth Century*

1. Thomas Jefferson, *Papers*, vol. 6, ed. Julian P. Boyd (Princeton, N.J.: Princeton University Press, 1951), p. 350.

CHAPTER 5
Manufacturing and the Work Force: *Industrialization and Clothing*

1. For extensive discussion of early industrial development in New England, see Bruce Laurie, *Artisans into Workers: Labor in Nineteenth-Century America* (New York: Farrar, Straus and Giroux, 1989).

CHAPTER 6
Communication and the Cult of Womanhood

1. Quoted in Caroline Bird, *Enterprising Women* (New York: W. W. Norton, 1976), p. 59.

CHAPTER 8
Dress Reform

1. Dee Brown, *The Gentle Tamers: Women of the Old Wild West* (New York: G. P. Putnam's Sons, 1958), p. 138.

2. Ibid.

3. Ibid., p. 143.

4. Lillian Schlissel et al., eds., *Far from Home: Families of the Westward Journey* (New York: Schocken Books, 1989), pp. 140–141.

5. Ibid., p. 105.

6. Brown, *Gentle Tamers*, p. 145.

7. Gairdner B. Moment and Otto F. Kraushaar, eds., *Utopias: The American Experience* (Metuchen, N.J., and London: The Scarecrow Press, 1980), p. 233.

8. *Review of Reviews* 7 (April 1893): 313.

9. Ibid., 314.

10. Ibid., 315.

11. Ibid., 316.

CHAPTER 9
Masters and Slaves: *Southern Hierarchy and Clothing*

1. Frederick Law Olmsted, *A Journey in the Back Country* (New York and London: G. P. Putnam's Sons, 1907), p. 7.

2. Ibid., p. 30.

3. St. Jerome, *Letters*, ed. James Duff (Dublin: Browne and Nolan, 1942).

4. Olmsted, *Journey in the Back Country*, p. 5.

5. Ibid., p. 81.

6. Ibid.

7. Ibid., p. 78.

8. Ibid., p. 154.

9. Ibid., p. 214.

10. Ibid., p. 161.

11. Ibid., p. 264.

12. Elizabeth Fox-Genovese, *Within the Plantation Household* (Chapel Hill and London: University of North Carolina Press, 1988), pp. 127–128. Fox-Genovese's study includes generous and excellent passages on clothing and the role of clothing in the plantation-based society.

13. Ibid., pp. 213–214.

14. Ibid.

15. Ibid., p. 224.

C H A P T E R 10
Western Frontier

1. Dee Brown, *The Gentle Tamers: Women of the Old Wild West* (New York: G. P. Putnam's Sons, 1958), p. 110. The "wampus," or "wamus," a heavy cloak, or "jumper," buttoning at the waist and neck and somewhat resembling a cardigan, was worn by both men and women.

2. Ibid., p. 107.

3. Ibid.

4. Everett Dick, *The Sod-House Frontier, 1854–1890* (Lincoln, Nebr.: University of Nebraska Press, 1979), p. 268.

5. Joanna L. Stratton, *Pioneer Women: Voices from the Kansas Frontier* (New York: Simon and Schuster, 1981), p. 65.

6. Ibid.

7. Lillian Schlissel et al., eds., *Far from Home: Families of the Westward Journey* (New York: Schocken Books, 1989), p. 148.

8. Dick, *Sod-House Frontier*, p. 268.

9. Stratton, *Pioneer Women*, p. 68.

10. Ralph Bowen, ed. and trans., *A Frontier Family in Minnesota: Letters of Theodore and Sophie Bost, 1851–1920* (Minneapolis: University of Minnesota Press, 1981), p. 47.

11. Ibid., p. 50.

12. Ibid., p. 80.

13. Brown, *Gentle Tamers*, p. 133.

14. Ibid.

15. Ibid.

16. Ibid., p. 137.

17. Ibid., p. 134.

18. Elizabeth Gedney, "Cross Section of Pioneer Life at Fourth Plain," *Oregon Historical Quarterly* 43 (1942): 14.

19. Brown, *Gentle Tamers*, p. 136.

20. Ibid.

21. Ibid., p. 59.

C H A P T E R 12
Conspicuous Consumption and Self-Consciousness

1. H. Jones, "Dress," *Cornhill Magazine*, n.s., 22 (April 1894): 406.

2. Ibid., 407.

3. Ibid., 410.

4. Ibid., 413.

5. Thorstein Veblen, "Economic Theory of Women's Dress," *Popular Science Monthly* 46 (December 1894): 198.

6. Ibid.

7. Ibid., 199.

8. Ibid.

9. Ibid., 200.

10. Ibid., 201.

11. Ibid., 203.

12. Ibid.

13. Ibid., 204.

14. Ibid.

15. Ibid.

16. Ibid., 205.

17. Ibid.

18. Ibid.

19. Ibid.

C H A P T E R 14
Clothing for the Ages

1. Sally Helvenson, "Advice to American Mothers on the Subject of Children's Dress: 1800–1920," *Dress* 7 (1981): 30.

2. Quoted in ibid., 32.

3. Quoted in ibid., 34.

C H A P T E R 15
The Roaring Twenties: *Dress Reform Redux*

1. Anna G. Noyes, "A Practical Protest Against Fashion," *The Independent* 63 (August 29, 1907): 503.

2. Ibid., 508.

3. Nina Wilcox Putnam, "Woman Who Has Upset the Tyranny of Feminine Fashion," *American Magazine* 75 (May 1913): 34.

4. Ibid.

5. Ibid., 35.

6. Ibid.

7. Nina Wilcox Putnam, "Fashion and Feminism," *Forum* 52 (October 1914): 580.

8. Ibid.

9. Ibid., 582.

10. Ibid.

11. Ethel Ronzone, "Standardized Dress," *Journal of Home Economics* 10 (September 1918): 426.

12. Ibid., 427.

13. Ibid.

14. Ibid.

15. Mary Alden Hopkins, "Women's Rebellion Against Fashions," *New Republic* 31 (August 16, 1922): 331.

16. Ibid.

17. Ibid., 332.

18. Ibid.

19. Ibid.

20. Ibid.

21. Ibid.

22. *Literary Digest* 70 (June 1921): 34.

23. Ibid.

24. Ibid.

25. Ibid.

26. Nina Wilcox Putnam, "Ventures and Adventures in Dress Reform," *Saturday Evening Post* 195 (October 7, 1922): 15.

27. Ibid., 93.

28. Ibid.

29. Ibid.

30. Ibid., 331.

31. Ibid., 332.

32. Ibid.

C H A P T E R 16
Sports

1. Kathrene Gedney Pinkerton, "Clothes for Woodswomen," *Outing* (July 1913): 18.

2. Ibid.

3. Grace Ober, "Camping and Tramping Costumes for Girls," *Home Progress* (July 1913): 40.

4. Lucille Eaton Hill, ed., *Athletics and Out-Door Sports for Women* (New York: The Macmillan Company, 1903), p. 14.

5. Ibid., p. 20.

6. Ibid.

7. Ibid.

8. Ibid., p. 30.

9. Ibid., p. 56.

10. Ibid.

11. Ibid.

12. Ibid., p. 58.

13. Ibid., p. 59.

14. Ibid., p. 63.

C H A P T E R 19
Consumerism and Communication

1. Russell Lynes, *The Tastemakers: The Shaping of American Popular Taste* (New York: Dover Publications, 1980), p. 300.

2. Robert S. and Helen Merrell Lynd, *Middletown, A Study in Contemporary American Culture* (New York: Harcourt, Brace and Company, 1929), p. 66.

3. Ibid., p. 78.

4. Ibid., pp. 82, 164.

5. Ibid., p. 166.

6. Ibid., p. 167.

7. Ibid., p. 164.

C H A P T E R 20
Diversity and Uniformity

1. Harold Koda, "Rei Kawakubo and the Aesthetic of Poverty," *Dress* 11 (1985): 5.

Bibliography

Ackroyd, P. *Dressing Up, Transvestism and Drag—The History of an Obsession*. New York, 1979.

Adams, James D. *Naked We Came: A More or Less Lighthearted Look at the Past, Present, and Future of Clothes*. New York, 1967.

Aikman, Duncan. *Calamity Jane and the Lady Wildcats*. New York, 1937.

Albrecht, Juliana, Jane Farell-Beck, and Geitel Winakor. "Function, Fashion, and Convention in American Women's Riding Costume, 1880–1930." *Dress* 14 (1988): 56–67.

Alpert, George. *The Queens*. New York, 1975.

Anderson, Ruth Matilda. *Hispanic Costume 1480–1530*. New York, 1979.

Anspach, Karlyne. *The Why of Fashion*. Ames, Iowa, 1960.

Ash, Juliet, and Lee Wright. *Components of Dress*. London and New York, 1988.

Axtell, James. *After Columbus*. New York and Oxford, 1988.

Bailey, Florence H. "The Influence of Gabrielle Chanel on the American Women's Fashions in the Twentieth Century." Master's thesis, University of Maryland, 1970.

Banta, Martha. *Imaging American Women: Idea and Ideals in Cultural History*. New York, 1987.

Barthes, Roland. *The Fashion System*. London, 1985.

Bartlett, Richard A. *The New Country: A Social History of the American Frontier, 1776–1890*. London and New York, 1974.

Batterberry, Michael and Ariane R. *Mirror, Mirror: A Social History of Fashion*. New York, 1977.

Becker, Vivienne. *Antique and Twentieth-Century Jewelry*. London, 1980.

Bell, Daniel. *The Coming of Post-Industrial Society*. Beverly Hills, Calif., 1981.

Bell-Metereau, Rebecca Louise. "Cross-Dressing and Sex Role Reversals in American Film." Ph.D. diss., University of Indiana, 1981.

Berendt, John. *Esquire Fashions for Men*. New York, 1966.

Bergon, Frank, ed. *The Journals of Lewis and Clark*. New York, 1989.

Bigelow, Marybelle S. *Fashion in Western History*. Minneapolis, 1979.

Blake, Forrester. *Riding the Mustang Trail*. New York, 1935.

Bliven, Bruce. "Flapper Jane." *New Republic* 44 (Sept. 9, 1925): 65.

Blum, Stella. *Victorian Fashions and Costumes from Harper's Bazaar, 1867–1898*. New York, 1974.

Blum, Stella, ed. *Everyday Fashions of the Twenties as Pictured in Sears and Other Catalogs*. New York, 1982.

Bodnar, John. *The Transplanted: A History of Immigrants in Urban America*. Bloomington, Ind., 1985.

Boehn, Max Von. *Modes and Manners: From the Middle Ages to the End of the Eighteenth Century*, 1909. Reprint. New York, 1932.

Bond, David. *Twentieth-Century Fashion*. New York, 1981.

Booth, Sally Smith. *The Women of '76*. New York, 1973.

Boucher, Francois. *20,000 Years of Fashion*. New York, 1966.

Bowen, Ralph, ed. and trans. *A Frontier Family in Minnesota: Letters of Theodore and Sophie Bost, 1851–1920*. Minneapolis, 1981.

Brandon, Ruth. *Singer and the Sewing Machine*. London, 1976.

Braun, L. *Costumes Through the Ages: The Evolution of Styles of Dress*. New York, 1982.

Bray, John. *All About Dress*. 1913. Reprint. Ann Arbor, Mich., 1957.

Brooke, Iris. *Dress and Undress*. Westport, Conn., 1958.

Brown, Dee. *The Gentle Tamers: Women of the Old Wild West*. New York, 1958.

Brownmiller, Susan. *Femininity*. New York, 1984.

Buck, Anne. *Victorian Costume*. 2d ed. Carlton, Bedford, 1984.

Caffrey, Kate. *The 1900's Lady*. New York, 1976.

Calasibetta, Charlotte Mankey. *Essential Terms of Fashion: A Collection of Definitions*. New York, 1986.

Caldwell, Doreen. *And All Was Revealed: Ladies' Underwear 1907–1980*. New York, 1981.

California Historical Society Papers, 1887–93. 10 vols. San Francisco.

Callister, Herbert. *Dress from Three Centuries*. Hartford, 1976.

Campbell, Patricia Warner. "Public and Private: Men's Influence on Women's Dress for Sport and Physical Education." *Dress* 14 (1988): 48–55.

Carter, Ernestine. *Twentieth-Century Fashion: A Scrapbook, 1900 to Today*. London, 1975.

Case, Victoria and Robert Armand. *We Called It Culture: The Story of Chautauqua*. Garden City, N.Y., 1948.

Casse, Catherine. "The Iroquois Moccasin: Its Utilitarian and Symbolic Functions." *Dress* 10 (1984): 12–24.

Clappe, Amelia K. *The Shirley Letters*. San Francisco, 1922.

309

Clark, Fiona. *Hats*. New York, 1982.

Coleman, Dorothy, Elizabeth Ann, and Evelyn. *The Collector's Book of Dolls' Clothes: Costumes in Miniature, 1700–1929*. New York, 1975.

Coleman, Elizabeth Ann. *Of Men Only: Men's and Boys' Fashions*. Brooklyn, 1975.

Coleridge, Nicholas. *The Fashion Conspiracy*. New York, 1988.

Colle, Dorece. *Collars, Stocks, Cravats: A History and Costume Dating Guide to Civilian Men's'Neckpieces 1655–1900*. Emmaus, Pa., 1972.

Copeland, Peter F. *Working Dress in Colonial and Revolutionary America*. London and Westport, Conn., 1977.

Courtney, Alice E., and Thomas W. Whipple. *Sex Stereotyping in Advertising*. New York, 1983.

Craig, Hazel T. *Clothing: A Comprehensive Study*. Philadelphia, 1973.

Crawford, Morris De Camp. *One World of Fashion*. New York, 1933.

————. *The Philosophy of Dress*. New York, 1925.

————. *The Ways of Fashion*. New York, 1941.

Curl, James Steven. *The Egyptian Revival: An Introductory Study of a Recurring Theme in the History of Taste*. London, 1982.

Daggett, Mabel Potter. "Then the Delineator Was Young: The Story of the First Butterick Pattern and How It Multiplied." *The Delineator* 76 (November 1910): 365–66.

Dalzell, Robert F., Jr. *Enterprising Elite*. Cambridge and London, 1987.

Dary, David. *Cowboy Culture*. Lawrence, Kans., 1989.

DeLano, Sharon. *Texas Boots*. New York, 1981.

Depew, C. M., ed. *One Hundred Years of American Commerce*. New York, 1895.

DeVoto, Bernard A. *Across the Wide Missouri*. Boston, 1947.

Dichter, Ernest. *Strategy of Desire*. Garden City, N.Y., 1960.

Dick, Everett. *The Sod-House Frontier, 1854–1890*. Lincoln, Nebr., 1979.

Dickson, Carol Anne. "Patterns for Garments: A History of the Paper Garment Pattern Industry in America to 1976." Master's thesis, Ohio State University, 1979.

Dorner, Jane. *Fashion in the Forties and Fifties*. Shepperton, 1975.

Dorner, Jane. *The Changing Shape of Fashion Through the Years*. New York, 1974.

Dryad, Sue Gibson, and Mary Frances Drake. "Andrew Johnson, the Tailor President." *Dress* 11 (1985): 77–88.

Dublin, Thomas. *Women at Work*. New York, 1979.

Earle, Alice Morse. *Child Life in Colonial Days*. 1899. Reprint. Detroit, 1989.

————. *Costume of Colonial Times*. 1924. Reprint. Detroit, 1975.

————. *Customs and Fashions in Old New England*. 1893. Reprint. Rutland, Vt., 1971.

Elting, John R. *Military Uniforms in America: The Era of the American Revolution, 1755–1795*. San Rafael, Calif., 1974.

Embleton, Gerald A., and Martin Winder. *Military Dress in North America*. New York, 1973.

Erwin, Mabel D., and Lila A. Kinchen. *Esquire's Fashion for Today*. New York, 1973.

Erwin, Mabel D., Lila A. Kinchen, and Kathleen A. Peters. *Clothing for Moderns*. 6th ed. New York, 1979.

Evans, Joan. *A History of Jewelry*. Boston, 1970.

Ewing, Elizabeth. *Dress and Undress: A History of Women's Underwear*. New York, 1979.

————. *A History of Twentieth-Century Fashion*. Totowa, N.J., 1985.

————. *Women in Uniform Through the Centuries*. London, 1975.

Faragher, John Mack. *Women and Men on the Overland Trail*. New Haven, Conn., and London, 1979.

Farrell, Warren. *The Liberated Man*. New York, 1974.

Fehr, Barbara. *Yankee Denim Dandies*. Blue Earth, Minn., 1974.

Feightner, Mia Mae. "Clothing and Accessories Available to Pioneers of Southern Indiana, 1816–30. Master's thesis, Iowa State University, 1977.

Finkel, Alicia. "A Tale of Lilies, Sunflowers, and Knee Breeches: Oscar Wilde's Wardrobe for His American Tour." *Dress* 15 (1989): 4–15.

Fogarty, Anne. *Wife Dressing*. New York, 1959.

Foote, Shelly Jayne. "Egypt in America: The Popularization of Ancient Egypt and Its Influence on American Jewelry, 1869 to 1925." Master's thesis, George Washington University, 1985.

Fox-Genovese, Elizabeth. *Within the Plantation Household*. Chapel Hill, N.C., and London, 1988.

Fraser, Kennedy. *The Fashionable Mind: Reflections on Fashions, 1970–1982*. Boston, 1985.

Gedney, Elizabeth. "Cross Section of Pioneer Life at Fourth Plain." *Oregon Historical Quarterly* 43 (1942): 14.

Gehret, Ellen J. *Rural Pennsylvania Clothing: Being a Study of the Wearing Apparel of the German and English Inhabitants in the Late Eighteenth and Early Nineteenth Century*. York, Pa., 1973.

Gertenrich, Caryl. "The Thomas Kay Woolen Mill in Salem, Oregon, 1900–1959." Master's thesis, Oregon State University, 1978.

Gilman, Roger, ed., *Romanticism in America*. Baltimore, 1940.

Ginsburg, Madeleine. *The Glass of Fashion*. Rochester, 1974.

_____. *Victorian Dress in Photographs*. New York, 1983.

Gold, Annalee. *Seventy-five Years of Fashion*. New York, 1975.

Goldstein, W. "Men's Garment Trade in Cincinnati, Ohio, in the Nineteenth Century: A Social, Economic, and Technological Study." Ph.D. diss., Ohio State University, 1981.

Goodrum, Charles, and Helen Dalrymple. *Advertising in America: The First Two Hundred Years*. New York, 1990.

Gorsline, Douglas. *What People Wore: A Visual History of Dress from Ancient Times to Twentieth-Century America*. New York, 1952.

Guild, Thelma S., and Harvey L. Carter. *Kit Carson: A Pattern for Heroes*. Lincoln, Nebr., and London, 1984.

Gummere, Amelia Mott. *The Quaker*. London, 1980.

Haack, Ellen J. "Clothing Worn by Iowa Residents in Professional and Business Classes Who Lived in Selected Small Towns Between 1870 and 1880." Master's thesis, Iowa State University, 1979.

Halttunen, Karen. *Confidence Men and Painted Women: A Study of Middle-Class Culture in America, 1830–1870*. New Haven, Conn., 1982.

Harting, Joan L., ed. *Fashion Plates in the Collection of The Cooper-Hewitt Museum*. New York, 1982.

Haweis, Elizabeth. *The Art of Beauty*. 1878. Reprint. New York, 1978.

_____. *Fashion Is Spinach*. New York, 1938.

Hawke, David Freeman. *Everyday Life in Early America*. New York, 1988.

_____. *Franklin*. New York, 1976.

Helvenson, Sally. "Advice to American Mothers on the Subject of Children's Dress: 1800–1920." *Dress* 7 (1981): 30–46.

_____. "American Children's Costume in the Period 1840–1885 and Its Relationship to the Child's Role in Society." Master's thesis, Florida A. & M. University, 1975.

Hendrickson, Robert. *The Grand Emporiums*. New York, 1979.

Hill, Lucille Eaton, ed. *Athletics and Out-Door Sports for Women*. New York, 1903.

Hill, Margaret Hamilton, and Peter A. Buchnell. *The Evolution of Fashion*. London, 1967.

Hillier, Bevis. *The Style of the Century, 1900–1980*. New York, 1983.

Hollander, Anne. *Seeing Through Clothes*. New York, 1978.

Hooper, S. E. "Rural Dress in Southwestern Missouri Between 1860 and 1880." Master's thesis, Iowa State University, 1976.

Hopkins, Mary Alden. "Women's Rebellion Against Fashions." *New Republic* 31 (August 16, 1922): 331.

Houch, C. *The Fashion Encyclopedia*. New York, 1982.

Hoxie, Frederick H., ed. *Indians in American History*. Arlington Heights, Ill., 1988.

Hurlock, Elizabeth R. *The Psychology of Dress: An Analysis of Fashion and Its Motive*. London, 1980.

Jachimowicz, Elizabeth. *Eight Chicago Women and Their Fashions, 1860–1929*. Chicago, 1978.

Jacobs, Lewis. *The Rise of the American Film*. New York, 1939.

Jefferson, Thomas. *Papers*. Edited by Julian P. Boyd. 12 vols. Princeton, N.J., 1952.

Jenkins, Alan. *The Twenties*. New York, 1974.

Johnston, Susan. *Fashion Paper Dolls from Godey's Lady's Book: 1840–1854*. New York, 1977.

Jonason, Linda. "Dressmaking in North Dakota Between 1890 and 1920: Equipment, Supplies, and Methods." Master's thesis, North Dakota State University, 1977.

Jones, H. "Dress." *Cornhill Magazine*, n.s., 22 (April 1894): 406–413.

Kahlenberg, M. H. *Fabric and Fashion*. Los Angeles, 1974.

Kartchner, Grace. "The Clothing of Mormon Girls, Ages One to Twelve, in the Great Salt Lake and Utah Valleys from 1847 to 1896." Master's thesis, Oregon State University, 1975.

Kauffman, Sandra. *The Cowboy Catalog*. New York, 1981.

Keenan, Brigette. *The Women We Wanted to Look Like*. New York, 1977.

Kennedy, Charyl Drews. "The Prince of Wales' Fashion Influence in the U.S. from 1920 to 1930." Master's thesis, Kent State University, 1979.

Kennett, Frances. *The Collector's Book of Fashion*. New York, 1983.

Kern, Stephen. *Anatomy and Destiny: A Cultural History of the Human Body*. New York, 1975.

Kidwell, Claudia Brush, and Valerie Steele. *Men and Women: Dressing the Part*. Washington, D.C., 1989.

Koda, Harold. "Rei Kawakubo and the Aesthetic of Poverty." *Dress* 11 (1985): 5–10.

Kohler, Carl. *A History of Costume*. New York, 1963.

Kreyche, Gerald F. *Visions of the American West*, Lexington, Ky., 1989.

Kulik, Gary, Robert Parks, and Theodore Penn, eds. *The New England Mill Village, 1790–1860*. Boston, 1982.

Langner, Lawrence. *The Importance of Wearing Clothes*. New York, 1959.

Larkin, Jack. *The Reshaping of Everyday Life, 1790–1840*. New York, 1988.

Larson, Joyce M. "Clothing of Pioneer Women of the Dakota Territory, 1861–69." Master's thesis, South Dakota State University, 1978.

Lauer, Jeannette C. *Fashion Power: The Meaning of Fashion in American Society*. Englewood Cliffs, N.J., 1981.

Laurie, Bruce. *Artisans into Workers: Labor in Nineteenth-Century America*. New York, 1989.

Laver, James. *The Concise History of Costume and Fashion.* New York, 1974.

Lewis, Lloyd, and Henry Justin Smith. *Oscar Wilde Discovers America.* New York, 1936.

Lubin, L. B. *The Elegant Beast.* New York, 1981.

Lucie-Smith, Edward. *The Story of Craft—The Craftsman's Role in Society.* New York, 1984.

Lurie, Alison. *The Language of Clothes.* New York, 1983.

Lynd, Robert S. and Helen Merrell. *Middletown: A Study in Contemporary American Culture.* New York, 1929.

Lynes, Russell. *More Than Meets the Eye: The History and Collections of The Cooper-Hewitt Museum.* New York, n.d.

————. *The Tastemakers: The Shaping of American Popular Taste.* New York, 1980.

Marchand, Roland. *Advertising the American Dream: Making Way for Modernity, 1920–1940.* Berkeley, Calif., 1985.

Martin, Linda. *The Way We Wore—Fashion Illustrations of Children's Wear, 1870–1970.* New York, 1978.

Maurice, Arthur B., and Frederick T. Cooper. *The History of the Nineteenth Century in Caricature.* 1904. Reprint. New York, 1970.

McClellan, Elisabeth. *A History of American Costume, 1607–1870.* Philadelphia, 1904.

McCormick, Barbara Howe. "A Study of Selected Women's Dresses Worn in Oklahoma from 1889–1907 as Influenced by Certain Economic, Socio-cultural, Religious, and Political Occurrences of the Time." Master's thesis, Oklahoma State University, 1971.

McFarland, Gerald. *A Scattered People: An American Family Moves West.* New York, 1985.

McMartin, Maria Barbara. "Dress of the Oregon Trail Emigrants: 1843–1855." Master's thesis, Iowa State University, 1977.

Meline, James F. *Two Thousand Miles on Horseback.* New York, 1867.

Melinkoff, Ellen. *What We Wore.* New York, 1984.

Mera, H. P., and Joe Ben Wheat. *The Alfred I. Barton Collection of Southwest Textiles.* Coral Gables, Fl., 1978.

Miller, Rita. "The Design and Construction of Women's Day Dresses from 1890 to 1940 in Relationship to the Advancement of Technology." Master's thesis, Florida A. & M. University, 1975.

Mills, Betty J. *Amanda Goes West: A Journal of Fashion History Through Paper Dolls.* Lubbock, Tex., 1983.

Minnegerode, Meade. *The Fabulous Forties.* New York, 1924.

Moase, S. MacDonald. "Dress of American Children from 1894 Through 1914 as Illustrated in the 'Delineator.'" Master's thesis, Iowa State University, 1972.

Molloy, John T. *Dress for Success.* New York, 1974.

Moment, Gairdner B., and Otto F. Kraushaar, eds. *Utopias: The American Experience.* Metuchen, N.J., and London, 1980.

Moncrieff, R. W. *Man-Made Fibres.* 6th ed. New York, 1975.

Moreau Collection Papers. Bibliothèque Nationale, Paris.

Morison, Samuel Eliot, Henry Steele Commager, and William E. Leuchtenburg. *A Concise History of the American Republic.* 2d ed. New York, 1983.

Nash, Roderick. *The Nervous Generation: American Thought, 1917–1930.* Chicago, 1970.

Newton, Stella Mary. *Health, Art and Reason: Dress Reformers of the Nineteenth Century.* London, 1974.

Norton, Thomas Elliot, and Robert Frank. *The Fur Trade in Colonial New York, 1686–1776.* Madison, Wis., 1974.

Noyes, Anna G. "A Practical Protest Against Fashion." *The Independent* 63 (August 29, 1907): 503.

Ober, Grace. "Camping and Tramping Costumes for Girls." *Home Progress,* July 1913, 40.

O'Connor, K. *The Anthropology of Fashion.* New York, 1974.

Ohanian, Gabriele, Elizabeth Paredes, and Nancie Balun. *Footloose: Not All Shoes Are Made for Walking.* New Brunswick, N.J., 1977.

Olian, JoAnne. *The House of Worth: The Gilded Age in New York.* New York, 1982.

Olmsted, Frederick Law. *A Journey in the Back Country.* New York and London, 1907.

Parsons, Frank A. *The Psychology of Dress.* 1920. Reprint. Detroit, 1975.

Payne, Blanche. *History of Costume.* New York, 1965.

Penn, William. *Some Fruits of Solitude.* New York, 1900.

Perlongo, Bob. *Early American Advertising.* New York, 1985.

Picken, Mary Brooks. *The Language of Fashion.* New York, 1939.

Pinkerton, Kathrene Gedney. "Clothes for Woodswomen." *Outing,* July 1913, 18.

Polhemus, Ted, and Lynn Procter. *Fashion and Anti-Fashion—Anthropology of Clothing and Adornment.* London, 1978.

Porter, Glenn, and Harold C. Livesay. *Merchants and Manufacturers.* Baltimore and London, 1971.

Powell, Mary Ann. "Ladies with Legs: An Historical Survey of the Social Acceptability of Pants on Women: 1851–1976." Master's thesis, University of Texas, 1977.

Putnam, Nina Wilcox. "Fashion and Feminism." *Forum* 52 (October 1914): 580–84.

————. "Ventures and Adventures in Dress Reform." *Saturday Evening Post* 195 (October 7, 1922): 15.

_____. "Woman Who Has Upset the Tyranny of Feminine Fashion." *American Magazine* 75 (May 1913): 34–36.

Raeburn, Antonia. *The Suffragette View*. New York, 1975.

Ratner, Elaine. "Levi's." *Dress* 1 (1975): 1–5.

Reutlinger, Dagmer. *The Colonial Epoch in America*. Worcester, Mass., 1975.

Richardson, Herbert. *Costume in History*. London, 1934.

Riesman, David, with Nathan Glazer and Reuel Denney. *The Lonely Crowd: A Study of the Changing American Character*. New Haven and London, 1961.

Roach, Mary Ellen, and Joanne Bubolz Eicher. *Dress, Adornment, and the Social Order*. New York, 1965.

Roach, Mary Ellen, and Kathleen Ehla Muse. *New Perspectives on the History of Western Dress (A Handbook)*. New York, 1980.

Robertson, Mary D., ed. *Lucy Breckinridge of Grove Hill: The Journal of a Virginia Girl, 1862–1864*. Kent, Ohio, 1979.

Ronzone, Ethel. "Standardized Dress." *Journal of Home Economics* 10 (September 1918): 426.

Rose, Clare. *Children's Clothes*. London, 1989.

Rosenberg, Adolph. *The Design and Development of Costume from Prehistoric Times up to the Twentieth Century*. London, 1925.

Rossi, William A. *The Sex Life of the Foot and Shoe*. New York, 1976.

Rubins, A. Alfred. *History of the Jewish Costume*. New York, 1973.

Rudofsky, Bernard. *The Unfashionable Human Body*. New York, 1974.

Russell, Douglas A. *Costume History and Style*. Englewood Cliffs, N.J., 1983.

Rust, Terrie Ellen. "A History of Swimwear Reflecting Some Sociological and Technological Changes." Master's thesis, San Jose State University, 1977.

Said, Edward. *Orientalism*. New York, 1978.

Saxon, Mary Kathleen "Aesthetic Dress of the Nineteenth Century: Principles and Practices." Master's thesis, University of Texas at Austin, 1981.

Schlissel, Lillian. *Women's Diaries of the Westward Journey*. New York, 1982.

Schlissel, Lillian, Byrd Gibbons, and Elizabeth Hampsten, eds. *Far From Home: Families of the Westward Journey*. New York, 1989.

Schoeffler, O. E., and William Gale. *Esquire's Encyclopedia of Twentieth-Century Men's Fashion*. New York, 1973.

Sears, Roebuck and Company Catalog (1898–1914).

Seebohm, Caroline. *The Man Who Was "Vogue": Life and Times of Conde Nast*. London, 1982.

Seelye, John. *Yankee Drover: Being the Unpretending Life of Asa Sheldon, Farmer, Trader, and Working Man, 1788–1870*. Hanover, N.H., and London, 1988.

Shine, Carolyn R. "Scalping Knives and Silk Stockings: Clothing the Frontier." *Dress* 14 (1988): 39–47.

Silver, Pat Beverlee. *The Effects of Leisure on American Women's Clothing: A Survey from 1850–1974*. San Diego, 1974.

Simmons, William S. *Spirit of the New England Tribes: Indian History and Folklore, 1620–1984*. Hanover, N.H., 1986.

Snyder, C. M. *Dr. Mary Walker: The Little Lady in Pants*. New York, 1962.

Sosin, Jack M. *The Opening of the West*. Columbia, S.C., 1969.

Spruill, Julia Cherry. *Women's Life and Work in the Southern Colonies*. New York, 1972.

Squire, Geoffrey. *Dress and Society, 1560–1970*. New York, 1974.

Stamper, Anita, ed. "Clothing and Textiles in the Nineteenth-Century South" (Special Issue), *The Southern Quarterly, A Journal of the Arts in the South* (University of Southern Mississippi) 25, no. 1 (Fall 1988).

"The Stetson Story." *American Heritage*, Spring 1953, 28–31.

Stewart-Abernathy, Judith C., Louise Terzia, and Swannee Bennett. *Life Threads: Clothing Fashions in Early Arkansas, 1810–1870*. Little Rock, Ark., 1989.

Stowell, Donald C. "The New Costume in America: The Ideas and Practices of Robert Edmund Jones, Norman Bel Geddes, Lee Simonson and Aline Bernstein, 1915–1935." Ph.D. diss., University of Texas at Austin, 1972.

Strasser, Susan. *Satisfaction Guaranteed*. New York, 1989.

Stratton, Joanna L. *Pioneer Women: Voices from the Kansas Frontier*. New York, 1981.

Sutherland, Daniel E. *The Expansion of Everyday Life, 1860–1876*. New York, 1989.

Taylor, Lisa, ed. *The Phenomenon of Change*. New York, 1984.

Thomas, Tony. *Hollywood and the American Image*. Westport, Conn., 1981.

Thompson, Charles John. *The Mysteries of Sex: Women Who Posed as Men and Men Who Impersonated Women*. New York, 1974.

Tomerlin Lee, Sarah, ed. *American Fashion*. New York, 1976.

Torbet, Laura. *Clothing Liberation: Out of the Closet and Into the Street*. New York, 1973.

Tranquillo, Mary D. *Styles of Fashion: A Pictorial Handbook*. New York, 1984.

Tucker, Barbara M. *Samuel Slater and the Origins of the American Textile Industry, 1790–1860*. Ithaca and London, 1984.

313

Tyrell, Anne M. "The Relationship of Certain Cultural Factors to Women's Costume in Boston, Massachusetts, from 1720–1740." Master's thesis, Virginia Polytechnic Institute, 1975.

Uhlrich, Pamela. "Clothing Needs of Columbus, Georgia, 1850–1900, as Met by External and Internal Resources." Master's thesis, Auburn University, 1980.

Veblen, Thorstein. "Economic Theory of Women's Dress." *Popular Science Monthly* 46 (December 1894): 198–205.

Vreeland, Diana. *American Women of Style*. New York, 1975.

Wald, Carol, and Judith Papachristou. *Myth America: Picture Women, 1865–1945*. Westminster, Md., 1975.

Walker, Isaac. *Dress: As It Has Been, Is and Will Be*. 1885. Reprint. Ann Arbor, Mich., 1964.

Warwick, E., H. C. Pitz, and A. Wycoff. *Early American Dress: The Colonial and Revolutionary Periods*. New York, 1977.

Watkins, Josephine. *Fairchild's Who's Who in Fashion*. New York, 1975.

Waugh, Norah *The Cut of Men's Clothes: 1600–1900*. New York, 1964.

—————. *The Cut of Women's Clothes: 1600–1930*. New York, 1975.

Weitz, John. *Man in Charge: The Executive's Guide to Grooming, Manners, Travel*. New York, 1974.

White, E. A. "Silhouette Characteristics of Women's Day Dresses in the U.S. from 1900–1920." Ph.D. diss., Iowa State University, 1970.

Whyte, William H., Jr. *Is Anybody Listening?* New York, 1952.

Wilcox, R. Turner. *The Dictionary of Costume*. New York, 1969.

—————. *Five Centuries of American Costume*. New York, 1963.

Woolson, Abba G., ed. *Dress Reform: A Series of Lectures Delivered in Boston—Dress As It Affects Health of Women*. 1874. Reprint. New York, 1974.

Worrell, Estelle. *Children's Costume in America, 1607–1910*. New York, 1981.

—————. *Early American Costume*. Harrisburg, Pa., 1975.

Wright, Louis, ed. *The Elizabethans' America*. Cambridge, Mass., 1965.

Index

A

abolitionism. *See* slavery

Ackerman, Rudolph, 43*n*

Adams, Samuel, 31

advertising, 69, 73, 91, 110, 125, 204, 274–275; using sports figures, 3, 192, 221–222, 267, 276; sewing machine, 77, 108, 283; post–World War II, 135, 170, 270; 1920s, 212, 263–266; vacuum cleaner, 268–269

Agatz, Cora Wilson, 80

age and clothing, 49, 189–201, 213, 302, 303. *See also* children's clothing; young people

Alamo, The (film), 106

Alcott, William A., 192

Amadas, Philip, 10

American Baseball League, 226

American Professional Football Association, 226

American Revolution, 32, 36

Andrews, Julie, 237

androgynous clothing. *See* gender, politics of

anklets. *See* stockings (bobby socks)

Anthony, Susan B., 82*n*

Apache Indian chiefs, 279

aprons. *See* overalls

Arena magazine, 73

Arrow shirts. *See* shirts, dress

Articles of Confederation, 31–32

Astaire, Fred, 131, 161, 302

automobile, the, 147, 151, 222, 265

Autry, Gene, 298

aviation, 164, 222

B

Baltimore, Lord (George Calvert), 15

Barlow, Arthur, 10–11

barter (of clothing), 62, 98

baseball, 226, 228. *See also* sports clothing

bathing suits, 59, 151, 204, 223, 225, 233–235; bikini, 235

Battle of Grandsome (1476), 21

beach pajamas, 234. *See also* leisure clothing

beards, 290; Native Americans and, 8, 17

beatniks, 135

Beautiful and Damned, The (Fitzgerald), 207

Beecher, Catherine, 192

Bergen, Edgar, 148

bicycles, 51, 79, 85, 205

bifurcation, 238

Black Baseball League, 226

blacks, 32, 41, 135, 176; employment for, 76, 145, 152; clothing for, 87, 145, 283, 285, 287; in sports, 226; and "hipness," 283. *See also* slavery

Blass, Bill, 116

Bliven, Bruce, 207

Bloomer, Amelia, 79

bloomers, 42, 78–84 *passim*, 238, 243; for sports, 223, 230, 231, 233

blouses ("waists"), 123, 126; Gibson girl, 55, 143; "Russian," 212; Peter Pan, 259

blue jeans, 184, 186, 261, 267, 290, 303; "designer," 116; patched or cut off, 178, 181; for children, 197. *See also* denim; Levi's

bobby socks. *See* stockings

body-painting, 1; of Native Americans, 10, 16, 17, 95, 121; for protection against glare, 102

bombast, 20

boots. *See* footwear

Bost, Sophie, 108

Boston Machine Works, 55

Boston Tea Party, 31

bow ties, 101, 267

boys' clothing, 54, 73, 125, 133, 191, 195–199 *passim*, 238, 265; advertised, 192, 267. *See also* children's clothing

Brando, Marlon, 298

brassieres: abandonment of, 207; burning of, 249; "training," 267. *See also* underwear

breeches: worn by natives, 16; colonial, 18–22 *passim*, 26, 28, 33, 41, 43; slashed, 20–21, 26; replaced by trousers, 32, 33, 238; invention of, 238. *See also* trousers

Brereton, John, 16

Brief and True Report of the New Found Land of Virginia (Harriet), 11

Bringing Up Baby (film), 247

Brown, Mrs. H. Fletcher, 215

Brown, Moses, 63–64

Brown, William Almy, 64

Brummell, George Bryan "Beau," 238, 295

Bryan, William Jennings, 156

Bryn Mawr College, 253

buckskins. *See* leather clothing

Budge, Don, 228

buffalo hides. *See* leather clothing

Bush, George, 222, 303

businessmen's clothing, 133. *See also* suits, men's

bustles, 82, 84, 109, 111

Butterick, Ebenezer, 77

buttons, 13, 21, 26, 152, 195; improvement of, 42, 43*n*

C

Calamity Jane, 237

Calamity Jane (film), 107

California Indians, 10. *See also* Native Americans

315

321

323

Picture Credits

Bourquin Collection, Kansas Collection, University of Kansas Libraries — back jacket bottom center, 241 right

The British Museum — 11, 12 left, top center, right, bottom

Courtesy of the John Carter Brown Library at Brown University — 6

Carnation Company — 133, 142 bottom

Jimmy Carter Library — 185

Caterpillar Co. — 53 bottom right, 141 bottom, 168 bottom, 243 top

Colorado Historical Society — back jacket bottom right and left, viii, 92, 103, 117 bottom, 118–119, 226, 278, 280–281, 285

Des Plaines Historical Society, Des Plaines, Illinois — 72, 190, 191 left, 198 left, right, 199 left, 201 right, 225, 229 top

Eastern Air Lines — 164 top, 165

Courtesy Elmira College Archives — 220, 253, 257 left, 259 top right

Courtesy Essex Institute, Salem, Massachusetts — 22, 23, 24 bottom, top right, 25 top, bottom

From the Collections of Henry Ford Museum & Greenfield Village — 146, 147 top right, bottom right, 171, 265 bottom

General Mills, Inc. — 266 left, right

Hoover Historical Center, The Hoover Company — 268, 269 top, bottom left, center, right

State Historical Society of Iowa — 49, 54, 57 right, 132 top, 134, 155, 200 left

Lyndon Baines Johnson Library — 113

John Fitzgerald Kennedy Library — 174

Lafayette, Colorado, Miners Museum — 62, 63, 213 top left, bottom left, right, 240 right, 241 left

Levi Strauss & Co. — 114, 116 left, right, 265 top, 274 right, 275 top and bottom

Library of Congress — front jacket top left, bottom center and right, back jacket bottom center, 3, 19, 30 far left, top left, top right, bottom, 32 right, 33 left, 40, 42, 43, 56, 59, 66 left, right, 67, 74, 78, 83, 84, 85, 86, 90, 94, 95, 96 top, 97 top, 99 top, bottom, 100, 104, 105, 106 center, 108, 110, 111, 122, 130, 136, 137 left, right, 138, 139, 140, 143, 144, 149 right, 150, 151 top, bottom, 152, 153, 154, 156, 158 bottom, 160, 173, 176, 182–183, 187, 188, 191 right, 193, 194, 195, 196, 197 left, right, 199 right, 200 right, 201 left, 204, 205, 206, 208, 209, 215 left, 219, 222, 227 right, 232 left, 239 left, right, 258, 283, 284

Courtesy Lynn Historical Society, Lynn, Massachusetts — 48, 50, 51 top, 52 right, 55 bottom left, 60, 65, 120, 124, 141 top

Massachusetts Historical Society — 24 left

Memphis State University — 261 top

Movie Star News — back jacket top right, 89 top, bottom, 244, 246, 247, 249 left, 267, 287, 294, 296, 297 top, bottom, 300 left, right, 301 left, right

National Archives — 170 bottom, 243 bottom, 271, 272, 273 top, bottom

New York Public Library — 73

Courtesy of the New York State Museum — 13

City of Norfolk, Virginia — 167 top, bottom

Jerry Ohlinger — front jacket top center, 88, 106 left, right, 107, 112, 148 left, right, 149 left, 161, 162 left, right, 163, 217, 236, 245

Oshkosh B'Gosh — 142 top

Courtesy of J. C. Penney Archives — 178 right, 210 top right and left, bottom center, and left, 211 top left and right, bottom left, center, and right, 270 left, right

Joseph Pennell Collection, Kansas Collection, University of Kansas Libraries — 51 bottom, 145, 192

The Historical Society of Pennsylvania — front jacket top right, 9, 14, 27

Pennsylvania State University Archives — 227 left, 228 left, right, 232 right, 252 bottom, 254, 261 right

Plymouth Plantation — 28 top left, right, bottom, 29 top left and right, bottom left and right

Franklin Delano Roosevelt Library — 157, 158 top, 159, 166

Rutgers, The State University of New Jersey — 260

Santa Fe Trail Center — 109

Sears, Roebuck and Co. — 126, 127, 210 top left, 214, 274 left

The Division of Costume, The National Museum of American History, Smithsonian Institution — x, 32 left, 33 right, 34 left, center, right, 35 left, center, right, 36 left, right, 37 top, bottom, right, group — left, center, right, 44 left front, left behind, center, right, 45 left, right, 46 left, right, 47 left, right, 52 left, 53 top left and right, bottom left, 55 top right, 57 left, 96–97 bottom, 117 right, 123, 147 left, 172 left, 172 right, 175, 178 left, center, 179 left, 184 left, center, right, 215 right, 232 center, 233 left, right, 234 left, center, right, 235 left, right

The Division of Costume, The National Museum of American History, Smithsonian Institution, Advertising Collection — 55 top left, bottom right, 58, 70, 71, 77, 81, 91, 102, 125, 170 top, 207, 210 bottom right, 224, 240, left, 262 left, right, 264

Library, Texas Women's College — 230 top, 231 bottom, 255 top, 257 right, 259 bottom

Trinity College, Hartford, Connecticut — 229 bottom, 251, 252 top

The University of North Carolina at Greensboro — 231 top, 255 bottom, 259 top left

Historical Photographs Collections, Washington State University Libraries — front jacket bottom left, 230 bottom, 250, 256 left, right

Wide World Photos — back jacket top left, 168 top, 169, 177, 179 right, 180–181, 186, 202, 242, 248, 249 bottom, 277, 282, 286, 288, 289, 290, 291, 292, 293, 298, 299